W9-DIM-869

WITHDRAWN FROM LIBRARY

Reading and Writing Women's Lives
A Study of the Novel of Manners

Literature Advisory Boards

Challenging the Literary Canon

Consulting Editors

Nina Baym
*University of Illinois
at Urbana-Champaign*
Henry Louis Gates, Jr.
Cornell University
Carolyn G. Heilbrun
Columbia University
Amy Ling
Georgetown University
J. Hillis Miller
University of California at Irvine

Nineteenth-Century Studies

Juliet McMaster, Series Editor
University of Alberta

Consulting Editors

Carol Christ
*University of California
at Berkeley*
James R. Kincaid
University of Southern California
Julian Markels
Ohio State University
G. B. Tennyson
*University of California
at Los Angeles*

Studies in Speculative Fiction

Eric S. Rabkin, Series Editor as of 1989
University of Michigan
Robert Scholes, Series Editor 1984–1988
Brown University

Challenging the Literary Canon

Other Titles in This Series

*Ink in Her Blood:
The Life and Crime Fiction
of Margery Allingham*
Richard Martin

*Toward a New Synthesis:
John Fowles, John Gardner,
Norman Mailer*
Robert J. Begiebing

*Charlotte Perkins Gilman:
The Woman and Her Work*
Sheryl L. Meyering, ed.

*Working-Class Fiction in
Theory and Practice:
A Reading of Alan Sillitoe*
Peter Hitchcock

*Form and Meaning in the
Novels of John Fowles*
Susana Onega

*Simone de Beauvoir and
the Demystification of
Motherhood*
Yolanda Astarita Patterson

*Articulated Selves:
Attainment of Identity
through Storytelling in
Twentieth-Century
American Fiction*
John Kalb

William Styron's Sophie's
Choice: *Crime and
Self-Punishment*
Rhoda Sirlin

MONTGOMERY COLLEGE
ROCKVILLE CAMPUS LIBRARY
ROCKVILLE, MARYLAND

Reading and Writing Women's Lives
A Study of the Novel of Manners

Edited by
Bege K. Bowers
and
Barbara Brothers

U·M·I Research
Press

Ann Arbor / London

AAX 3670

OCT 1 0 1991

Copyright © 1990
Bege K. Bowers and Barbara Brothers
All rights reserved

Produced and distributed by
UMI Research Press
an imprint of
University Microfilms Inc.
Ann Arbor, Michigan 48106

Library of Congress Cataloging in Publication Data

Reading and writing women's lives : a study of the novel of manners / edited by Bege K. Bowers, Barbara Brothers.
p. cm.—(Challenging the literary canon)
Includes bibliographical references.
ISBN 0-8357-2029-2 (alk. paper)
1. English fiction—History and criticism. 2. Women and
literature—Great Britain. 3. Manners and customs in literature.
4. Women in literature. I. Bowers, Bege K., 1949- .
II. Brothers, Barbara, 1937- . III. Series.
PR830.W6R4   1989
823.009'355—dc20   89-20348
                                                                          CIP

British Library CIP data is available.

The paper used in this publication meets the minimum requirements of
American National Standard for Information Sciences—Permanence of Paper for Printed
Library Materials, ANSI Z39.48-1984. ⊗ ™

To Our Parents:
Yvonne Howell Bowers and John L. Bowers, Jr.
Mary Ella Bingham Hoover and William Hoover

One goes into the room—but the resources of the English language would be much put to the stretch . . . before a woman could say what happens when she goes into a room. . . . How should it be otherwise? For women have sat indoors all these millions of years, so that by this time the very walls are permeated by their creative force, which has, indeed, so overcharged the capacity of bricks and mortar that it must needs harness itself to pens and brushes and business and politics.

Virginia Woolf, *A Room of One's Own*

Contents

Acknowledgments

We want to thank our contributors for writing essays especially for this book. Special note needs to be taken of the 1985 Modern Language Association panel on the novel of manners—Barbara Brothers, Gloria Sybil Gross, Maureen T. Reddy, and Mary F. Sisney—in which this book had its inception; the 1987 College English Association panel—Bege K. Bowers, Barbara Brothers, Janet E. Dunleavy, Marylea Meyersohn, and Maureen T. Reddy—which contributed to further rethinking of the tradition; to James R. Kincaid for his appreciation of the novel of manners and critical acumen; and to Joseph Wiesenfarth for allowing us to draw on his study of Henry James and the Gothic tradition. Three grants from the Youngstown State University Research Council supported the costs of the bibliographic research and preparation of the manuscript, including funding an assistant, Lisa Davis, who so expertly and promptly dealt with all tasks asked of her, and Sandra Chiles, who so ably prepared the index and helped with proofing. Doris Knapp, student, also assisted in checking quotations. We owe much to our students, especially those in a graduate seminar in the novel of manners; our colleagues (particularly Sandra W. Stephan, Charles Nelson, and Clyde Hankey); our department secretary, Mary Louise Quisenberry; the research librarian, Hildegard Schnuttgen; and Louis A. Zona, Executive Director, Butler Institute of American Art. We are also indebted to those women scholars whose work has preceded ours, particularly those of the early twentieth century, such as Bridget MacCarthy and Charlotte Morgan, whom we discovered in writing the first chapter. Barbara also wants to thank her husband Larry and her children, Mark and Jill, for their support and understanding.

Introduction

What Is a Novel of Manners?

Barbara Brothers and Bege K. Bowers

It may surprise you, as it did us, to learn that the term *novel of manners* did not come into existence concurrently with *Evelina, Pride and Prejudice,* or any of the other books we so often associate with the early novel of manners. Ironically, the term does *not* appear in the *Oxford English Dictionary*—although it is used with some frequency to describe the works of such *present-day* writers as Barbara Pym and Anita Brookner. And while both of these authors are English, and English authors are most often cited as originators of the form, no historical or critical study of the English novel of manners as such has been written, except for Joseph Wiesenfarth's recently published study examining how the novel of manners tradition melds with that of the Gothic novel to form the Gothic novel of manners.[1] Since 1972, James Tuttleton, Gordon Milne, and Jerome Klinkowitz have sought to establish the tradition as it exists in American literature, and in 1981 Hanna Charney published *The Detective Novel of Manners,* a study describing popular detective fiction in terms of the older tradition. Yet, of all these writers, only Tuttleton seems to recognize that what *kind* of novel the novel of manners is, what novels the term *includes* or *excludes,* may not have been established. Tuttleton, however, addresses that question solely within the context of American literary and social history. That the question has not been addressed in a critical or historical study of the English novel of manners reflects a tacit dismissal of the tradition, which in its eighteenth-century inception and nineteenth-century practice has been identified with women writing about women's lives.

Critics and literary historians agree on only two matters: Jane Austen wrote novels of manners, and such novels present something of the "social customs, manners, conventions, and habits of a definite social class at a particular time and place" (Holman, *Handbook to Literature*).[2] Such agreement might seem to be adequate, but, in fact, it is not. The definitions that commentators on the novel of manners freely extrapolate from these two points of agreement are fundamentally different. What is more, the commentators do not address their differences or agree to disagree: Is a novel of manners as much a study of character as of society? Or if a novel focuses on what is morally right and not just on what is socially proper—if it is as much psychologically as "sociologically oriented" (Tuttleton 11)—is it then a novel of a different kind? Is it a novel of manners only if the class presented is upper class? Must it be limited to the domestic world and deal just with the problem of finding a husband? Can it accommodate serious social or political issues? Must the presentation be "realistic," or can it be stylized and exaggerated in the mode of the comedy of manners?

That quite dissimilar authors have been cited as precursors of the tradition illustrates the lack of agreement as to whether the individual in relation to society or society alone is the subject of the novel of manners. Some critics, such as Gordon Milne, who refers to Tuttleton's study, suggest that Henry Fielding wrote the first novel of manners, whereas others—and it is important to note who those others are—principally Henry James and Charlotte Morgan, author of *The Rise of the Novel of Manners,* feel that it is in Samuel Richardson's works that features of the novel of manners were first combined.

While Tuttleton would grant that a novel of manners may have more than just manners and manners alone as its subject, others, such as Fred Millett, editor of the eighth edition of *A History of English Literature* (1964), limit the scope of the novel of manners to "paint[ing] contemporary society"—no ideas, no character study. Millett identifies three kinds of novels in the nineteenth century: romantic-historical novels; novels of manners; and realistic social novels, or novels with a "purpose." Only Fanny Burney and Jane Austen, according to Millett, wrote true novels of manners. Maria Edgeworth introduced "social purpose" into the genre; Elizabeth Gaskell wrote social problem novels; George Eliot created novels of psychology and morals; Anthony Trollope recounted histories, combining romance with realism; and Henry James and George Meredith drew upon the elements of the novel of manners, which for Millett is a genre in which the characters' "chief business [is] . . . social duties; their chief interest . . . matrimony" (340–75). In short, Millett claims that a novel of manners is circumscribed within the domestic and that it treats only questions of social propriety. One would also have to conclude that Millett sees the domestic as a realm separate, and thus separable, from the public (and male) world of politics and value judgments encoded in a society's way of conducting its business, including how it classifies and defines its peoples (gender, class, race) and what it establishes as the "proper" relationships among and within those groups.

Further confusion in defining the novel of manners results from its association with another term, *comedy of manners*. Sources such as the *Harper Handbook to Literature* state that the novel of manners is an "adopted" form of the comedy of manners. Some critics write as if the two terms were synonymous. For them, the novel of manners focuses on aristocrats or the elite of society. Milne contends that both forms, the novelistic and the dramatic,

> employ a carefully patterned structure; both offer a balanced, chiseled polished style; and both are written in the vein of urbane, sophisticated humor. They evoke the same upperclass world as well, carefully describing its handsome drawing rooms, using appropriate imagery (e.g., mausoleum or formal garden figures) to suggest its flavor, and adroitly reproducing the brittle dialogue of its inhabitants. (13)

A novel such as Evelyn Waugh's *A Handful of Dust* might fit such a definition, but not Jane Austen's *Emma*. At issue here is the class of society focused upon—aristocrats—as well as narrative style, depiction of character, and treatment of dialogue. Neither in manner nor in setting and class depicted, we contend, does the novel of manners correspond to the comedy of manners, with its "chiseled polished style" and aristocratic drawing rooms.

What links the two traditions is simply the word *manners*. Yet, the differences in the ways critics use the word *manners* suggest that the link is a tenuous one indeed. Even those critics for whom *manners* is the only essential word define the term differently: "good manners," or the manners of the upper class (Millett); or, almost antithetically, as a synonym for *mannerism* (Milne); or, at times, in the more general sense of conventions governing behavior (Tuttleton). In spite of these quite divergent views of the form and content of a novel of manners, however, literary critics and historians agree that Jane Austen is *the* novelist of manners.

While we would not argue with the contention of Tuttleton or the writers of some literary handbooks that for a novel to be a novel of manners it must present in some detail the "actualities of the social world" in which the characters live (Tuttleton 18), we would point out that the realistic depiction of character is equally essential. The novel of manners narrates the actions of *characters*, not the character *types* that the comedy of manners dramatizes. As Quentin G. Kraft has stated in discussing Samuel Richardson's *Clarissa*, the title of the novel signals the fact that "proper names . . . were beginning to be written with a difference." That difference, the "stress . . . moving from the family name to the given name," marks a shift to "individualized characters," characters who change, grow, and develop in the course of the narrative. Rather than sketching the "generic characters of prior fiction," the novel begins with Richardson to trace the life of an "individual" (45). That shift is precisely marked by the titles of some of the first novels identified as novels of manners: Burney's *Evelina*, Austen's *Emma*, and Edgeworth's *Helen*. The novel of manners is as much a study of *character*, in the sense of the portrayal of an individualized self, as it is a study of social conventions.

We the editors and authors of the present study perceive the novel of manners as focusing on the individual in relation to society. It is not more about one than about the other; it does not take as its subject merely the particular manners and customs of a specific social class at a given place and point in time. Instead, the novel of manners offers a perspective on the nature of the *self* as shaped but not entirely determined by social forces; as expressing itself in relation to, but not necessarily in accord with, the values of a society embodied in outward conventions. Informed by the conception that only through studying and analyzing social context can we interpret what lies beneath or is revealed through the gestures, words, and actions of a given character, the Janus-like novel of manners examines both the psyche of the individual and the social world in which the individual lives.

While the self as depicted in the novel of manners does not transcend its social milieu and is interpreted through the community's understanding of what is right and proper, the individual does not necessarily define his or her being as would the community within which that individual interacts and by which that individual is judged. The "ideological pressure" of manners (see James Kincaid's essay), however, is everywhere, even when the artificiality or the power of a society's conventions is not the focus of the story. Manners are always more than a matter of propriety—of which woman should pour the tea, what sex should be bound in stays or a cinched-waist dress, who is to arrive first at a village party, or who should marry whom. Manners reveal not just how a society conducts its business but also what it considers that business to be. Novels of manners are concerned with selfhood and morality within a cultural context and thus depict the inevitable conflict between private and public personas and between illusion (imagination and desire) and the actualities of daily existence. In fact, they are so concerned with the details of everyday life that some critics and readers have dismissed them as "trivial," "unimaginative," or "dull." But Pym's portrayal of the novelist of manners as a kind of anthropologist reminds us of how significant such quotidian matters are.

What no historians and critics of the novel of manners have done is to take seriously the form and content of Austen's novels as central to a definition of the genre, nor have they taken into consideration those writers of the nineteenth century whose practice of novel writing was viewed by their contemporaries as being similar to Austen's. That most academics who have written on the American novel of manners have paid so little attention to the broader tradition may be attributed to their overriding concern: to claim the existence of worthwhile examples of the form in *American* literary history. Explicitly or implicitly, these critics have been responding to Richard Chase (*The American Novel and Its*

Tradition, 1957) and others who regard the romance as defining the "great tradition" for America. The question of whether America had "groups with recognizable and differentiable manners and conventions" (Tuttleton 13)—that is, whether it had groups with "observable manners" (17)—forms the context in which American literary critics and historians have discussed the novel of manners.

Tuttleton cites Lionel Trilling's definition of manners ("Manners, Morals, and the Novel"): "culture's hum and buzz of implication[,] . . . the whole evanescent context in which its explicit statements are made[,] . . . that part of a culture which is made up of half-uttered or unutterable expressions of value . . . [and in which] assumption rules" (Trilling 200–201). But though Tuttleton concurs with Trilling's definition of manners, he ignores Trilling's statement that the novel of manners concerns itself with both inner and outer reality, with looking closely at society, observing both class distinctions and differences in manners, in order to "catch the meaning of every dim implicit hint" of the "largest intentions of men's souls as well as the smallest" (205). (That women's souls were always felt to be different from men's souls and that women writers, taking women and their lives as their subjects, were the first to write in that genre dubbed the novel of manners are unnoted by Trilling. Nor does he understand that the novel of manners is as much if not more about the snobbery of gender than about that of class.) Tuttleton rightly places Trilling on the side of Chase, who argues that few American authors have written novels of manners, a claim Tuttleton wishes to dispute.

The problem with Tuttleton and other commentators on the novel of manners is that their definitions are based on overtly "partial" readings of literary history. To the extent possible, definitions should be descriptive, not prescriptive or unduly influenced by personal biases. Both the novels of the nineteenth century and the commentary upon them need to be examined in order to formulate a more descriptive definition of the genre. Such an examination is also necessary in challenging the existing valuation of the contributions of nineteenth-century novelists of manners to the English novel and in rereading twentieth-century women writers, including black women writers, who have responded to the tradition in their novels.

Though the word *manners* appears often in the reviews of novels by Burney, Austen, Edgeworth, and later nineteenth-century novelists, Henry James may have been the first to use the longer term, *novel of manners*. In his review of *Felix Holt,* written for the *Nation* in 1866, James classifies *Felix Holt, Adam Bede,* and *Romola* with "a kind of writing in which the English tongue has the good fortune to abound—that clever, voluble, bright-colored novel of manners which began with the present century under the auspices of Miss Edgeworth and Miss Austen" (*Literary Criticism: Essays* 911). But what were the characteristics identified by nineteenth-century critics, reviewers, and writers in their critical comments on Austen and the other writers such as Edgeworth that they grouped with her?

Sir Walter Scott hailed the "new style" of novel (*CH* 63, 87) crafted by Austen for its characterization, its depiction of the life and speech of ordinary people, and its eschewing the improbabilities of the romance—even for its comic parodying of the characters, situations, and plots of those stylized heroic fictions.[3] That character portrayal was early on deemed the significant and remarkable aspect of Jane Austen's novels is evident not just in Scott's statements but also in other reviews written during the first seventy years of the nineteenth century. In fact, so excellent was Austen at delineating the nuances of human motivation and action that numerous critics—including Richard Whately, George Henry Lewes, and Thomas Macaulay—compared her to Shakespeare. Macaulay notes that none of her characters has a "hobbyhorse" like Sterne's characters nor a "ruling passion, such as we read of in Pope" (*CH* 122). Whately contends that the conversations of Austen's characters are conducted "with a regard to character hardly exceeded even by Shakspeare [*sic*] himself" (*CH* 98), while Richard Simpson, a Shakespearean scholar, echoes the comparison and elaborates on Macaulay's list: "nor a humour, like Ben Jonson, nor a trick, like Mr. Dickens" (*CH* 249). But it was not just Austen's characters who were described as "happily delineated and admirably sustained" (*CH* 109). The reviews also stressed Edgeworth's depiction of character: her characters were notably real and finely drawn.

Reviewers praised not just the expertness and depth of character portrayal in these early novels but also the use of "realistic" dialogue, which played for the first time in the novel of manners and its precursors a sustained and central role in narrating a story. Unlike the "brittle" dialogue characteristic of the comedy of manners, dialogue in the "modern reformed school of novels" (*CH* 145)—another label used for novels by Austen, Edgeworth, and Gaskell— reproduces the speech of "commonplace people" (*CH* 81). Burney's *Evelina,* identified by Bridget MacCarthy and Edward Wagenknecht as the "pioneer" of the novel of manners,[4] was praised for its dialogue. Although Burney employed the epistolary form, the "letters" in *Evelina* are often scenic demarcations; events are reported not in summary form but in the words exchanged by characters. Rather than an "endless affectation of sentiment," William Hazlitt contends, the "common dialogue" of this, Burney's "best" novel captures "intuitively" the "idiom of character and manners" (6:124). Not just Austen but Edgeworth, too, in Whately's view, "draws character and details conversations, such as they occur in real life, with a spirit and fidelity not to be surpassed" (*CH* 93). Whately goes on to observe that Austen "say[s] as little as possible in her own person, and giv[es] a dramatic air to the narrative, by introducing frequent conversations" (*CH* 97–98). Henry Crabb Robinson writes of Austen's "perfectly colloquial style of . . . dialogue" (*CH* 85); others comment on her "skill in making her personages speak characteristically" (*CH* 121); and George Henry Lewes calls attention in *Blackwood's Magazine* to her "dramatic ventriloquism" (*CH* 162). All in all, the reviewers suggest that how characters *express* themselves in what we now call the novel of manners is as important as what they *do* to reveal their particular natures and situations. Rather than merely portraying the manners of a particular class, dialogue distinquishes the psyche of one character from that of another.

What interested contemporary reviewers, however, was not just the detailed, realistic portrayal in these novels, which they frequently compared to a Hogarth print or the Flemish school of painting, but also the *kinds* of characters portrayed. "Common" and "natural" (*CH* 97), drawn from the "ordinary walks of life," these fictional creations "conduct themselves upon the motives and principles" that "readers may recognize as ruling their own [lives]" (Scott, *CH* 63–64). Rather than emerging from the upper-class, aristocratic drawing rooms of the comedy of manners (cf. the Branghtons and Mr. Smith in Burney's *Evelina*), the characters come from country villages, the middle class, and, on occasion, the lower class.

Though the mode of presentation was considered realistic and mirrorlike, "[delineating] with great accuracy [both] the habits and the manners" of a given group of people and those of a particular character or characters (*CH* 72), reviewers also noted the comic and the ironic elements. Some reviewers emphasized the gentle mocking of the individual: in Austen's novels, "one's own absurdities [are] reflected back upon one's conscience; . . . the follies . . . she holds up to us, are, for the most part, mere follies, or else natural imperfections; and she treats them, as such, with good-humoured pleasantry; mimicking them so exactly, that we always laugh at the ridiculous truth of the imitation" (*CH* 81). Austen's "playful humour," her "subtle and lively power of ridicule" (*CH* 121), her parodying in *Northanger Abbey* of "the unnaturalness, unreality, and fictitious morality, of the romances she imitate[s]" (Simpson, *CH* 242), as well as her playful exposure of her society's conventions of courtship and marriage, delighted many of her contemporaries. Throughout her fiction, "Miss Austen [takes an ironic stance] against whatever is affected or perverted, or merely sentimental, in the province of love" (*CH* 137). Hazlitt had observed earlier, in an essay attacking the heroes of romance, a similar strain in Burney's *Evelina*, in which—while much of the sentimental still reigns—the situations of romantic fiction and the idea of "romantic love" as the basis for marriage are gently mocked: her "*forte* is ridicule," he wrote, and "no one had ever much less of the romantic" (17:252).

To examine the artistry and complexity of Austen's fiction or to demonstrate the numerous subthemes that later novelists of manners have recast for different times and places exceeds the scope of our volume. What we feel needs to be reasserted is the subtlety and complexity of her delineation of individual characters and her ironic and playful questioning of both the individual and society. Two essayists in this volume explore Austen's character portrayal and use of dialogue—Gloria Gross, who illustrates the "psychodynamic texture" of Austen's novels, the "remarkable congruity" between Austen's novels and modern psychological realism, and Marylea Meyersohn, who examines Austen's manipulation of speech to reveal character and "the relationship of the individual and society." For it is not just Austen's contemporaries who find depth in her presentation of characters and skill in her manipulation of dialogue. Writers and readers of women's lives have returned over and over again to her fictions.

In the essays on other novelists identified by nineteenth-century reviewers and critics as writing in the same school as Austen—Maria Edgeworth, Elizabeth Gaskell, Anthony Trollope—Janet Dunleavy, Maureen Reddy, and James Kincaid focus both on defining the place of these authors in the novel of manners tradition and on refuting twentieth-century dismissals and oversimplified readings of their novels. Dunleavy analyzes Edgeworth's narrative techniques and character portrayal, "her inventive manipulation of [the novel of manners'] conventions." Most reevaluations of Edgeworth's work, she suggests, suffer from an overemphasis on the biographical, contributing to a misconceived view of the novelist as a "fair authoress" able to write only because of her father's influence and help. Dunleavy also makes a case for the importance of ideas in Edgeworth's novels: one can be both a novelist of manners and a novelist of "social purpose."

Ideas are important in Gaskell's novel *Wives and Daughters* as well, even though this novel is not usually grouped with Gaskell's social problem novels. Reddy writes: "In *Wives and Daughters*, the social problem is actually the entire society itself, which Gaskell explores in terms of manners. The central question is this: How is the individual, especially the individual woman, to find a way to live in a society that seems hostile to individual desires . . . ?"

But society is not kind to male desires, either, unless those desires conform to accepted conventions. Part of what the novel of manners examines is those accepted conventions, their artificiality as well as the ways in which they thwart individual desires. Kincaid argues that in exposing the artificiality of some manners, Trollope's novels raise questions about the "naturalness" of all manners. He also explores Trollope's representation of the "private" and "public" realms, noting in particular how *The Duke's Children* reveals that "[m]arriage and love are . . . patently affairs of class, politics, and cash," the "private realm . . . riddled through with political forces." Trollope's novels are in this sense as domestic as Austen's are political histories. Like Gaskell's, Edgeworth's, and Austen's, Trollope's novels raise questions about society while portraying moral dilemmas. Perhaps the domestic setting of the novel of manners is not so trivial after all. Most certainly the essays in this volume should put to rest classification systems such as that of Millett, who would create a separate category for novels that combine a critique of society with a study of individual character.

What is at issue in the present study is not just a definition of the novel of manners but also the value of the tradition. The subject matter of the novels led Ralph Waldo Emerson to complain in his journals: "[M]arriageableness. All that interests in any character introduced is still this one, Has he or [she] the money to marry with, and the conditions conforming?" (9:337, brackets in the original). And William Forsyth, in *The Novels and Novelists of the Eighteenth Century, in Illustration of the Manners and Morals of the Age* (1871), bemoans the "constant husband-hunting . . . displayed in Miss Austen's novels." "Are we to think," he asks, "that husband-hunting was the sole object in life of daughters, and the sole object for which mothers existed?" (337, 334–35). To be sure, it was a personal and economic necessity that a husband be found. How Forsyth could have missed the fact that British society labeled unmarried women "redundant" and wrote essays and books addressing the problem of "superfluous" women is a mystery!

Usually, and not always favorably, the world of the novel of manners was perceived as a woman's world, viewed from a woman's perspective. Manners, as Hazlitt says of Burney, are presented "with a consciousness of [the female] sex, and in that point of view in which it is the particular business and interest of women to observe them" (6:123). Like Hazlitt, Whately writes that "one of Miss Austin's [*sic*] great merits in our eyes . . . [is] the insight she gives us into the peculiarities of female character" (*CH* 100). What we find among characters and practitioners of the genre is not so much an abundance of "old maid[s]," ridiculed by Henry James through one of his fictional mouthpieces (*Literary Criticism: Essays* 962), as the "singular" number of female names noted in T. B. Shaw's *Outlines of General Literature* (1849; *CH* 129). The names of women characters frequently became the titles of the novels—*Evelina, Cecilia, Camilla, Helen, Almiera, Leonora, Emma*—though the heroines are not drawn larger than life. They are neither "fiends" nor "angels" (Whately, *CH* 100) nor "heroes," either, as Hazlitt observes approvingly of Edgeworth's characters (17:252).

While twentieth-century readers may consider Austen a major novelist, she was not a particularly popular writer in the nineteenth century, nor did all early reviewers find the "domestic novel," "the common-life novel," the "novel of real life," or the "novel of society" (*roman de société*)—other terms by which the early novel of manners was called—interesting or imaginative. Some found the novels boring: "They show us too much of the littlenesses and trivialities of life, and limit themselves so scrupulously to the sayings and doings of dull, ignorant, and disagreeable people, that their very truthfulness makes us yawn" (*CH* 145–46). The subject, some felt, was mundane; the central characters were women; the plot turned on courtship and marriage or how one lives if one is *not* married.

Subtly but surely, a number of factors—the gender of many of the novelists plus their focus on domestic concerns, the posture on the part of some that social novels should be concerned with large (masculine) problems of class, material- ism, and ethics (that is, if one could concede that the novel should concern itself at all with actualities and not just with aesthetics), developing concepts of "canon"—all conspired to give the novel of manners a passing nod except from those eager to say that Americans could write something other than romance. Only in the last decade—since contemporary reviewers have begun to use the term *novel of manners* as a label for novels by such authors as Pym and Brookner and since feminist literary critics have called attention to the ways in which the writing and reading of women's lives have been suppressed by the patriarchal and aesthetic values of those who have controlled the conventions of the academic literary community—have the problems of definition and the question of the value of the novel of manners tradition become issues in English literary history.

Accustomed as we have become in the last ten years to the rediscovery and reevaluation of women writers, we perhaps need to recall how much of a barrier female gender, either as author or as subject of a novel, presented in securing a place in literary history. Ernest Baker opened his chapter entitled "Some Women Novelists" in *The History of the English Novel* (1939) by asserting: "The woman of letters has peculiarities that mark her off from the other sex as distinctly as peculiarities of race or ancestral tradition. Whatever variety of talent, outlook, or personal disposition may be discernible in any dozen women writers taken at random, it will be matched and probably outweighed by resemblances dis- tinctly feminine" (10:199).

James, in his preface to *The Portrait of a Lady*, reflects on how unusual it is to think of endowing "with the high attributes of a Subject" someone like Isabel Archer, "the mere slim shade of an intelligent but presumptuous girl." Yet, as James suggests, "George Eliot has admirably [and self-consciously accomplished] it—'In these frail vessels is borne onward through the ages the treasure of human affection'" (*Literary Criticism: French* 1077). To critics such as James, the strength of women writers was their portrayal of *women;* Eliot's Will Ladislaw, he says in derision, is a "woman's man" (*Literary Criticism: Essays* 961). In another instance, he singles out Gaskell's portrayal of Doctor Gibson and Squire Hamley in *Wives and Daughters;* unlike her other male characters, these are "strongly marked, masculine, middle-aged men . . . as forcibly drawn as if a wise masculine hand had drawn them" (*Literary Criticism: Essays* 1061). Reflected in James's remarks are the gender assumptions of his society, even though James chose to follow in his English literary mothers' tradition and exhibited an appreciation for and sensitivity to the lives of women, not just "by showing what it means for an American girl to become a lady in European society," but even more fundamentally by portraying the problem posed for a female who tries to grow up "without giving up being her *self*" (see Wiesenfarth's essay on *Portrait of a Lady* in this volume).

James, of course, was too fine a reader of novels to be guilty of relegating all writing by women to a separate genre, as did Ernest Baker, but James's comments on women writers (e.g., they are above all "patient observers") reflect his view that the female gender is wanting in imagination. (How this view accords with Ann Radcliffe's *The Mysteries of Udolpho* or with other Gothic tales is not a question he addresses.) Even in his discussion of Trollope's novels, James clearly identifies the novel of manners as a "feminine" genre: "His great, his inestimable merit was a complete appreciation of the usual. This gift is not rare in the annals of English fiction; it would naturally be found in a walk of literature in which the feminine mind has laboured so fruitfully. Women are delicate and patient observers; they hold fast their noses close, as it were, to the texture of life" (*Literary Criticism: Essays* 1333). While not questioning the literary qualities of the novel of manners, James nevertheless relegates it to the ranks of a lesser and "feminine" art, something like the painting of teacups. As he remarks concerning Austen, Eliot, and others of their sex, "if women are unable to draw, they notoriously can at all events paint, and this is what realism requires" (*Literary Criticism: Essays* 827).

Without, it seems to us, meaning to, James set the stage for the pejorative connotation that the novel of manners has acquired in the twentieth century.[5] Jane Austen is, in his words, "instinctive and charming" (*Literary Criticism: French* 333). Though delivered as praise, the comment is damning; the implication is clear. Austen lacks not only imagination but also the critical acuteness of the male intellect: "with all her light felicity, [she] leaves us hardly more curious of her process, or of the experience in her that fed it, than the brown thrush who tells his story from the garden bough" (*Literary Criticism: French* 117). Instinctive rather than learned, observers rather than imaginative artists, Austen and other women writers (and alas poor Trollope, too) failed, in James's view, to contribute to the development of the novel from a craft into an art. For that development, the (male) critical spirit was necessary. "[T]he novel is so preponderantly cultivated among us by women, in other words by a sex ever gracefully, comfortably, enviably unconscious (it would be too much to call them even suspicious) of the requirements of form" (*Literary Criticism: French* 333), James wrote, that it is small wonder they did little to make the public aware of the "artistry" of fiction.

Though implicitly critical of authors like Austen who did not write explications or justifications of their fictional practices, James was not willing to ignore their accomplishments. In what seems almost a contradiction, he remarks that they achieved "as great results as any" (*Literary Criticism: French* 333). Nevertheless, for a later age that was to limit "literariness" to self-conscious, self-reflexive works of formal experimentation, restricting even further what was deemed worthy of being called art, James's attitude toward what women wrote in the nineteenth century damned them to the realm of the second-rate, if not worse.

That there has been no critical-historical study of the British novel of manners, except for Wiesenfarth's study of the relationship between the Gothic and the novel of manners, reflects the extent to which the kinds of questions asked about literature are limited by twentieth-century concepts of "canon," and of what is "literary." For example, the New Critics defined "literature" as a self-enclosed system encoded in a special language of symbol, image, and motif, irrelevant to and independent of actualities outside literature. No virtue at all could be found in accurate and faithful observation of people, place, and manners! The New Critics' definition of literature implicitly dismissed questions about the "ideas" of a work of literature and even about changes and developments in formal devices—all great art shared the same characteristics. Subject was irrelevant; "poetic" language (not the "everyday" language of the novel of manners) was the "matter" for literary criticism.

Likewise, F. R. Leavis's *The Great Tradition* (1948)—which subsumed all questions about literary history within the allegedly larger, but paradoxically extremely limited context of imaginative novels that take "seriously" life's moral questions—had a formidable impact on the focus of historical and critical writing. Such kings as Henry James and only two attendant queens, Austen and Eliot, fell into the Leavisite hierarchical line. And since literature had moralizing, cultural work to do, no time could be wasted on novels that had appealed to the mistaken tastes of an earlier generation or on works that Leavis felt had served merely as grist for the minds of true literary greats, those whose works were "universal" and those works that transcended the particulars and idiosyncrasies of a certain place and time.[6] Leavis's dispute with the advocates of the purely "aesthetic" value of literature did little to further the cause of evaluating the contributions of nineteenth-century writers in the novel of manners tradition. Nor did it help to identify those writers in the twentieth century who drew upon the tradition.

Writers of the thirties and later writers such as C. P. Snow, most of whom proclaimed the social value of literature and criticized the elitism of a literature written by a few to be read only by the elect, took up the banner for a literature of ideas, commitment, and/or class issues. But the novel of manners is not a "propaganda" novel or a sociological novel. Lionel Trilling, like Virginia Woolf earlier in "The Leaning Tower," describes these newer genres as lacking insight into the characters they portray, as exhibiting a great distaste for social injustice but little taste for or understanding of those to whom social justice needs to be extended, and as presenting well the distinctions and discriminations of class but not the complexities of character.

What readers and critics attend to reflects their conceptions of what is significant form in art, what are significant issues in life, and what is the nature of the self. Certainly, part of the recent renewal of interest in the novel of manners is the heightened perception, stimulated by Marxist and feminist critics in particular, of the interplay of forces inside and outside the individual such that the very categories "private" and "public" are called into question. Authors and readers, like characters within the fictions, are neither outside nor inside society but *within* it. Gestures, words, and actions—the dark glass through which we attempt to peer into the souls of others—are constantly defined and redefined through acts of interpretation, which is to say that for characters *in* as well as readers *of* the novel of manners, interpretation is of crucial concern.

The question of "reading," or interpretation, is especially relevant to the novel of manners, for the shaping forces of social and historical contexts—the constructs through which we read ourselves and others—are reflected in the subject matter of the novels themselves. Some novels of manners, as Bege Bowers and James Kincaid point out in their essays on Eliot and Trollope, examine the very nature of manners, becoming "meta-novels" that expose the dangers inherent in interpreting and defining, as well as the artificiality of all customs and their transformation into prescriptive rules or ideologies. From "accommodation" to "subversion," novels of manners explore all the means of coping, of attempting to resolve conflict, identified by Marxist and feminist critics of the last few decades.[7] And if, at times, the resolutions seem forced or tenuous, we must at least give the novels credit for raising much more difficult and complex questions than some critics have been ready to acknowledge. The difficulty and complexity of those questions as James addressed them in *The Portrait of a Lady* as well as the tradition's relationship to the Gothic novel are the subjects of Wiesenfarth's essay, an enlargement of a chapter from his published study.

George Eliot's novels meet the test of formal rigor and self-consciousness required by Leavis and others for inclusion in the "canon" of serious literature, but for some critics this very seriousness excludes her novels (and such is also frequently the case for James's novels) from the tradition of the novel of manners (cf. Millett), a view that this study attempts to refute. Eliot's novels are generally not discussed as novels of manners; Virginia Woolf's never are. If Eliot placed too much stress on philosophical or moral ideas to be classed among the mere observers of society, Woolf attended too much to the aesthetic, becoming, in the view of many, another modernist absorbed by experiments in form. Meanwhile, for those who exclude the psychological study of character from the purview of the novel of manners, Eliot's attention to the inner lives of her characters and Woolf's enlarging the presentation of the subjective alienate them from the tradition. We, however, would argue that Woolf's modifications of the conventions of fictional narration are just that, and that form is not her subject but the means to an end that is in harmony with the novel of manners tradition. Certainly, the attention of both authors to character is consistent with the tradition.

Both Eliot and Austen attend to the customs, manners, and habits of particular social groups and the mundane details of everyday life. They do so because they portray the self as understanding itself through social realities. Thus, Virginia Woolf is linked to Jane Austen by more than choosing to write of the trivialities of day-to-day existence, of parties and pageants (see Mark Hussey's essay in this volume). In Woolf's novels, the details of a particular time and place may not always be provided by an omniscient narrator—Woolf's objections to the space given in the novels of her immediate predecessors to those details is well known—but the "manners, social customs, folkways, conventions, traditions, and mores" (Tuttleton 10) in which "assumption rules" (Trilling 201) are reflected in the thoughts and actions of her characters. By making the presentation of manners more internal than external, Woolf perhaps ascribes to manners an even greater power than did her predecessors. Whatever is a woman (or a man) to do given the constraints on gender and class? This question might be said to run through all Woolf's novels; certainly the question echoes clearly throughout *Mrs. Dalloway* and *Between the Acts,* the novel that Hussey focuses on in this volume. Hussey documents Woolf's attention to manners not just in *Between the Acts* but also in her diaries; he also notes that the Leavises rejected her for her presentation of a "privileged, 'civilized' milieu." That the social world of the privileged and educated elite forms the milieu of Woolf's novels does not indicate her approval of their values. Certainly, the gender distinctions that Woolf attacked in her novels were not an abstract concept but, as she demonstrated, an integral part of the hierarchical exclusivity of the British class system that Woolf documented with historical accuracy.

Carolyn Heilbrun argues in her essay that, among other things, historical accuracy is a convention of the novel of manners and that the upper-class milieu found in Woolf's novels and many nineteenth-century British novels of manners is essential for the detective novel of manners. To write of a gang of thieves or the Mafia is to leave the world of the detective novel of manners because there is no code of civilized behavior, there are "no social or moral norms" corresponding to those of "the English system of class and race and gender," faulty as it was. There is indeed no ordered everyday life to be disturbed by a crime, "reprehensible chiefly because it amounted to a betrayal of . . . trust" resulting from "a world where certain modes of behavior were trustfully anticipated." For Heilbrun, Dorothy Sayers's *Gaudy Night* may have been the last detective novel of manners, the last to reflect a historical presentation of rather than a nostalgic desire for community. That nostalgic desire is, of course, reflected in other novels labeled by reviewers as novels of manners, novels that are set in the past or the present and that seriously or comically depict a pseudo-historical social world—for example, the novels of Angela Thirkell. In such novels, manners have become mannerisms, superficial and lacking the power to inflict personal harm, and thus the novels are essentially sentimental or farcically comical.

But if the upper- or middle-class worlds of the landed gentry, the educated, or the privileged have largely dissolved as identifiable communities in twentieth-century life and fiction, the worlds marginalized by that white male society have not, at least not in the historical social setting of England in the period bounded by the fifties and eighties in which Barbara Pym's novels take place. Not only does Pym establish that men and women still inhabit different communities in spite of women's incursion into the universities and work places of contemporary English life; but in her novel *Jane and Prudence,* which Barbara Brothers chooses as the focus for her essay in this volume, Pym also suggests that generational differences in manners and mores may have become great enough to label different generations as distinct *classes.* What Brothers focuses upon, however, is the fact that the gender roles established by "the social expectations and mannerisms that grew out of the Victorian public text of work and the private text of marriage" still act to divide men and women into two distinct classes.

That men and women were, and perhaps still are, two distinct classes in the "heterosexual plot on which the class system and patriarchy generally rested" (Heilbrun) is perhaps best illustrated in Mary Sisney's essay on black novels of manners. The black women novelists she examines have, as she observes, "more in common with the works of such literary ancestors as Edith Wharton and Jane Austen than with those written by such black contemporaries as Claude McKay and Countee Cullen." An understanding of the tradition of the British novel of manners, not merely the black novel of manners, helps to explain the power with which Gloria Naylor's *Linden Hills* speaks to both black and white readers about the lives of women (and of black men) enmeshed in the cultural values of a patriarchal, bourgeois society. The black novel of manners exposes the "ideological pressure" of society's "hum and buzz" and reveals the sinister underside of the right way to behave.

John Wilkinson's essay, with which this volume concludes, addresses the problem of definition by examining the contemporary academic novel, a type of novel that also takes as its focus manners. Yet, it would seem that these novels have more in common with the comedy of manners than with the novel of manners: characters are most often caricatures; class is pitted against class; and the novels focus on the values of the two classes rather than on the values of the individual in relationship to the community to which he or she belongs. The definition of a tradition can be tested by its ability to exclude as well as include. We have maintained that a novel *about* manners is not necessarily a novel *of* manners given the practice of the novelists to whom the term was first applied, and that though some have considered the novel of manners a daughter of the comedy of manners, the conventions of the two traditions are so different—more profound than what might be attributed to the two different media, the drama and the novel—that one must not assert too strong a family resemblance. Certainly, writers of the British novels of academic life have not taken the domestic or the lives of women as their focus; rather, they depict how British white male society is still divided into distinct classes.[8]

All definitions and traditions are problematic, of course: descriptions and classifications even of natural phenomena plunge us into the depths of contradictory minutiae. What is more, statements of the boundaries and constituent conventions of literary periods, genres, and subgenres shift imperceptibly from the descriptive to the prescriptive mode; qualifiers such as "according to Aristotle" and "Greek" are dropped, the statement becoming "tragedy *is.* . . ." The process is perhaps inevitable. Seemingly inevitable, too, is the reading of an author through the conventions of the tradition in which he or she has been placed. Our questioning of the boundaries and conventions established by earlier readings of the novel of manners, our exposing the assumptions and values underlying those readings, is intended both to redefine and to reassess the novel of manners. Past discussions of these novels, as is true of our own, frequently reveal as much about literary traditions, about particular literary critics, *their* values, and *their* societies, as about the novels themselves. Redefinitions and revised literary histories—such as we are proposing here—are themselves restricted by their frame(s) of reference. Yet, by placing works in new or revised contexts, by altering the "windows" through which we observe the "familiar" (James, *Literary Criticism: French* 1075), they make a significant difference in whom, what, and how we read.

Notes

1. A number of the novels we are considering here have, however, been discussed under other rubrics, such as the domestic novel, the middle-class novel, and novels by women writers. See, for example, Colby's *Yesterday's Woman* (1974); Voss-Clesly's *Tendencies of Character Depiction in the Domestic Novels of Burney, Edgeworth, and Austen* (1979); Tomlinson's *The English Middle-Class Novel;* and Poovey's *The Proper Lady and the Woman Writer* (1984). Morgan's *The Rise of the Novel of Manners,* as the title suggests, focuses on precursors to the novel of manners.

2. Austen is thus the author we have chosen to treat in the first two essays, even though some of the Edgeworth novels that Janet Dunleavy discusses in her essay were published before Austen's and even alluded to by Austen in her novels (*Belinda,* for example, in *Northanger Abbey*).

3. Our source for most of the commentary of nineteenth-century reviewers and critics of Austen's work is B. C. Southam's *Jane Austen: The Critical Heritage,* parenthetically documented in our essay as *CH.*

4. For another discussion of Burney in the context of the novel of manners, see Voss-Clesly.

5. Austen may be recognized by most literary historians as a great writer, but they then consider her to be more than a novelist of manners. Even in Austen's case, however, the label "miniaturist" has stuck, creating the illusion that her novels are necessarily something less than those written by "serious" and "strong" masculine hands such as James's.

6. In *Literary Theory,* chapter 1, Terry Eagleton discusses the relationship between Leavis's "great tradition" and formalism.

7. See, for example, Karl's *The Adversary Literature* (1974); Gilbert and Gubar's *The Madwoman in the Attic* (1979); Newton's *Women, Power, and Subversion* (1981); Eagleton's *Literary Theory* (1983); and Poovey's *The Proper Lady and the Woman Writer.*

8. One should also note the illustration *A Political Discussion* (fig. 4), in which woman is present only as a photograph that overlooks the men rapt in heated conversation. That the British academic novel places male characters at the center—female characters, academically employed or not, are peripheral—is a function of both the class struggle that is portrayed and the sexist definition of that struggle. Compare, for example, any literary history of the 1930s: class battled class, but women were not seen as a class; they were simply not seen. See also B. Brothers's essay in this volume.

Figure 1. Ben Shahn (1898–1969), *Inside Looking Out*, 1953
*(Collection of the Butler Institute of American Art,
Youngstown, Ohio)*

1

Jane Austen and Psychological Realism: "What Does a Woman Want?"

Gloria Sybil Gross

"The great question . . . which I have not yet been able to answer, despite my thirty years of research into the feminine soul, is 'What does a woman want?'" (Jones 2:421). Freud's famous question might well be referred to Jane Austen, who, writing in the early nineteenth century, is generally esteemed as one of the original and most brilliant novelists of manners. Her works present fully imagined human beings with the rich texture of emotional life: her characters come alive to a degree not entirely attempted before by her eighteenth-century predecessors in the novel. Austen knew what women—and what men—want, and she traced the pattern of their souls, much as Freud did, through the concrete, direct experience of everyday life. A word, a gesture, a look, a tone of voice, these significant small details of social intercourse are the clues to the deepest sources of feeling. With an informed and attentive eye to human behavior, Austen exposed profound unconscious dynamics and their powerful influence upon conscious life. Her achievement attests to the remarkable congruity between the novel of manners and modern psychological realism, as they originated and developed in the late eighteenth and nineteenth centuries.

By the turn of the eighteenth century, the groundwork was already being laid for the new discipline that we call modern psychology. Deriving in large part from eighteenth-century empirical philosophy, in the tradition of John Locke, Bishop Berkeley, David Hartley, David Hume, and others, the new analysis of the mind was founded on the assumption that mental functioning could be known through observation and assessment of one's experience; hence, the emphases on examination of motives, on the association of ideas, and on attempts to find linkages between internal and external states. Following these directions, two fundamental hypotheses begin to take form: the principle of psychological determinism or causality—that in the mind, as in physical nature, nothing happens by chance or in a random way—and the proposition of the unconscious—that important mental processes take place, of which the individual him- or herself is unaware. Significantly, the novel of manners came into being in an inchoately modern world, secular and individualistic, affected by a zest for the immediate and experiential—this, in marked contrast to the old world view of supernatural and institutional agencies, dominated by transcendent authority. As people began to see themselves as they are, not as they ought to be, they also began to conceive of themselves as psychological rather than exclusively moral beings. Psychodynamic issues increasingly came to influence heretofore solely doctrinal forms in religion, politics, society, and philosophy.[1] An early novelist of manners, Jane Austen successfully grappled with the new concept of psychological realism as, more often than not, she radically defied conventional myths about marriage, sex, the family, friendship, and the like: she exploded the credence and dogma once taken for granted about these complex human relationships, and she did so in a manner thoroughly advanced for the times.

If Austen was significantly influenced by the eighteenth-century empirical tradition, perhaps her most celebrated intellectual hero was Samuel Johnson, her acknowledged favorite author in prose (Austen-Leigh 89). Himself a pioneer in the new psychological analysis of human nature, Johnson directed assiduous attention to the study of human character and the dimensions of an inner life, and it is very likely that he helped to inspire the psychodynamic texture of Austen's writings. Indeed, following the Austen heroine's long travail of mishap and adversity, one is often struck by affinities to Johnson's writings; his caveats against the "dangerous prevalence of imagination," his penetrating inquiries into hidden origins of emotion, his ardent pursuit of the truth about people.[2] Presumably, Austen knew the famous stricture about Richardson's *Clarissa*, that "there is always something which she prefers to truth" (Hill 1:297), for it seems to articulate her predominant analytical intent. Johnson's statement, contradicting the proposal that Clarissa was a "perfect heroine," is an important psychological inference, as he appears to recognize in Richardson's storyline the deeper level of self-evasion, i.e., the young woman's complicity in her own undoing.[3]

It is this profound awareness, or shrewd analytical faculty, that resounds so intensely in Austen's novels as she taps her characters' innermost being. A remarkable short piece from her collection of juvenilia seems to indicate an early predilection for psychological realism. Entitled "A Letter from a Young Lady, whose feelings being too strong for her Judgement led her into the commission of Errors which her Heart disapproved," the essay appears to be a spoof of popular sentimental palaver on human nature. But beneath the drollery and wit, one cannot help but sense the chilling coherent picture of severe psychopathology, replete with treachery, murderous rage, estrangement, and denial:

Many have been the cares and vicissitudes of my past life, my beloved Ellinor, and the only consolation I feel for their bitterness is that on a close examination of my conduct, I am convinced that I strictly deserved them. I murdered my father at a very early period of my Life, I have since murdered my Mother, and I am now going to murder my Sister. I have changed my religion so often that at present I have not an idea of any left. I have been a perjured witness in every public tryal for these last twelve years; and I have forged my own Will. In short there is scarcely a crime that I have not committed—But I am now going to reform. (*Minor Works* 175)

The "heroine" decides to reform because she has just helped Colonel Martin of the Horse Guards bilk his brother out of eight million pounds: "The Colonel in gratitude waited on me the next day with an offer of his hand—. / I am now going to murder my Sister. / Yours Ever, / Anna Parker" (176). Certainly here, in rudimentary form, are several of the psychological themes later refined and developed to become the high insignia of Austen's novels: familial discord; sadistic triumph; vicious, compulsive pursuit of selfish goals; topped off by coolly smug and comfortable self-deception. It is an astonishing glimpse into the human psyche by a young adolescent girl who was to become one of the foremost psychological realists in literature.

I wish now to turn to *Emma* (1816), perhaps of all the novels the most emotionally complex, by virtue of its stunning conceptual framework of an inward life. Austen's use of principles of psychological determinism and the unconscious in this mature work is one of the most remarkable analyses before Freud of psychodynamics and problems of human relationship.

For his conundrum at Box Hill, cheerful, shallow Mr. Weston asks and immediately answers, "What two letters of the alphabet are there, that express perfection? . . . M. and A.—Em—ma.—Do you understand?" (371; vol. 3, ch. 7). It is a scene of one of the more costly of Emma's painful reckonings, for she has just insulted Miss Bates, and she will be severely reprimanded by Mr. Knightley before returning home. For the only time in the story, she "felt the tears running down her cheeks almost all the way home, without being at any trouble to check them, extraordinary as they were" (376; vol. 3, ch. 7). This is a critical turning point in a story fraught with secrets, intrigue, riddles, and charades, a story in which people's motives are craftily hidden, often hardly known to themselves, let alone to the outside world. The characters in *Emma* dissemble famously, to greater and lesser degrees of detection: from flagrant, self-flattering, parading Mrs. Elton of the ubiquitous barouche-landau and Maple Grove connections, which, as far as we know, never materialize, and her *caro sposo*, Mr. Elton, a kind of gigolo *manqué* who might not be so bad had Emma not drawn him out, but who under her and Mrs. Elton's tutelage can only be more foolish and insipid than before; to more subtle, friendly, and charming Frank Churchill and aloof and reserved Jane Fairfax, whose masquerades fool everyone into thinking that Frank is in love with Emma and Jane is destined for service as a governess; to most opaque, gentle, kindly, infirm Mr. Woodhouse, whose plenitude of ailments assures him nearly complete dominion over his daughter, not to mention everyone else in his society—the Bateses, the Westons, the Knightleys, even Mr. Knightley—over whom he presides.

Speaking of Frank and Jane, and unwittingly of herself, Emma appears to sum up the situation in words that express the inner dynamics operating to greater and lesser incriminating degrees through each character: "What has it been but a system of hypocrisy and deceit,—espionage, and treachery?—To come among us with professions of openness and simplicity; and such a league in secret to judge us all!" (399; vol. 3, ch. 10). Mr. Knightley expresses the same, also when speaking of Frank Churchill, as he reflects on the evils of deluding oneself and others: "Playing a most dangerous game. . . . Always deceived in fact by his own wishes, and regardless of little besides his own convenience. . . . His own mind full of intrigue, that he should suspect it in others.—Mystery; Finesse—how they pervert the understanding!" (445–46; vol. 3, ch. 15). In *Emma,* no one is fully exempt from Mr. Knightley's charge, and certainly not the heroine, whom only silly Mr. Weston and her father could call "perfect." Emma's case, in fact, becomes the rather literal rendering of Johnson's criticism of Clarissa, that "there is always something which she prefers to truth." The other preferences lie deeply hidden, of course, and become accessible only if we follow the intricate chain of Emma's action in the world, of events thoroughly deterministic, as she carries out the wishes of her unconscious life. This deepest level of the heroine's soul, her innermost desires and fears, can be understood through her most important relationships: with her father, Mr. Woodhouse; her friend, Harriet Smith; and her lover, Mr. Knightley.

To live with Mr. Woodhouse, as the name might imply, is to remain barricaded from the outside world, in a kind of ritualized imprisonment. The strict observance of locking people in at Hartfield is Mr. Woodhouse's special care, and whenever reality in the form of hazardous weather, unsympathetic other people, and especially love and marriage threatens his devotions, as it were, he is sure to have it kept at bay. All of his friends and relations are at his service to suppress drafts, appetites, and themselves: a nice basin of thin gruel, a large fire in mid-summer, his own especial set around him, and Mr. Woodhouse is in his element. His particular objects are those who unhappily slip in and out of his purview: "poor Mrs. Weston" and "poor Isabella," neither of whom he ever gives up on detaining, even after marriage, and, of course, Emma. But he himself is the revered first object, the principal one to be guarded in the face of continue risk, while in turn he guards everyone else from the vicissitudes of life, much to the sacrifice of their personal growth and fulfillment. For in spite of all its protectiveness, Hartfield every so often gives us glimpses into real terrible loneliness, as Mr. Woodhouse and Emma sit unvisited and, for all they know, unloved. At one of her most depressed moments, when she fears the loss of Mr. Knightly, Emma seems almost to understand the implicit danger. Shut up in the house on a cold, rainy July afternoon with the ever-downcast, ever-inconsolable Mr. Woodhouse, Emma envisions the bleakest of futures:

> The weather affected Mr. Woodhouse, and he could only be kept tolerably comfortable by almost ceaseless attention on his daughter's side, and by exertions which had never cost her half so much before. It reminded her of their first forlorn tête-à-tête, on the evening of Mrs. Weston's wedding-day. . . . The prospect before her now, was threatening to a degree that could not be entirely dispelled—that might not be even partially brightened. If all took place that might take place among the circle of her friends, Hartfield must be comparatively deserted; and she left to cheer her father with the spirits only of ruined happiness. (422; vol. 3, ch. 12)

Emma cares for Mr. Woodhouse as for a helpless child, whose condition must always be watched closely. She assuages his nervous agitation, which on the surface appears most amusing: the horrors of nine at a dinner table, underboiled asparagus, precipitously flung-open windows and doors. But on a more serious level, the very life of Mr. Woodhouse depends upon Emma's attendance at Hartfield, a fact that Mr. Knightley understands; even he will not take her from her father. That Mr. Woodhouse requires constant attention lest he fall sick and die is an axiom of Emma's conscious as well as unconscious life. Her beloved father must ever be rescued, and what a burden for a young woman just entering the world, with compelling feelings and appetites of her own! It is a frustrating conflict, for she never can completely be rid of the object she must at once cherish and regret. The difficulties of managing Mr. Woodhouse are alluded to unwittingly by Isabella when, speaking of the irksome Mrs. Churchill to the party of her father's friends at Randalls, she remarks, "To be constantly living with an ill-tempered person, must be dreadful. It is what we happily have never known any thing of" (121; vol. 1, ch. 14). (No doubt her own husband's Mr. Woodhouse-like xenophobia is not exempt from the irony here). Emma herself comes closer to knowing what can only be deeply suppressed anger toward her father after she roundly insults Miss Bates, another Mr. Woodhouse-type personage, tedious and troublesome in her own way. Mr. Knightley upbraids her, "How could you be so unfeeling to Miss Bates?" (374; vol. 3, ch. 7), reminding her of duties incurred from earliest childhood. As she reflects upon the incident with increasing guilt, Emma's thoughts turn at once to her father: "As a daughter, she hoped she was not without a heart. She hoped no one could have said to her, 'How could you be so unfeeling to your father?' " (377; vol. 3, ch. 8). Clearly, Emma's unwonted cruelty is displaced from her father, for whom it is intended, to Miss Bates: he arouses her wrath and indignation, but it is a hostility she dare not own.

While her resentment is deeply concealed, Emma's love for her father is openly expressed in the playing of Mr. Woodhouse's favorite game, the mission of rescue. As over and over Emma saves her father from the dire trespasses of the outside world, she is rewarded and indeed seems most pleased to accept his doting adulation, his ascribing to her almost magical powers.[4] So it is that the loving relationship between them is established: in return for the pains of custody over Mr. Woodhouse, Emma acquires a kind of omnipotence. She is almightily and undeniably perfect in her father's eyes—the most beautiful, accomplished, clever, and delightful young woman alive. As she exults early on over her presumed matchmaking skills, here the marriage of Mrs. Weston, Mr. Woodhouse pays her his typical adoring tribute: "Ah! my dear, I wish you would not make matches and foretel things, for whatever you say always comes to pass" (12; vol. 1, ch. 1). On another occasion, reflecting on the previous evening's dinner party at Hartfield for Jane Fairfax and Mrs. and Miss Bates, Mr. Woodhouse vouches for Jane's good time, fondly observing to Mr. Knightley, "She must have found the evening agreeable, . . . because she had Emma" (171; vol. 2, ch. 3). The irony is not lost on Mr. Knightley, who has just reproved Emma for her cool feelings toward Jane. He knows of the rivalry between the two women, marked on Emma's side by envy of Jane's real achievements in art, music, literature, and personal elegance, all of which put Emma's own foolish affectations to shame. (At times Emma even comes dangerously close to an affinity with the egregious Mrs. Elton, a caricature of vulgar pride.) He replies in a tone that can only be semimocking, "True, sir; and Emma [had a good time], because she had Miss Fairfax" (171; vol. 2, ch. 3). Ever laboring to undo the fatuous idolization, Mr. Knightley particularly aims to deflate Emma's preposterous superiority, which she owes so integrally to her father. Mr. Woodhouse is the source of her elevation above the rest, but at the same time, of her exclusion from the rest, a difficult and painful predicament for any young woman. Emma has her father's worship, but at the price of enormous self-sacrifice, for she does not know her real self or other people.

This problem is well illustrated when Emma resolves to decline the Coles's dinner invitation on no firmer principles than her imaginary ascendancy: "Nothing should tempt *her* to go. . . . The Coles were very respectable in their way, but they ought to be taught that it was not for them to arrange the terms on which the superior families would visit them" (207; vol. 2, ch. 7). But upon reflecting that all of her friends will be there, and particularly handsome Frank Churchill, she is torn by indecision: even the prospect of "her being left in solitary grandeur . . . was but poor comfort" (208; vol. 2, ch. 7). Emma's grandiosity, so pathetic in spite of its ridiculousness, is the outcome of her relationship to her father. Giving almost all in exchange for magical dominion at Hartfield, she is bereft of real integrity and self-knowledge. She understands little of the conflicts, of the warring internal factions deep inside her, which erupt in frustrating external events to cause her sorrow and unhappiness.

Perhaps the aspect of herself that Emma understands least is her sexual needs, her natural desire for relationships with men. She protests that she will never marry, yet a twenty-year-old woman who specializes in "arch" and "saucy" looks, who teases and rather notoriously strings along the eligible young men of her circle, who concocts an elaborate series of love intrigues, seems little to know her real motives. Securely locked up at Hartfield with Mr. Woodhouse, in a strange way the kept as well as the keeper, Emma cannot return the amorous feelings she must inspire. She takes up Harriet Smith in order to help rid herself of these feelings, all the more uncomfortable as they find objects in Mr. Elton, Frank Churchill, and Mr. Knightley. She projects her sexual fantasies about these men onto her friend Harriet in order to avoid acknowledging them in herself:[5] thus she disowns powerful, unacceptable impulses by attributing them to another, to "a very pretty girl," who is "short, plump and fair, with a fine bloom, blue eyes, light hair, regular features, and a look of great sweetness" (23; vol. 1, ch. 3), in short, the proverbial milkmaid, the buxom gratification of every man's dream. (It is no coincidence that Harriet at last finds her rightful place on Mr. Martin's farm.) Emma represses the erotic side of her personality and adopts Harriet as a kind of surrogate who can freely indulge prurient interests. To Emma, Harriet's magnetism is inestimable, just as Emma must experience her own sexuality, albeit repressed. So it is that she blindly and necessarily sets up the imbroglios to come. Speaking of Harriet's irresistible charms, she says "playfully" to Mr. Knightley: "I know that such a girl as Harriet is exactly what every man delights in—what at once bewitches his senses and satisfies his judgment. Oh! Harriet may pick and choose. Were you, yourself, ever to marry, she is the very woman for you" (64; vol. 1, ch. 8).

When contemplating Harriet, Emma generally means herself—she is the very woman for Mr. Knightley, just as she is for Mr. Elton, for Frank Churchill, for who can predict how many others, in an implicitly erotic sense. But she cannot acknowledge these low feelings; and thus Harriet becomes her deputy, as it were, a fitting role for the younger woman, "the natural daughter of somebody," whose origins are shrouded in illegitimacy. Significantly, Emma feels vastly superior to Harriet, and it would be difficult to miss the real condescension in the endless "Miss Woodhouse-ing" and "Harriet-ing" of their ludicrous tête-à-têtes. But Emma believes she can raise the girl to her own high station, and with this in mind, she advises her little protégée to refuse Mr. Martin, whose offer of marriage she considers degrading. It is clear that Harriet must not be allowed to be Harriet, simply and naturally at home with her pretty little Welch cow at Abbey-Mill farm. The emblem of sexual desire and desirability, she cannot be set free to realize her true inclination, for to do so would betray the raw and shocking demands of physical appetite. And so Emma keeps Harriet to herself, professedly to elevate and dignify, much as she paints the portrait for Mr. Elton, all out of proportion. In Emma's mind, Harriet's only acceptable image is lofty and elegant, just as she imagines herself to transcend every influence of vulgar sensuality. But really Emma succumbs to the amorous "Harriet" within her, and through the agency of the little milkmaid, flirts audaciously with Mr. Elton, Frank Churchill, and even Mr. Knightley. None of them can help but take the bait, though there are mixed reactions as to what "Harriet" means. To inane Mr. Elton, the invitation is most attractive, but he later protests that he "never cared whether [Harriet] were dead or alive" (130; vol. 1, ch. 15), and to conceited Frank Churchill, likewise, the temptation is great, but he also pleads obliviousness, so wrapped up is he in his own selfish little world. It is only Mr. Knightley who can accept Harriet's true nature, in short, the fundamental need to love and be loved, and though initially somewhat stunned, he comes to admire her. To Emma, "his praise of Harriet, his concession in her favour, was peculiarly gratifying" (332; vol. 3, ch. 3), and she heartily accepts his sanction.

As Mr. Knightly proposes marriage to her, Emma is confronted once and for all by the elaborate charade and self-deception of her vicarious relationship to Harriet. Having worked herself into a frenzy for fear that Mr. Knightley loves Harriet, she now hears that he loves Emma herself, and that he has interpreted her fears of Harriet as rejection:

> While he spoke, Emma's mind was most busy, and, with all the wonderful velocity of thought, had been able—and yet without losing a word—to catch and comprehend the exact truth of the whole; to see that Harriet's hopes had been entirely groundless, a mistake, a delusion, as complete a delusion as any of her own—that Harriet was nothing; that she was every thing herself; that what she had been saying relative to Harriet had been all taken as the language of her own feelings; and that her agitation, her doubts, her reluctance, her discouragement, had been all received as discouragement from herself. (430–31; vol. 3, ch. 13)

Here is the culmination of some astonishing psychological insights, for we see Emma, probably for the first time, without Harriet's cover, open to the effects of her own powerful sexual feelings. Mr. Knightley wants her and not her surrogate, and he in fact reads correctly "her agitation, her doubts, her reluctance, her discouragement." Ostensibly, she has been afraid that he would ask for Harriet and is relieved that he asks for herself; but on the deeper level, her distress comes from real fears of liberating the "Harriet" she must now own, truly the erotic, the passionate, the daemonic side of loving. That Mr. Knightley wants this, that he cherishes her most outrageous, vulnerable self, makes him Emma's perfect lover.

"What does a woman want?" Why, Mr. Knightley, of course. And so Emma accepts him, calmly and graciously, saying "just what she ought. . . . A lady always does" (431; vol. 3, ch. 13). The absolute rightness of the moment would seem to belie all the difficulty, the real vicissitudes of their courtship. And indeed, preying on Emma's mind are the two other major relationships of her life as yet unresolved: her father at Hartfield and Harriet still at large. We are reminded: "Seldom, very seldom, does complete truth belong to any human disclosure; seldom can it happen that something is not a little disguised, or a little mistaken; but where, as in this case, though the conduct is mistaken, the feelings are not, it may not be very material" (431; vol. 3, ch. 13). If Emma's conduct has led her astray, then her feelings bring her back to the man able to accept the full range of her womanliness. With Mr. Knightley, she need not pretend, for he knows her intimately: from the anguished caretaking of fidgety old Mr. Woodhouse; to the bungling supervision of Harriet; to the madcap flirtation with Frank Churchill; to the desperate slap at poor Miss Bates. It is ever Mr. Knightley's role to help Emma out of these difficulties, and it is clear that her life would be intolerable without him. Indeed, he is the only one who faithfully and entirely attends to Emma, herself the attendant on far too many others. At her most poignant self, she appears to be virtually the sole provider either for those who turn out not to need her at all—Frank Churchill, Jane Fairfax, even the Westons and John Knightleys—or for those who need her too much—Harriet and her father, together with the frail, lost denizens with whom he associates. As befits his name, Mr. Knightley rescues Emma from a life that could only grow more forlorn and more oppressive, as she tries to take control over the increasingly uncontrollable machinery of events she puts in motion.

In an early conversation with Mrs. Weston, Mr. Knightley assesses the state of Emma's feelings, that is, before she and Harriet conspire to pursue Mr. Elton, Frank Churchill, and indeed Mr. Knightley himself: "There is an anxiety, a curiosity in what one feels for Emma. I wonder what will become of her! . . . It would not be a bad thing for her to be very much in love with a proper object. I should like to see Emma in love, and in some doubt of a return; it would do her good. But there is nobody hereabouts to attach her; and she goes so seldom from home" (41; vol. 1, ch. 5). During this same dialogue, when he disapproves of Emma's growing friendship with Harriet and regrets the peculiar dominion at Hartfield, Mr. Knightley, in effect, sums up the principal failure of Emma's life: the lack of a truly loving relationship. He senses and identifies the barriers to such in Harriet and, more discreetly, in Mr. Woodhouse. As he soon must see it, Mr. Knightley's mission is to break through these barriers and rescue the maiden entrapped within. But seldom was there a maiden so loath as Emma, for her defenses are formidable. Only when Mr. Knightley seems to be slipping away does she understand that she is living as in a stifling, soulless prison, and she desperately lets down the guard. Thus, Mr. Knightley's prediction comes true: Emma falls in love when she is most humbled.

Emma's humility does not come easily, and she blunders through many a compromising escapade before giving up her grandiose delusions. The successive fiascoes in trying to outwit, outshine, and manipulate her peers wreck her fancied superiority, her goddesslike pose in the face of real people and real life.

All but abandoned when everyone else pairs off, or seems to—Mr. and Mrs. Weston, Mr. and Mrs. Elton, Jane Fairfax and Frank Churchill, Harriet and Mr. Knightley—Emma confronts the bleak prospect of having no one for herself. Only now does she throw off the absurd prerogatives of controlling those around her, of directing and assisting their every move. She realizes that she needs to be supported herself, not interminably supporting, and she needs to excel in one man's eyes, not every man's. In a flash of insight, Emma understands Mr. Knightley's tender and exclusive attentions to her, and she knows that he loves her:

> Till now that she was threatened with its loss, Emma had never known how much of her happiness depended on being *first* with Mr. Knightley, first in interest and affection.—Satisfied that it was so, and feeling it her due, she had enjoyed it without reflection; and only in the dread of being supplanted, found how inexpressibly important it had been. . . . She had herself been first with him for many years past. She had not deserved it; she had often been negligent or perverse, slighting his advice, or even wilfully opposing him, insensible of half his merits, and quarrelling with him because he would not acknowledge her false and insolent estimate of her own—but still, from family attachment and habit, and through excellence of mind, he had loved her, and watched over her from a girl, with an endeavour to improve her, and an anxiety for her doing right, which no other creature had at all shared. In spite of all her faults, she knew she was dear to him; might she not say, very dear? (415; vol. 3, ch. 12)

That Emma loves Mr. Knightley and always has is the ultimate secret in a history dominated by pretense and suppression of genuine human emotion. She experiences love as removing all barriers, as complete accessibility: thus, she surrenders the noxious guise of hypocrisy and evasion to trust in herself and to meet her natural responsibility: "High in the rank of her most serious and heartfelt felicities, was the reflection that all necessity of concealment from Mr. Knightley would soon be over. The disguise, equivocation, mystery, so hateful to her to practise, might soon be over. She could now look forward to giving him that full and perfect confidence which her disposition was most ready to welcome as a duty" (475; vol. 3, ch. 18). In this context, Emma's "duty" is the fidelity and respect that is owed to herself. Mr. Knightley has successfully stormed the citadel, and Emma is free. Even the lurking dragons of Mr. Woodhouse and Harriet are dispelled as Mr. Knightley sacrifices his stronger person to the former and sees that the latter is safely tucked away where she belongs. By living at Hartfield, he will assume the guardianship of Mr. Woodhouse, and as for "Harriet," the voluptuous, tantalizing alternate-Emma, he places her at his own Abbey-Mill farm to be gratified at last. Mr. Knightley reaches Emma on the deepest level of her emotional life, setting right the intricate internal discord that has led to her folly and liberating her most deserving self. She cannot but love him.

In psychodynamic terms, the plot and characterization of Jane Austen's other major novels, *Sense and Sensibility* (1811), *Pride and Prejudice* (1813), *Mansfield Park* (1814), and *Persuasion* (1818), appear to share similar organizing themes related to unconscious mental processes.[6] As in *Emma*, we are led to discover the pattern of an inward life, that is, the heroine's deeply suppressed unconscious wishes projected upon external reality, much to her own cost and sorrow. In each case, these wishes are found to be the effect of stifling, distressful family relationships. It is inherently a burden of existence that Mr. Woodhouse or any of his manifold counterparts, often more formidable, act as the official saboteurs of powerful human emotions, and so it is that the suppression of rage, sexual desire, envy, and the like leads to severe conflict and misdirection of normal aims and instincts. Generally, the problematic family members in Austen's novels are, at best, dead (Mrs. Woodhouse, Mrs. Elliot, Mr. Henry Dashwood); at middlemost, self-centered (Mr. Woodhouse, Aunt Bertram) or foolish (Mrs. Dashwood, Mrs. Bennet) or remote (Uncle Bertram, Mr. Bennet); and, at worst, cruel (Mr. Elliot, Aunt Norris). While Emma, Elinor and Marianne Dashwood, Elizabeth Bennet, Fanny Price, or Anne Elliot may secretly resent, even reject, the precepts of incompetent parental authorities, she is at the same time subject to their arbitrary rule. Moreover, in the peculiar bargain that has been struck, she becomes the caretaker of seriously flawed, rather weak-minded specimens of failure and unhappiness, as her nobler spirit is offered up, as it were, to the caprice and wretchedness it is her duty to assuage.

Austen's heroines labor under continual agitation and duress that would shatter less sturdy souls: Elinor and Marianne suffer varying degrees of chagrin and remorse for their mother's lack of good judgment and romantic folly, particularly as she pushes the latter into the arms of the reprobate Willoughby. While Elinor cautions her sister against increasing involvement and indiscretion, "Mrs. Dashwood entered into all their feelings [Marianne and Willoughby's] with a warmth which left her no inclination for checking this excessive display of them. To her it was but the natural consequence of a strong affection in a young and ardent mind" (*Sense and Sensibility* 54; vol. 1, ch. 11). Elizabeth cringes during the famous supper scene at Netherfield, while her mother rattles on with mounting gaucherie about the would-be acquisition of Bingley's fortune for Jane (and rather incidentally, Bingley along with it), and her father sits amused and detached. The blundering antics of the rest of the family, compounded by the haughty superiority and critical eye of Mr. Darcy, are such that "Elizabeth blushed and blushed again with shame and vexation" (*Pride and Prejudice* 100; vol. 1, ch. 18). Fanny is mortified and abused throughout her young life by the patently malignant Aunt Norris, always brandishing her vicious charges and reminding everyone of the girl's humble origins. When Fanny begs to be excused from the raucous private theatricals at Mansfield, Aunt Norris retaliates: "I shall think her a very obstinate, ungrateful girl, if she does not do what her aunt and cousins wish her—very ungrateful indeed, considering who and what she is" (*Mansfield Park* 147; vol. 1, ch. 15). Anne trembles at her father's tyrannical selfishness and callous neglect of all but his own empty little affairs. Of his stony-hearted reaction to her past unsuccessful engagement to Captain Wentworth, we are told, "Sir Walter, on being applied to, without actually withholding his consent, or saying it should never be, gave it all the negative of great astonishment, great coldness, great silence, and a professed resolution of doing nothing for his daughter" (*Persuasion* 26; vol. 1, ch. 4). And of course Emma ever teeters on the brink of disaster lest her dear father's phobic universe be invaded. Even the welcome company of their own especial set is fraught with difficulty. Considering Mr. John Knightley's occasional ill-humor, for example, Emma nervously anticipates the dire effects on her father of "a sharp retort equally ill bestowed. It did not often happen; for Mr. John Knightley had really a great regard for his father-in-law; and generally a strong sense of what was due to him; but it was too often for Emma's charity, especially as there was all the pain of apprehension frequently to be endured, though the offence came not" (*Emma* 93; vol. 1, ch. 11).

If the Austen heroine is systematically enmeshed and enthralled by a troubled family life, here also are the origin and development of internal discord, and thus we discern the psychologically deterministic pattern of present difficulties. Unable to satisfy compelling human needs, the heroine expresses frustration by any number of evasive maneuvers: psychosomatic illness, phobic isolation, paranoia, and vain and foolish strategies to control others. Moreover, as the chief of her deprivations is sexual, so it is that she becomes compromised to varying degrees by a dangerously erotic young man—Willoughby, Wickham, Henry Crawford, William Elliot, Frank Churchill. With the likes of these, any hope of serious attachment can only bode more sorrow and unhappiness. It seems a desperate dilemma: on the one side, complete, if short-lived sexual bliss, followed by the necessary falling off of affection, by infidelity, betrayal, and eventual abandonment and loss; on the other side, continued toleration of increasingly intolerable circumstances. The latter choice, in effect, embodies the Austen heroine's celebrated "self-command," which analytically suggests radical suppression of all but overwhelming primary instincts and emotions, a condition inevitably leading to serious impairment.

In the midst of these equally bleak and ill-favored prospects, the hero appears on the scene, in a mythic sense, as it were, to redeem what could only come to intense grief. Colonel Brandon, Edward Ferrars, Mr. Darcy, Edmund Bertram, Captain Wentworth, and Mr. Knightley all reach their respective heroines on the deepest level of consciousness as, Perseus-like, they break the chains that bind these women to grotesque inner demons, while they provide the loving acceptance and passionate commitment so desperately craved. It is a supreme and far-reaching attempt at ordering not only the individual but also the collective psyche, the society itself, as each reflects the other through Austen's remarkably modern psychological vision of human life. During one of the most deeply moving scenes in all the novels, Anne Elliot, the only heroine with a "past," and perhaps for this reason the most desperately alone and pitiable, receives a final note from Captain Wentworth, and we are told, "On the contents of that letter depended all which this world could do for her!" (*Persuasion* 237; vol. 2, ch. 11). The profound reverberations of that moment and the next, which joyfully makes known a "true attachment and constancy among men" (237), strike to the very heart of the novel of manners. Anne is at last to be fulfilled by her marriage to Captain Wentworth, and the event, in turn, fulfills our own need for moral order, intelligibility, and the integrity of life. Here are the ideological assumptions of the novel of manners, fully articulated through the special province it takes as its own, the individual coming into accord with the society.

Generating unique interest in exploring and utilizing the new psychological realism, the great nineteenth-century novel of manners attempted to make sense of pictures of everyday life by finding the hidden motivations, the interior chains of causality, that influence people to behave as they do.[7] Moreover, the genre helped bridge the gap between the old moral-absolutist and the new experiential-ist-psychological worlds, as we apprehend moral order in analytical terms. We perceive the rudiments of a scale of psychical development as individuals attain greater and lesser degrees of self-knowledge and relationship to the outside world. Not least in a tribute to Jane Austen's genius is her ability to create and put to use such a scale for the characterizations in her novels. In each case, we mark distinctly ascending levels of personal fulfillment and social adjustment: from the dangerously erotic young man's wild, unregulated impulses and rather total disregard of everyone around him, to the opacity and unreliability of impaired parental authorities, to the waiflike insecurity and morbid isolation of the heroine, to the almost perfect self-respect and trustworthiness of those who provide genuinely loving support and hope for the future.

Unlike many of her eighteenth-century predecessors in the novel, Austen is not interested in characters' moral-punitive ordeals, in their suffering physical abuse or vicious reproach for the consequences of their so-called "evil" acts. In contrast to, say, the heroes and heroines of Richardson, Fielding, Smollett, Mackenzie, or Radcliffe, Austen's characters' real punishment or reward, as the case may be, is just being themselves, and this is a thoroughly modern point of view. If Jane Austen's heroines get "what a woman wants"—what any person wants—it is to come closer into accord with self and with society; in effect, to see the error of their self-destructive ways, to be amenable to change, and thereby to move up the scale of psychic development. Only with this goal can they partake of the richest possibilities for personal freedom, higher understanding, and the pleasures of love.

Figure 2. Junius Brutus Stearns (1810–85), *The Marriage of Washington*, 1849 *(Collection of the Butler Institute of American Art, Youngstown, Ohio)*

Notes

1. For a helpful discussion of the origins of modern psychological principles in eighteenth-century empirical philosophy, see Keener, particularly 15–31, "The Chain of Being, the Chain of Events, and the Chain of Becoming." Keener writes of the eighteenth-century "psychologized" world:

    The truly knowable chain of becoming is the chain of mental processes in the knower. The project of a science of man based upon observation of his behavior as it really is has turned into the project of a science of the enchainment of events in the mind, that enchaining a process with its own natural series, its own proper sequences of causes and effects, its own principles of change. . . . The ancient counsel "Know Thyself" has first acquired unprecedented urgency and then inexplicable complexity. (23)

2. The affinities between Austen and Johnson have been often remarked, from relationships of moral philosophy, to satiric technique, to rhetorical style. For specific commentary, see, for example, Bradbrook and Scholes.

3. Ian Watt's classic discussion of Johnson's criticism of *Clarissa* explains the "truth" as Clarissa's sexual feeling for Lovelace, which she dares not show (228). As I intend to suggest, sexual feeling is one of several significant latent themes in Austen's novels.

4. Paris also traces Emma's "perfectionism" and "narcissism" to the relationship with her father and their peculiar bargain: her catering to his weakness in exchange for the status of perfect daughter (81–83).

5. Fleishman (249–51) takes a similar position, though I would not go as far as he does to suggest a "homosexual component" in Emma's projection.

6. Though it shares certain psychological features with the other novels, I have excluded *Northanger Abbey* from the following discussion, in view of its chiefly parodical intent.

7. It seems natural to try to locate the analytical context for Austen's novels in her own time. This essay suggests certain principles about the psychological study of character through the traditional medium of classical psychoanalysis, itself an outgrowth of late eighteenth- and nineteenth-century epistemology. The "new psychology," originating in eighteenth-century empirical philosophy and culminating in the Freudian Age, was clearly understood and utilized by Austen, who frequently acknowledged a high regard for some of its early leading exponents, including Johnson, Hume, Sterne, Richardson, Burney, and others. For a more extensive discussion of the historical and philosophical origins of modern psychology, with special reference to Austen, see Keener (243–307) and Jean Hagstrum. In his book on Austen, John Halperin specifically discusses *Emma's* "psychological" aspects as deeply rooted in an eighteenth-century background (267–78).

    Readers interested in exploring current developments in feminist as well as in French neo-Freudian and neo-Freudian feminist literary theory as applied to Austen may look into the intriguing analyses in Sandra Gilbert and Susan Gubar and in Joseph Litvak. The former discuss Austen's "subversion" of the repressive ideology her novels seem to endorse and note that her characters reclaim authority by asserting their "irrepressible interiority" and their "belief in female subjectivity" (179). The latter, recalling the Lacanian model of a feminist antilogocentric discourse in which female sexuality disrupts the tyranny of unitary meaning and logocentric discourse, finds Austen at her most subversive when her characters are seen in an "endless circuit of fiction, interpretation, and desire, with its dynamic and reciprocal relations between men and women" (771).

2

Jane Austen's Garrulous Speakers: Social Criticism in *Sense and Sensibility, Emma,* and *Persuasion*

Marylea Meyersohn

Although no one really knows what the novel of manners is, it is universally acknowledged that its chief practitioner is Jane Austen. She would have liked the irony, that she was writing something for which there is no precise definition. Perhaps she would have accepted Trilling's notion that the novel of manners takes society as its "field of research" and the development of individual character as its object, although heaven knows what she would have made of its being "an indication of the direction of man's soul" (205). Surely, it was the direction of woman's soul that interested her. Surely, she was demonstrating how women could, as Frank Bradbrook has pointed out, live in "inferior" society—one of the chief topics of the novel of manners—and finding exactly the right literary techniques to indicate the relationship of the individual and society.

Tony Tanner has called her overriding concern "the nature of true utterance" (*Jane Austen* 6), and indeed the full weight of meaning in Austen is carried by speech.[1] The dialogues of Austen's characters, therefore, offer remarkable insights into Austen's beliefs about the social function of rational discourse to enhance civility. Among the many grammatical or linguistic markers of speech that Austen uses, speech length lends itself particularly well to dialogic analysis. In general, Austen is biased against wordy speakers in all her novels save *Persuasion* (which is different at any rate from the others in many ways), and she uses garrulity as an example of irrational social discourse. Her garrulous speakers destroy social happiness, and their words, not merely idiosyncratic, not merely single comic voices, indicate systematic distortions in communication. I should like to observe Austen at work on the problem of the right and appropriate number of words for the social context, by examining the speeches of characters who speak at length—over 250 words in a single speech—in *Sense and Sensibility* and *Emma*. In addition, I should like to note some changes in the uses of the long speech in *Persuasion*.

What we find when we examine the long speeches of both men and women is the language of gender definition: that is, speakers at length are *stereotypically* masculine or feminine; they do not represent the mixing that Austen so loved in human nature (*Northanger Abbey* 200; vol. 2, ch. 10).[2] Men who speak at length are usually pompous or overbearing; women who speak at length are vulgar or dependent. We hear them, although they do not hear themselves, as the author's parodic presentation of male or female speech undilutedly conventional. Particularly in the earlier novels, *Northanger Abbey* and *Sense and Sensibility*, we find the male monologue that Austen is mimicking. The long utterances of General Tilney, John Thorpe, and Henry Tilney all ring out as one form or another of male "presentation self"; Colonel Brandon, Edward Ferrars, and John Willoughby are variations on the same, although *Sense and Sensibility* will present at the conclusion of the novel a conventional female voice in Marianne Dashwood.[3] In *Emma,* Austen will take up the "idle (or powerless) discourse" of the female voices, creating that garrulous list—Harriet Smith, Miss Bates, Mrs. Elton, stereotypes of female speakers as timid maids, poor spinsters, vulgar wives.[4] In effect, Austen derides in males their abuse of linguistic power through the overproduction of words, and she derides in females their absence of linguistic power, again through the overproduction of words.

The long speeches of males in Austen, with few exceptions, do not bond the speaker to the hearer; they alienate, and another voice is heard beneath the speaker's: that of the author who has entered into her own dialogic contact with the reader, to demonstrate the literary uses of boring speakers. What is missing from the scenes in which men make long speeches is the proper condition for discourse, what has been envisioned by Jürgen Habermas in "Towards a Theory of Communicative Competence" as "the ideal speech situation," which has no requirement save reciprocity and freedom from constraint. Since men and women rarely have the same chance to initiate and perpetuate discourse, ideal speech situations between the sexes occur in Austen only in the few happy unions, the Crofts, for example, and between some of the heroines and their future husbands, those whose marriages seem especially blessed linguistically: the Darcys, the Knightleys, and the Wentworths. Men who talk more frequently and at greater length are always a source of ridicule in Austen, even such husbands-to-be as bewildered Edward Ferrars, adorable Henry Tilney, or the mentor, Edmund Bertram. The men from whom Austen's heroines can expect a reasonably equal—and a reasonably passionate—relationship, on the other hand, learn to use vocabularies equal in length and assertion to those of their women.

For the true range of male eloquence, we must turn to *Sense and Sensibility* and its language-display texts: Brandon, Ferrars, and Willoughby.[5] Colonel

Brandon, who describes himself correctly as an "awkward narrator" (204; vol. 2, ch. 9), is the maker of the longest speeches in the novel. Austen offers an extraordinary irony in the length and breadth of his self-disclosures. Male speakers are traditionally held to be chary of self-disclosure; it is part of their masculinity—part, indeed, of the "true manly style." For Brandon and Edward Ferrars to disclose themselves is a way for Austen to satirize them, demasculinize them, since males' inexpressiveness is held to be part of their power.[6] Brandon is a supreme narcissist. He will give, he says, a "short account of himself" (205; vol. 2, ch. 9), and six pages of remarkable self-aggrandizement follow; he tells repeatedly how *he* has suffered, how pained *he* has been in witnessing the sufferings of others—"What I endured in so beholding her" (207; vol. 2, ch. 9). He deprecates his role and his importance and yet manages to be in the forefront of the story he tells. Colonel Brandon cannot tell a story straight, which is not necessarily a major offense in storytelling since the discursive or shapeless mode is attractive and often indicates truthfulness, but the way he tells the story modifies and lessens the tragedy and the suffering of the two Elizas and of Marianne, too.[7]

The real story beneath Brandon's seduced-and-abandoned plot is a story about rivalries among men. Beside it, the sufferings of women pale. "[I]mperfectly have I discharged my trust!" (211; vol. 2, ch. 9), he says, but he does not seem quite to believe himself. (Does he expect Elinor to contradict him, as a deferential womanly gesture in conversation?) His story is a ritualistically delivered tale of how men treat women, as seducers or protectors like Brandon himself; the women themselves have no lives to speak of except to be spoken of. They are objects of fraternal, oedipal warfare (Brandon and his brother and his symbolic brother Willoughby), but the men have all returned "unwounded" (211; vol. 2, ch. 9) from the wars; only the women have scars.

Indeed, women do not have stories to be told. Throughout the novel, Elinor Dashwood guards her secrets, and her silences indicate her "sense." Austen rewards her linguistic behavior and systematically punishes her sister Marianne's excesses of speech, which derive from her absence of "self-command." Therefore, it is particularly interesting to see that Marianne's only truly lengthy speech comes after she has learned *not* to express herself directly, not to tell the truth of her feelings. She broods over feelings in a silence that "gave more pain to her sister than could have been communicated by the most open and most frequent confessions of them" (212; vol. 2, ch. 9).

Marianne's long speech (345–46; vol. 3, ch. 10) arises out of her rebirth after sickness. She has been "deprogrammed," as it were, and her words strike us as the mea culpa of the redeemed sinner. Her long speech is a female confessional, with a female model of expiation—withdrawal from the world. Here, Austen seems to suggest two opposing lines of thought. On the one hand, she is suggesting that women who talk in lengthy monologues lose their female integrity. On the other hand, she confounds us by punishing Marianne for the extraordinary breadth of her desires and demonstrates that Marianne remains excessive to the end. Even her mea culpas are excessive; they are expressions of the same narcissism that colors the utterances of Brandon or Willoughby. Narcissism, therefore, is sometimes male and sometimes female. Still, we have a subversive message here as well: women who take up the male monologue form—except to give information—are doomed.

Willoughby's long speeches—narrative and confessional—are not boring. His description of himself and his folly (320–24; vol. 3, ch. 8) is interrupted, actually, by some sizable responses from his listener, Elinor. In effect, he displays a narcissism appropriate to his physical attractiveness. What he wants of Elinor, he says, is very modest actually (not the total acceptance that Colonel Brandon seems to demand): that she should find him guilty by "one degree less than [she] do[es] now" (319; vol. 3, ch. 8) and not that she should think better of him when she has heard him out. He persuades her that he is not diabolical but, rather, the product of his society. When Austen wishes to forgive personal flaws, she often invokes society: an inadequate education, a vain and extravagant world, the wearing down of the spirits of the weak. Willoughby was not born to be poor, but he has expensive tastes; thus, his villainy.

The form of Willoughby's narrative wins him some measure of expiation. He speaks with warmth. The other male speakers are for the most part listless and when they do exert themselves have the vitality not of warmth but of agitated depression. The flow of Willoughby's discourse is what distinguishes it from Brandon's, which lacks the true verbal stream; Willoughby is "feeling" what he is saying. Although, like Elinor, we grow impatient for his departure, it is not out of boredom. He animates the story he tells by his physical presence. His discourse is alive because he describes the processes by which relationships between men and women grow or wither, not a boring topic to Austen. We do, indeed, hear "the whole of the story," but it is told by a character who had a chance to become good and lost that chance, a far better story than Brandon's. His "story" interests Austen; it is Henry Crawford's story, the story of the possible regeneration of a Don Juan. Brandon's narrative, on the other hand, is an attempt to reconstruct the past to his own historical advantage. The reason there is no flow to Brandon's discourse is that he must "pause" to repress the hidden in his narrative (his relation to his brother). His construction of reality adds up to verbal failure because the length of the speech cannot hide the psychology of his motives.

There are some correctives in this novel to women's listening to men: (1) Elinor's free indirect discourse; and (2) the presence of two women makers of long speeches. The latter are such an unusual pair that we learn something of the talking-listening conflicts of the novel through their speeches: that female vulgarians, in this case Mrs. Jennings and Miss Steele, have a better chance of being listened to than overly genteel males do—Austen's deconstruction of sense over sensibility. These women speak out when they have a mind to and seem to represent a view of sense and silence that modifies Elinor's.

Mrs. Jennings's tale describes the engagement of Edward and Lucy (258–60; vol. 3, ch. 1). It is an interesting form of reporting—kindly meant and wrong, with that paratactic quality that Austen's women have when they talk without being stopped (cf. Miss Bates). The words do not move along a straight plot line, and yet the basic thread is maintained to inform and elaborate the message: money is not important in a marriage if one of the partners is willing to help out, or if one of the partners' mothers can help out, an accommodated view of marriage coming out of Mrs. Jennings's own experience. The tale is at the same time gossip at its best: a revealing picture of the John Dashwoods at home, of the relationship between the Steele girls, with delicious details, for example, the Harley Street physician being called in to minister to hysterics, a kind of portrait of marriage à la mode out of Hogarth. It has its full share of "fragmentation," fillers to keep the conversation going and questions to draw the hearer into the narrative—"Could you have believed such a thing possible?" (258; vol. 3, ch. 1). Mrs. Jennings's words are not narcissistic presentations of self, and although she misreports the truth, her compassion and lack of avarice mark her for the future a reliable moral witness. Her long speech stands in direct contrast to John Dashwood's version of the Ferrars-Steele connection, a soft-hearted description of the events versus a hard-hearted version; neither is quite right, but the female version is livelier to read than the male version, and Mrs. Jennings is not presented as a bore.

The real story gets out because Miss Nancy Steele cannot keep a secret; this sister talks too much—the comic inversion of Marianne's expressiveness, as Lucy Steele mimics the silences of Elinor. Miss Steele, however, controls several full pages, which, despite their usage errors, tell a real story, as a comic turn. The tale must be so, she says, because she heard him say it all. She gives a kind of below-stairs version of true love, authenticated by her eavesdropping, as the starcrossed lovers pledge fidelity to one another in the next room (274–76; vol. 3, ch. 12).

Edward Ferrars, on the other hand, is boring because he has only one story to tell: how it was that he fell for Lucy Steele. It is the only thing that has ever happened to him (all we need him for, of course, since as the novel suggests several times, once in the mouth of Robert Ferrars, "want of employment" led him into a too-early erotic life). Without a profession, he had nothing to do but make love. In his confessional, Edward is not very likeable because he blames women for his foolishness: first his mother, for not providing him with a career, and then Lucy, for bewitching him when he was at loose ends. His self-examining speeches, like Brandon's, stand in contrast to the self-examination of Elinor. Can we really believe what Austen tells us about the conversations of "lovers"

(363–64; vol. 3, ch. 13) when we consider his conversation? No wonder they were "neither of them quite enough in love to think that three hundred and fifty pounds a-year would supply them with the comforts of life" (369; vol. 3, ch. 13).

Our last long speaker is Robert Ferrars, the General Tilney of *Sense and Sensibility*. He laces his talk with details on rooms, food, furniture, and name-dropping and becomes so boring a narrator that Elinor does not think he even deserves "the compliment of rational opposition" (252; vol. 2, ch. 14).

The one person who does not make long speeches in *Sense and Sensibility* is Lucy Steele, although a good deal of critical interest has gone into looking at her conversation for its vulgarity and ungrammaticality.[8] Still, for a girl with an unsure grasp of the past participle and of the uses of the relative pronoun, she does very well, indeed—the one figure in the novel with upward social mobility. She does much better than other parvenues, Isabella Thorpe or Harriet Smith, although her language is worse than theirs. Lucy is not entirely reprehensible, and "Lucy Steele's English" may mean rather less after her marriage to Robert Ferrars: perhaps her usages will become "hypercorrect." The speech of wives clinging uncertainly to newly acquired status is always "genteel."[9]

Female monologuists abound in *Emma,* including the heroine herself, whose self-talk provides the coda to the major events of the novel. The free associations of Miss Bates, the tales of Miss Smith's adventures at Ford's establishment, the social snobberies of Mrs. Elton (Lucy Steele grown up?) provide a spectrum of female conversational stereotypes just as earlier works exhibit male patterns.

The males in *Emma* are rarely lengthy monologuists, not even Mr. Woodhouse. For example, Mr. Knightley never speaks at length. Even his famous admonishment of Emma for her rudeness to Miss Bates—the "were she your equal" speech (*Emma* 375; vol. 3, ch. 7)—contains not quite 250 words despite its extraordinary effect of silencing Miss Woodhouse. There are, of course, male conversational stereotypes in *Emma:* There is Mr. John Knightley, the grumpy voice of reason, waiting perhaps for a "very true, my love" (113; vol. 1, ch. 13) from his wife. (The other women characters in *Emma* who say "very true" are Mrs. Elton, Harriet Smith, and Miss Bates, dependent women all.) And there is Mr. Woodhouse, the elderly tyrant of drafts and soups. Despite their differences, however, Mr. Knightley and Mr. Woodhouse talk about the same things. Neither of them wishes to leave the house on a snowy evening to visit other people or to venture outside the family group. Mr. Knightley will perhaps grow into Mr. Woodhouse; he has, of course, a certain "penetration" or insight that Mr. Woodhouse may never have had, but, still, they talk about the same things. Too much domesticity, perhaps, infects the speeches of both

London lawyers and hypochondriacal country squires. The satire lies not so much in speech length, therefore, as in speech content.

But how the women do run on. We have in *Emma* examples of what are held to be stereotypical female language-display texts: fillers, disfluency, illogical speech, unfinished sentences, statements as questions, stroking of the partner, introduction of topics.[10] What the women's speeches reveal is the speaker's rank within the social system; all these women speakers rank below Emma, and they struggle to communicate with her since they are dependent upon her. Emma, so sensitive to Frank Churchill's inability to speak up frankly to Mrs. Churchill, upon whom he is "dependent," does not, of course, recognize her own abuse of linguistic power over dependent women. One of the marks of dependency is clumsiness in using the rules of conversation; these women have trouble taking turns, and they lack the power of verbal irony. They do not hear themselves.

These three examples of distorted communication—Harriet, Miss Bates, Mrs. Elton—represent "ideal types" of female roles: the maid, the spinster, and the wife. (The other wives in the novel are related to Emma, Isabella, and Mrs. Weston, and although they are parodied, they are too close to the Emma circle to be used as types.) Miss Smith, Miss Bates, and Mrs. Elton are the very figures that haunt male images of women's discourse. Their words also serve the special function of making Emma's discourse look even more like "male" discourse in its wit, brevity, intelligence, and ability to abstract, to reinforce the reader's uncomfortable awareness of Emma's alienation from other women. These women will remain frozen in their female role assignments. They demonstrate anxiety of status, and their lengthy repertoires are "discourse strategies" against that anxiety.

When Harriet, the timid maid, describes at length her meetings with Robert Martin and his sisters at Ford's, we see the double bind in which she finds herself (177–79; vol. 2, ch. 3). To have to describe the encounter to Emma is a fearful burden. The main metaphor she uses here is entrapment, referring of course to both Emma and the Martins. She cannot get away, she says; she must wait out the rain. The main actor in the scene is Robert Martin, whose graceful conduct is described quite gracefully by Harriet although Emma denies "the value of Harriet's description" (180; vol. 2, ch. 3).

Harriet's language is a parody of stereotypical female speech. Harriet incorporates Emma, the listener, into her experience, not as a storyteller's device but as a bid for compassion. Harriet's anxiety intensifies as she speaks: she fears punishment from the Martins, whom she has rejected, and she must ward off Emma's anger, too. Actually, the Martins are extremely "delicate" in their behavior, Robert going so far as to continue to look out for her, and she says at the conclusion of her speech that "there was a sort of satisfaction in seeing him behave so pleasantly and so kindly" (179; vol. 2, ch. 3). Indeed, there was. Harriet has escaped whipping because of Robert Martin's sensibilities.

"The value of Harriet's description" adds to our respect for Robert Martin's "power of speech" and gives us a hint of Harriet's possible power of speech, too. She pleads with Emma to "make me comfortable again" (179; vol. 2, ch. 3), as direct a plea for dependence as we have in the book, and presents herself, perhaps disingenuously, as utterly unable to act without Emma's guidance. Harriet cannot stop talking about the encounter with the Martins. To stop the clearly obsessive flow of talk, Emma cuts it off by telling her very untenderly about Mr. Elton's defection, producing a higher order of despair. Later, however, Harriet will find the right words to claim Mr. Knightley's affection. An unequal relationship encourages such stratagems in the weaker person: it is part of the structure of the relationship.

When Emma mimics Miss Bates to Mrs. Weston (225; vol. 2, ch. 8), it is the subject's free association that causes the hilarity. The connectors are lost (frequent in the speech of older people), and the sentences exist without ballast; they float away on their own subject matter, but the subject matter is very restricted. Miss Bates has only one story to tell; anxiety dominates all—apples, spectacles, soups, Jane—the anxiety that others will not know how grateful she is for their attention to her, to her mother, or to Jane. Mr. Knightley has sent apples to the Bateses. They are grateful, but at once there is anxiety that they have used up all his apples. Frank fixes the spectacles of Mrs. Bates; still, one should have two sets of spectacles. In fact, anxiety produces and hangs on every revelation, which also frequently exposes the hostility bred by the anxiety. While reading aloud to her mother, Miss Bates is unluckily "off her guard enough" to alarm her by revealing that Jane is sick. Or, talking of Mr. Elton's marriage to the unknown Miss Hawkins, Miss Bates free-associates:

> What is before me, I see. At the same time, nobody could wonder if Mr. Elton should have aspired—Miss Woodhouse lets me chatter on, so good-humouredly. She knows I would not offend for the world. How does Miss Smith do? She seems quite recovered now. (176; vol. 2, ch. 3)

Or, letting the cat out of the bag:

> Then the baked apples came home, Mrs. Wallis sent them by her boy; they are extremely civil and obliging to us, the Wallises, always—I have heard some say that Mrs. Wallis can be uncivil and give a very rude answer, but we have never known any thing but the greatest attention from them. (236–37; vol. 2, ch. 9)

Or, Miss Bates's entrance to the ball at the Crown: she is nervous about appearing in society, and yet what can be the meaning of her comments on the correct social procedures to be observed?

Must not compliment, I know—(eyeing Emma most complacently)—that would be rude—but upon my word, Miss Woodhouse, you do look—how do you like Jane's hair?—You are a judge.—She did it all herself. Quite wonderful how she does her hair!—No hairdresser from London I think could. (323; vol. 3, ch. 2)

Or, it turns out that Mr. Woodhouse's collation for Miss Bates is not quite right:

There was a little disappointment.—The . . . fricassee of sweetbread and some asparagus brought in at first . . . sent . . . out again. Now there is nothing grandmamma loves better than sweetbread and asparagus—so she was rather disappointed, but we agreed we would not speak of it to any body, for its getting round to dear Miss Woodhouse, who would be so very much concerned. (329–30; vol. 3, ch. 2)

And always—to mark her speech—the dash, indicating, according to Chapman, the beginning of a parenthesis. The parenthetical is, of course, Miss Bates's strong point.

Miss Bates's last long speech, however, when Emma visits, has no slips.[11] It reveals her grandeur, not her silliness; her tremendous struggle to keep up appearances, her efforts to protect her mother and her niece. Emma shrinks before her, fearing for an instant that she will be denied forgiveness: "She had a moment's fear of Miss Bates keeping away from her" (378; vol. 3, ch. 8). An extraordinary conversational reversal: Emma has overheard Miss Bates saying to Jane in the moving, talking, and stirring that accompany Miss Woodhouse's expiation visit, "I shall say you are laid down upon the bed" (379; vol. 3, ch. 8). Miss Bates describes Jane's condition to Emma, and she tells the truth, that Jane will not see her. At the same time, there is anxiety about keeping Emma waiting, and there is denial—two strong currents in Miss Bates's talk—especially about Jane's "fortune" in getting a governess's position; but, at this moment, Miss Bates, fierce protector, puts Jane's feelings above Emma's, and their earlier roles are then suspended. Emma becomes the supplicant and Miss Bates the dispenser. The latter even manages, a bit later, to let Emma know that that "indefatigable true friend" (380; vol. 3, ch. 8) and employment agent, Mrs. Elton, has fatigued them all at her evening party.

Miss Bates's grandeur in this speech brings to mind her extraordinarily *short* speech at the "large modern circular table" that Emma has introduced at Hartfield when the company is playing alphabet games and the word "Dixon" is constructed. Jane, her face averted from those who have made the attack, turns towards Miss Bates, who speaks at once:

"Ay, very true, my dear," cried the latter though Jane had not spoken a word—"I was just going to say the same thing. It is time for us to be going indeed. The evening is closing in, and grandmamma will be looking for us. My dear sir, you are too obliging. We really must wish you good night." (349; vol. 3, ch. 5)

She is polite but forceful here, as she is at the scene of Emma's visit, and both times she brings a dimension of equality into the little world. Her desire to protect Jane enables her to speak without anxiety. When the spinster becomes protector, she is momentarily rational—and brief.

The third of the anxious trio of maid, spinster, and wife is Mrs. Elton, whose narcissism is the female counterpart to that of male caricatures. Mrs. Elton's language display can be observed in her conversation with Mr. Weston; they speak the same language: presentation of self. When Mrs. Elton and Mr. Weston, wife and husband, converse in chapter 18, 305–10, we have a lesson in how not to converse from two persons distinguished by their having married into the Hartfield circle, despite Weston's ownership of Randalls. These two strivers violate all rules of talking and listening. Each speaks only to tell his or her story, she of her sister at blessed Maple Grove, he of his son at the Churchills', status-borrowing in both cases. She interrrupts him; he seizes the opportunity to break in when she has a slight coughing fit. And then at last, "they were interrupted," and Mr. Weston having "said all that he wanted, soon took the opportunity of walking away" (310; vol. 2, ch. 18). This conversation is one of the clearest indications we have of Austen's view that both sexes are foolish; verbal preening behavior is not limited to males.

It is very hard not to catch Mrs. Elton, one of literature's great monologuists, in the act of vulgarity. The reader is introduced early to most of her turns, but Austen reserves Mrs. Elton's true vulgarity for the long speech in which she exhibits the vulgarity of which both she and Emma are guilty—the patronizing of other women—Emma of Harriet, Mrs. Elton of Jane Fairfax. Austen brings them together in part to highlight Emma's errors, in part to separate the latter's meddlesome mischief from Mrs. Elton's sadism. In her speech, Mrs. Elton describes herself as one who dares to act (283; vol. 2, ch. 15)—and dares to presume that she and Emma are of equal social status. Persons who congratulate themselves are damned by Austen. We wonder as Mrs. Elton talks why she has not tried to marry Jane off to one of her "extensive acquaintances" rather than place her as a governess. We hear Mrs. Elton's persistence in forcing Jane out-of-doors, and at the same time we forgive Emma's persistence with Harriet, because Emma's goal has a kind of goodness—to raise Harriet's status—and Mrs. Elton's goal is mean—to lower Jane's. Mrs. Elton's own status anxiety causes her to attempt to proletarianize Jane, to play Lady Bountiful offering occasional rides in the barouche-landau. Hers is a very ugly speech demonstrating that the words of wives are far worse than the words of timid maids or impoverished spinsters. Wives derive some of their status from the position of unmarried women, Austen suggests, and thus are free to torment an unmarried woman, especially if she has "superiority both of mind and manner" (286–87; vol. 2, ch. 15).[12] As Knightley notes, "Such a woman as Jane Fairfax probably never fell in Mrs. Elton's way before—and no degree of vanity can prevent her acknowledging her own comparative littleness in action, if not in consciousness" (287; vol. 2, ch. 15). Alas, even Knightley underestimates Mrs. Elton.

It is generally agreed among critics—most famously Virginia Woolf—that *Persuasion* is a new direction for Austen. Among the differences from earlier novels is the absence of the dialogic, and for our purposes here, the changes in the uses of the long speech. In general, the linguistic implications in male utterances are more powerful indicators of language change than are those in female utterances. In *Persuasion,* however, the lengthy speech of a woman has a new quality. Its function is to reveal the woman's identity in the social world; its aim is truthfulness, to disclose the speaker's sincerity, by both factual and expressive means. A powerless woman, Mrs. Smith, makes a long, on-stage speech, a plot-altering narrative-confessional that indicates the rationality, not the irrationality, of female discourse. Mary Poovey calls her the "necessary secret agent" (*The Proper Lady* 233) and likens her to Mrs. Norris and Miss Bates, but Mrs. Smith's agency is openly rewarded. Earlier, the female alterers of plot—Mrs. Ferrars or Mrs. Churchill—were dragons who spoke off-stage, but had such women held forth in directly reported speech, their utterances might have misfired, like Lady Catherine de Bourgh's. In fact, Mrs. Smith's speech acts are part of the dominance of women's speech acts that marks *Persuasion* (see, for example, Nurse Rooke and of course Lady Russell).

Nursing her wounds, Mrs. Smith has prepared her speech and is at long last permitted to give it.[13] Mrs. Smith is almost thrown off at first, and she has to switch material at the last moment since she has been formulating her plea for assistance from Anne after her marriage to Mr. Elliot. She recovers at once. She, too, will give "the whole history" (198; vol. 4, ch. 9), but Austen permits her prolixity since she has suffered so deeply as a woman: "[Anne] had a great deal to listen to; all the particulars of past sad scenes, all the minutiae of distress upon distress, which in former conversations had been merely hinted at, were dwelt on now with a natural indulgence" (210; vol. 4, ch. 9). Her first long speech (198–99; vol. 4, ch. 9) is a highly wrought dramatic essay, which comments upon itself as a speech act during its presentation, with an introduction, an explanation for withholding talk, a transition, the decision to speak at last, and a presentation of thesis: Mr. Elliot is "without a heart or conscience . . . black at heart, hollow and black!" (199; vol. 4, ch. 9). The thesis will be buttressed with proofs: "Facts shall speak" (199; vol. 4, ch. 9).

There are, however, strains on credibility as the story pours out: "Facts or opinion which are to pass through the hands of so many, to be misconceived by folly in one, and ignorance in another, can hardly have much truth left" (205; vol. 4, ch. 9). Real information is very hard to come by in this world of shifting class structures, but Anne is eventually won over. Indeed, Mrs. Smith herself speaks of receiving information in a verbal stream: "It does not come to me in quite so direct a line as that; it takes a bend or two, but nothing of consequence. The stream is as good as at first; the little rubbish it collects in the turnings is easily moved away" (204–5; vol. 4, ch. 9). She says to Anne, "If there is anything in my story which you know to be either false or improbable, stop me" (206; vol. 4, ch. 9). A little later, she pauses in her narrative, but "Anne had not a word to say, and she continued" (206; vol. 4, ch. 9). She produces a letter of Mr. Elliot's as one of her proofs (209; vol. 4, ch. 9); Anne says she does not need to see it, but Mrs. Smith insists, to buttress her position as a reliable witness. In fact, all of chapter 9 hangs on the question of the reliable witness to the past and to the present. Anne is glad to have her instinctive dislike of Mr. Elliot rooted in proof, but ultimately she believes Mrs. Smith because she knew her before, because Mrs. Smith has palpably suffered, and because she is an intelligent older woman. Anne has outgrown Lady Russell at last.

Although Mrs. Smith has been "carried away from her first direction" (208; vol. 4, ch. 9) in telling the tale of Mr. Elliot, we are certainly not bored. It is a great relief to have some version of the truth at last, but the tale is above all good novelistic gossip about adultery and treachery. Mrs. Smith's long speeches carry the historical truth about the past, but they also carry the novel's gravest narrative truth, that the position and intention of the speaker determine the response of the hearer.

Nobody in *Persuasion* other than Mrs. Smith talks *that* much. The good ones, in general, do what sensible speakers do—give information, for instance, Admiral Croft reporting on Louisa's engagement to Benwick. Even the villains do not ramble on, as they do in the set pieces of the earlier novels. Sir Walter's verbal style is pinned down permanently in only one long speech in chapter 3 (19; vol. 1, ch. 3), as is Mrs. Clay's admirable piece of self-definition, her hilarious analysis of professions and looks (20; vol. 1, ch. 3). Even Anne's set piece—her defense of women's "loving longest" in the White Hart Inn—is de-speechified by Austen by being broken into dialogue with Captain Harville.

Conversation, which has been in some danger in *Persuasion,* grows strong again in the reconciliation, but we do know that both Frederick and Anne change their use of words: she was tongue-tied and then regained the use of speech;[14] and he did not use language to distinguish feelings although later he has a "recollection" of how stupid he was (247; vol. 4, ch. 11). Contemporary linguists would say that both Anne and Frederick use emotional language in equal quantities, but the devices they use are culturally defined and different.[15] He exaggerates the boundaries between them; she attempts to re-create the processes by which they reached their positions in order to soften the boundaries.[16] Both men and women struggle openly in *Persuasion* to find a language that will keep them together, but the women are far more aware of the linguistic hazards involved in the effort to sustain relationships.[17]

In effect, with *Persuasion* it would seem that the long speeches of single voices are disappearing from Austen's novel of manners, as indeed from other novelists' writing too. The nineteenth-century novel begins to play down individual differences among characters, to focus not so much on the single distinctive speaker as on the speaker who represents an idea, a class, an occupation, a type. Anne Elliot thinks that "every little social commonwealth should dictate its own matters of discourse" (43; vol. 1, ch. 4). Anne cannot possibly take Frederick into the world of her family, with her "consciousness of having no relations to bestow on him which a man of sense could value" (251; vol. 4, ch. 12). Their friends will be his friends, and their conversations his conversations, in part because his career will determine their social place, not her own lineage. Anne prefers good conversation to genealogy, anyway. Their conversations will be privatized and domesticated. Perhaps they will live aboard ship, perhaps not. Wherever they are, they will retreat into a private sphere of discourse. With *Persuasion,* conversation in Austen's novel of manners changes direction. We will not hear the long speeches that formerly defined character. In fact, we can hardly hear the speakers at all, in a novel as much about overhearing as about hearing, as they make their way through the streets of Bath.

Notes

1. See J. F. Burrows. This recent, brilliant statistical analysis of dialogue in Austen will influence all Austen scholars. Burrows analyzes the relative frequency of the thirty most common words in Austen in forty-eight of her principal speakers. Such "statistical analysis of the peculiarities of incidence makes it possible," writes Burrows, "to approach the whole penumbra of 'meaning' in a new and fruitful way" (40). And indeed from his evidence it is possible to differentiate among the idiolects of Austen's characters and yet to treat speakers in all six novels as belonging to one linguistic "neighbourhood."

2. In Austen's novels, the makers of long speeches are male, with seven notable female exceptions: two female vulgarians of *Sense and Sensibility*—Mrs. Jennings and Miss Steele—who are featured by Austen as comic, if mixed-up, storytellers, not as bores; the special case of Marianne Dashwood; the women of *Emma;* and Mrs. Smith of *Persuasion,* although no generalizations about speakers will apply to her.

3. Mr. Collins is, of course, the lengthy speaker of *Pride and Prejudice.* The speechifying persons of *Mansfield Park* are Sir Thomas Bertram and his son, Edmund, since this novel is in part about the redemption and salvation of the males of Mansfield.

4. Trevor Pateman defines "idle discourse" as "powerless" discourse (as opposed to radical discourse). Those who engage in powerless discourse accept their lot, "treat definitions as closed and not for rational dispute; they dodge meaning."

5. One must note, however, that some of the prolixities may result from earlier, possibly epistolary versions of the novel. See John Halperin, *The Life of Jane Austen,* and B. C. Southam, *Jane Austen's Literary Manuscripts,* who notes that twenty-one letters are mentioned or quoted in *Sense and Sensibility.*

6. See Jack W. Sattel.

7. Mary Poovey (*The Proper Lady* 192) feels that Brandon's excesses arise from another source—his "intense anxiety" over female sexual appetite, as exemplified by the two Elizas.

8. See, for example, K. C. Phillipps.

9. See William Labov, who finds that women are considered more careful to use correct forms in their formal speech (301–4). Peter Trudgill also describes women's affinity for standard forms, arising perhaps out of fearfulness or status anxiety, and men's affinity for nonstandard forms, perhaps to communicate masculinity—a kind of reverse swank.

10. Much research on female speech and feminist language theory has appeared in the last twenty years. See, for example, Thorne, Kramarae, and Henley; McConnell-Ginet, Borker, and Furman; Cameron; Hiatt; Lakoff; and Spender.

11. Attempts at pinning down Miss Bates's speech are yet another way to fall prey to the difficulties of *Emma*. See Adena Rosmarin, 337.

12. As Marilyn Butler notes, however, mistreatment of vulnerable single women occurs throughout the book consistently—and certainly not only by Mrs. Elton (*Jane Austen* 257).

13. K. K. Collins suggests that Anne's willingness to accept Mrs. Smith's story comes in part from "prejudice," not necessarily a bad thing in itself. Certainly, it is Anne's prejudice that allows Mrs. Smith license to speak.

14. See Janice Bowman Swanson.

15. See Mary Ritchie Key, 98.

16. See Thomas J. Farrell.

17. Judy van Sickle Johnson points out that this novel contains more physical contact than any other Austen novel but rather less dialogic.

3

Maria Edgeworth and the Novel of Manners

Janet Egleson Dunleavy

Celebrated in her lifetime as a perceptive novelist, an elegant essayist, a promising playwright, and a prolific author of stories for children, Maria Edgeworth (1767?–1849) was deferentially described by Sir Walter Scott as a literary lioness while he was still a cub; acknowledged by Jane Austen in *Northanger Abbey* as a talented contemporary; praised in *The Edinburgh Review* by its demanding and often crotchety critic, Francis Jeffrey; hailed in an 1826 Harvard University Phi Beta Kappa address by Judge Joseph Story; and regarded by John Lockhart, Scott's son-in-law and the editor of the *Quarterly Review,* as a standard by which later novelists might be judged (Butler 1, 399–41; Newcomer, *Maria Edgeworth* 1, 14–15). Edgeworth's writings, printed and reprinted throughout the nineteenth century for a loyal reading public in England, the United States, and Canada, were translated for readers on the Continent. Well before the end of the century, her place in literary history had been assured.

At the height of his own career, in his preface to the Collected Edition of his work, Sir Walter Scott frankly and publicly acknowledged his debt to Edgeworth (Newcomer 16–17). Her influence was a continuing matter of critical discussion and speculation during the development of Anthony Trollope's reputation. At the time of Ivan Turgenev's death in 1883, the London *Daily News* reported that the master of realism had declared himself her "unconscious disciple" (Murray 39). Marshaling a century of opinion-makers for the survey with which he begins his bicentennial study (*Maria Edgeworth* 1–8), James Newcomer leaves no doubt that to nineteenth- and even many early twentieth-century critics, readers, and fellow writers, she was "the great Maria."

Nearly two centuries after publication of the earliest reviews of her work, Edgeworth is still regarded by literary historians as an important contributor to the development of the modern novel. Scholars who focus on separate facets of the genre's history of the past two hundred fifty years point to her pioneer work in what are now called the regional novel, the historical novel, the family saga novel, the novel of ideas, the novel of doctrine or social purpose, and the domestic novel, or novel of common life. But the loyal reading public of the nineteenth century has not renewed itself, and twentieth-century critics, as Newcomer points out (2–8), have been neither fair nor kind. A dusty figure in the wax museums of literature, today Maria Edgeworth is known *of* but little known. Among the titles in her long and impressive canon, only *Castle Rackrent* earns the spark of recognition that keeps it consistently in print. A few others flicker in and out of fashion and the public consciousness; the rest are consigned to darkness or doctoral dissertations.

What happened?

In part, critical failure in the twentieth century to see in Edgeworth's work the irony, conflict, and ambivalence now acknowledged as the strengths of a Jane Austen, *or* the refracted vision of an Elizabeth Bowen, a Virginia Woolf, or a Barbara Pym, *or* even the wry political commentary of an Anthony Trollope reveals the continuing impact of the opinions of Henry James, who regarded the literary corpus of the nineteenth century as a near-corpse, a body of work so lacking in intellectual and aesthetic nourishment that it could not possibly satisfy the sophisticated tastes and intellectual appetites of twentieth-century readers (cf. Brothers and Bowers, introductory chapter). In part, it reflects the fact that, irresistibly drawn to the drama of Maria Edgeworth's life, modern critics have given short shrift to her art. In part, the enduring popularity of *Castle Rackrent,* a first novel so fixed in literary history as her "best" book and so insistently and erroneously discussed as "unique," has discouraged independent study of its successors. In part, twentieth-century attitudes are almost certainly the result of a twentieth-century bias against nineteenth-century "fair authoresses." Patronizingly applied in the late eighteenth century to popular women writers considered lacking in insight and high seriousness, a hundred years later, in a practice not entirely discontinued today, the term was extended to almost all women writers—especially those whose works have been further trivialized by pejorative use of the term *novel of manners.*

Examples of the extent and crippling effect of such cumulative critical bias are found even in recent studies by those genuinely interested in Edgeworth's work. Richard Lovell Edgeworth has been a particularly stubborn obstacle to fair assessment of his daughter's writing. A myth of modern scholars—hard to dispel or dismiss despite evidence to the contrary—is that following her unassisted writing and publication of *Castle Rackrent* in 1800, Maria Edgeworth, a promising young author among the fair authoresses of her time, was so dominated by her well-meaning, overbearing, moralistic, and single-minded father, Richard Lovell Edgeworth, that thereafter she was never free to produce anything of comparable quality or significance but devoted herself to the production of moral tales that illustrated his theories of education.

Challenging, for example, the "stale and second-hand opinions" of predecessors (whom he wittily discredits simply by quoting their blatant inaccuracies), James Newcomer has been particularly eloquent in his defense of Maria Edgeworth as an "author of . . . distinguished novels of manners." Yet, leaving her somewhat in the position of a distinguished painter of teacups, he makes no case for more serious treatment of either the genre to which he links her reputation or her inventive manipulation of its conventions but diminishes her achievement with the specious declaration that "lacking . . . the effects of her father's training," she "would probably never have become the artist that she was" (5, 12–13). Further undercutting his own thoughtful reexamination of her work, especially his informed and informative analysis in the final chapters of his bicentennial study of the structure, irony, and narrative art of *Castle Rackrent*, Newcomer concurs in the critical opinion that has labeled this novel "unique" in her canon, an item unlike any other (164).

Nor does Marilyn Butler, author of the most recent full-length biography (1972), rescue Maria Edgeworth from either the antipathy of early twentieth-century critics or the ambivalence of later ones. Although she acclaims Edgeworth as "a key figure in the development of the English novel," contributes significantly to an understanding of that development from a biographical point of view, and deplores the myths that have obscured judgments of the Great Maria, she fuels these same myths, for she stresses the biographical content of Edgeworth's writings over the artistic synthesis to which they were subjected by the author and divides her study into three parts, one devoted to Edgeworth's literary apprenticeship *to* her father, one to Edgeworth's "partnership" *with* her father, and one to Edgeworth's "independence" *from* her father. This last section consists of two chapters, "Living without Her Father" and "Writing without Her Father." In both, emphasis on the word "without" suggests that Maria's independence, personal and artistic, was dearly bought.

Patrick Murray also divides his *Maria Edgeworth: A Study of the Novelist* (1971) into chapters that feature the father and diminish the daughter. His first chapter is devoted wholly and exclusively to a chronological sketch of the life of Richard Lovell Edgeworth; Maria is scarcely named. The second is a biographical sketch of Maria in which Richard Lovell Edgeworth is frequently named. A third chapter, on the novelist's Irish stories, singles out the "unique" *Castle Rackrent* for extended if not entirely favorable discussion, then allots less than half the same number of pages, like crumbs, for division among remaining works *(Ennui, The Absentee, Ormond)* identified as having an Irish focus. Edgeworth's other novels and tales (i.e., *Belinda, The Modern Griselda, Leonora, Madame de Fleury, Almeria, The Dun, Manoeuvring, Vivian, Emilie de Coulanges, Patronage, Harrington,* and *Helen*) plus her plays, translations from the French, children's stories, and short fiction for adults are disposed of in a brief fourth chapter entitled "The English Novels and Miscellaneous Writings." A fifth and final chapter—"Father and Daughter: The Literary Partnership"—returns to the subject of Richard Lovell Edgeworth, to the books and essays he wrote in collaboration with his daughter, and to her memoir of his life and work.

By 1973, in a second study intended primarily as an introduction to Edgeworth's fiction for readers unfamiliar with her work, even James Newcomer seems to have been drawn away from what first had attracted him—her sheer storytelling ability, her modifications of Richardson's and Fielding's precursors to the novel of manners, her narrative art—to the "elusive" truth of the "exact . . . relationship between father and daughter" (82).

Fortunately, as noted by Brothers and Bowers (cf. introductory chapter), changes in critical approaches to the novel have invited reevaluation of the work of just such authors as Maria Edgeworth. For example, while acknowledging that nineteenth-century concepts of the genre favor mimetic art, Lionel Trilling in *The Opposing Self* has challenged the notion that therefore nineteenth-century literature focuses on society to the exclusion of the individual. Rather, observes Trilling, authors and readers of the period regarded depictions of society and the individual as mirrors in which each could be studied as a reflection of the other. Thus, nineteenth-century novels of manners reveal, on the one hand, human failings that corrupt society; on the other, corrupt societies that feed on human failings.

From a different perspective, concerned less with sociological aspects of literature, more with authorial intent and narratology, John Halperin's analyses of the meditative narrative discourse in nineteenth-century British fiction (cf. *The Language of Meditation*, 1973; *Egoism and Self-Discovery in the Victorian Novel*, 1974) support Trilling's thesis. Corroborating Halperin in her 1979 treatise, *Tendencies of Character Depiction in the Domestic Novels of Burney, Edgeworth, and Austen*, Patricia Voss-Clesly traces simultaneously accessible twin discourses, objective and subjective, in selected texts. These and similar reexaminations of nineteenth-century literature by twentieth-century critics have encouraged reassessment of the genre broadly labeled *novel of manners*, a term that at one time or another has been used to encompass in whole or in part all the various novel forms (regional, historical, family saga, novel of ideas, novel of doctrine or social purpose, and domestic novel or novel of common life) identified in Maria Edgeworth's canon. A concerted effort on the part of feminist critics to examine particularly all literature dismissed as the work of "fair authoresses" and to make newly available those titles that, long out of print and never published in paperback, have been removed from the public consciousness also has been a significant factor in encouraging reassessment.

The Edgeworth novel that most needs reexamination, to remove the disguise that conceals its irony and to establish the unity of the author's work, is paradoxically the one that is least in need of introduction: *Castle Rackrent*

(1800). A cleverly conceived fiction usually labeled historical or regional and sometimes read as a pioneer family saga, it draws upon aspects of the eighteenth-century romantic novel, manipulates conventions of the domestic novel, and adds a touch of the Gothic to construct a mirror of the social and political realities of Ireland at the beginning of the nineteenth century. Cast as a memoir recorded by an Ascendancy class editor from the oral account of an uneducated steward of an Irish Big House, it brings together a sophisticated and an unsophisticated narrator in a text that consists of the fictional editor's preface, notes, and glossary (these are *not*, as some critics have mistakenly thought, the "additions" of the author but an integral part of the novel) and the fictional steward's history of the last four generations of the Rackrent family.

As in most novels of manners, plot is negligible. Setting—compounded, writes Newcomer, of "whiskey, decay, rot, guttering candles, tobacco, damp, horse dung, and dust" (155)—creates mood as well as sense of place, preparing an appropriate ground against which characters, the chief focus of attention, are paraded. Action is for the most part a function of thought, speech, and recollection. The editor's time is identified as the author's present by the fact that Ireland is about to lose "her identity by an union with Great Britain" (vi). (The Act of Union joining Great Britain and Ireland was passed by Parliament in 1800, the year the novel was published; it became effective January 1, 1801.) The steward's time is the past, from the years of his youth to the end of his service to the Rackrents, when, with the last Rackrent master on his deathbed, he watched his own son Jason, a successful attorney, put the finishing touch to his attempts to become the new master of the Castle. About the present he is ambivalent: the son he obliquely confesses to having aided and abetted in his rise to "high gentleman" now "never minds what poor Thady says"; his own achievement in having risen to steward from son of a driver (not a coachman but a man who drives to the pound the cattle of tenants behind in their rent) is forgotten (2).

These two narrator/characters of *Castle Rackrent*—in the foreground, Thady Quirk, the "illiterate old steward" reputed to be the author of the memoir; in the background, the unnamed editor, putative author of the preface—are linked within the world of the novel by the fact that some years ago the latter had persuaded Thady to allow his account of the history of the Rackrent family to be committed to writing. It is for the benefit of potential readers of this account, declares the editor, especially the *"ignorant* English reader" for whom Thady's story otherwise might be at worst "scarcely intelligible," at best merely "incredible," that he has written an introduction, constructed a glossary, and appended explanatory notes (v). These additions are required, he explains, because what old Thady tells are "tales of other times." The manners portrayed, he assures readers, "are not those of the present age." The race of the Rackrents (actually, the O'Shaughlin-Rackrents, for the direct Rackrent line died out in

Thady's childhood)—the convivial Sir Patrick, the litigious Sir Murtagh, the crafty Sir Kit, the profligate Sir Condy—"has long since been extinct in Ireland." No one is left, he avows, who might be offended by representation in print, for "[n]ations, as well as individuals, gradually lose attachment to their identity, and the present generation is amused, rather than offended, by the ridicule that is thrown upon its ancestors" (vi).

That the past is not so distant as the editor would have readers believe is evident from history (it is but two years since the Rising of 1798) and from Thady's chronology of events at Castle Rackrent. All Thady tells has happened within his lifetime; it is some seven years, perhaps, since his son Jason, having seized opportunities provided by the dissolute Sir Condy, acquired everything but the now-disputed jointure held by Sir Condy's widow. More to the point, as Newcomer makes clear (144–51), *what* Thady tells of milord and milady is scarcely the story the editor thinks it is, of a loyal Irish servant devoted to a Big House family. Like the resident magistrate of Lady Gregory's *Spreading the News,* the editor of *Castle Rackrent* is too biased, too sure of the validity of his own stereotypical attitudes toward landlord and servant, to see in Thady the intellect, the complexity of emotion, the self-respect, and the strength that he indeed possesses. The same may be said of most critics of the novel. As beguiled as the editor by Thady's *manners,* they have let the old boy—or was it the fair authoress?—fool them.

An interesting device first used by Maria Edgeworth to accomplish her ironic purpose in *Castle Rackrent* and thereafter employed in almost all her fiction is bitonality. As described by Robert B. Heilman in a study of the theory of the novel, it is introduced when one insistent tone that directs the attention or claims the sympathies of a reader is challenged by another (321). If intended and successful, it is artistic; if accidental and unsuccessful, it results in just so much static. For Maria Edgeworth, bitonality is always intentional. In *Castle Rackrent,* it both derives from and reinforces competition between editor and putative author for control of the novel by emphasizing the opposition of preface and memoir and the linguistically distinct verbal constructions of each. In his struggle to maintain supremacy, the editor reinforces his preface with pedantic notes and a glossary. But Thady's memoir includes an arsenal of possessive pronouns—"I and mine," "my duty," "my lady," "my advice," "for my part," "my late master and mistress," "my son," "my story," "my judgment"—against which, given the impotence of "the agent" and "your middle man," surely the editor could not hope to mount a defense. If the editor thinks to reassert his control over the old steward's narrative with the line he fires in conclusion— "The Editor could have readily made the . . . history more dramatic and more pathetic, if he thought it allowable to varnish the plain round tale of faithful Thady" (63)—it is because, like the critics who have misunderstood the novel, he is unaware of this statement's irony.

Thady's disguise is, of course, the disguise of the novel as a whole. As long as he is regarded as faithful, *Castle Rackrent* may be read as a historical or regional novel steeped in the atmosphere described by Newcomer. The irony perceived, *Castle Rackrent* is a modification of the novel of manners, "an amalgam of improvidence, stupidity, cupidity, pride, subservience, animosity, sentimentality, brutality, and perversity" (155) in which the private and public behavior of four generations of a politically influential and socially prominent family is revealed. If there is a moral to this story (and critics seem predisposed to find a moral in every Edgeworth story), it is perhaps an unstated but implied warning to new landlords like Jason that such behavior can finish them off within the lifetime of one old family steward, just as it brought an end to the tenure of the O'Shaughlin-Rackrents. Says Thady, whose ambiguous remarks have led perceptive critics to call *Castle Rackrent* a "novel of social purpose," "there's nothing but truth in [the story] from beginning to end" (63). The question is, whose truth? What Thady tells or what the editor *thinks* he knows? In his preface, the editor confides to the reader (has ever the innuendo of the novel of manners been used with more art?) that "We cannot judge either of the feelings or of the characters of men with perfect accuracy, from their actions or their appearance in public; it is from their careless conversations, their half-finished sentences, that we may hope with the greatest probability of success to discover their real characters." That he himself has not sought truth through the clues to Thady's real character in the very narrative before him provides the central tension of the novel.

Between 1782 and 1800, the political, social, and economic concerns related to the Irish Question synthesized by Maria Edgeworth in *Castle Rackrent* were not only under hot debate in England and Ascendancy Ireland but also earnestly discussed even on the Continent. For the subject of her second novel, *Belinda* (1801), Edgeworth turned to another controversial issue of the period: the proper role of women in private and public life. Years earlier, Edgeworth herself had been personally affected by the controversy, for in 1782, with an eye toward publication encouraged by her father, she had begun work on an English translation of *Adèle et Théodore*, a Rousseauistic treatise by Mme. de Genlis. The project had drawn strong disapproval in 1783 from her father's close friend, Thomas Day, who hitherto had been a sympathetic supporter of her education (Butler, *Maria Edgeworth: Biography* 147–49). Heated public arguments had been stirred in 1787 and again in 1792 by questions raised in Mary Wollstonecraft's *Thoughts on the Education of Daughters* and *A Vindication of the Rights of Woman*. Among the literary responses were Edgeworth's own *Letters for Literary Ladies* (1795), a slim volume of three short satiric pieces that anticipate Virginia Woolf's tongue-in-cheek irony, and *Emma Courtney* (1796), a fictional treatment of eighteenth-century feminist issues by Mary Hays, a disciple of Mary Wollstonecraft, that incorporates influences from the

Continent. *Emma Courtney,* in turn, inspired Edgeworth's "Angelina," a cautionary tale of an adolescent girl who to her disadvantage takes Mary Hays's heroine as her model. Begun as a play some time before 1799 but never produced, "Angelina" was rewritten in prose for publication in *Moral Tales,* which appeared in the same year as *Belinda* (Butler 165; Luria 8); it provides additional evidence of Edgeworth's consistent and sustained interest in issues that some critics have dismissed as of no concern to her.

Superficially more conventional in form, subject, and treatment than *Castle Rackrent* (that is, superficially more like the novels that had been popularized by Fielding, Richardson, and Smollett forty to sixty years earlier), *Belinda* therefore continues within Maria Edgeworth's canon the precedent of using the familiar forms and themes of the novel of manners in what some critics have described as the novel of doctrine or the novel of social purpose—a step in the history of the genre that was to lead to the political novels of such disparate authors as Anthony Trollope and C. P. Snow. Certainly, its cast of characters is appropriate: a young and unworldly woman (Belinda) sent to London to compete in the highest circles of the marriage market by a well-meaning and socially ambitious aunt (Mrs. Stanhope); an adept and experienced lady of fashion (Lady Delacour) selected by the young woman's aunt to provide proper social connections and advice on modish dress and behavior; attractive bachelors unwilling to marry (e.g., Clarence Hervey); unattractive bachelors willing to marry (e.g., Sir Philip Baddely); a wise man to whom all but the foolish defer (Dr. X); a virtuous lady whom all but the wicked admire (Lady Anne Percival). The simple and familiar plot (borrowed in part, like that of earlier novels of manners, from medieval romance) requires that Belinda undergo a number of trials to display her appropriate virtues as she perseveres in her quest for a husband—and that the author sustain the interest of the reader, again in the manner of medieval romance, through episodes that amuse, titillate, startle, arouse curiosity, and elicit sympathy on her behalf. All is accomplished according to pattern, but with an exaggeration that at times borders on caricature. A gentler irony convinces Belinda, the closer she comes to success, that a serious proposal from an eligible and affluent bachelor is a prize of uncertain value.

Belinda was, of course, a work-in-progress during the time when *Castle Rackrent* was being prepared for press. It would be curious if, as most critics have argued, it contained little or nothing to identify it as a product of the same artistic imagination. The fact is that similarities are evident, most obviously in Edgeworth's choices of structure and technique that underscore the polemic nature of the issue at the heart of each story: In *Belinda,* as in *Castle Rackrent,* twin discourses, each employing linguistic and stylistic devices suitable to its particular deployment, compete for the reader's sympathies and attention. At the center of one of these discourses is the unsophisticated, uncomplicated, and charmingly honest Belinda; at the center of the other is the sophisticated, complex, and fascinatingly devious Lady Delacour. Stylistically defined parallel structures within the narrative of each of these principal figures contrast private and public personae. Although the title of the novel suggests that Belinda is the primary principal figure, a sustained bitonality, accomplished by narrative and dramatic focus as well as by character development, establishes the equal significance of Lady Delacour.

Belinda's character, in private as in public, is stable and predictable. Shyness, modesty, prudence, and good manners all contribute to her public reserve. The public persona created by that reserve, like her aunt's green baize carpet covering, is interpreted by those around her as evidence that something deeper and wiser lies beneath. In fact, just as Mrs. Stanhope's green baize covering conceals nothing more extraordinary than an old, still serviceable but well-worn carpet, so beneath Belinda's reserve there is nothing more extraordinary than a simple, trusting, and affectionate nature, true virtue, and old-fashioned values.

Lady Delacour's character is far more complex. Once she may have been a Belinda, but her moral armor was insufficient to the tests she had to undergo. The woman she now is in the world of the novel is duplicitous. She is dependent on a range of situational masks, private and public, to hide unwelcome truths from herself as well as from others, to deny to others what she cannot hide even from herself, and to manage and manipulate family members, friends, and acquaintances, all to her temporal and temporary advantage. For her, openness and honesty require effort; self-serving, dissembling, and deceit are almost second nature. Yet, there is enough left of the woman she once was to cause her discomfort at times, if not pain, with consequential adverse effects on her self-confidence.

As Lady Delacour knows, her rapidly changing moods and emotional highs and lows (evidence of an internal ambivalence that she can neither control nor ignore) create a public impression of a vacillating nature. In fact, as Edgeworth makes clear, life is for this character a deadly serious game in which it is necessary to be ever alert, to have a ready plan of action, and to be warily suspicious, especially of those who, while insisting on their loyalty and affection, inexplicably (to her mind) ask nothing in return. Her strategies are thus calculated responses not to the actions and public poses of those around her but to what she observes of unconscious gestures, suppressed responses, careless remarks, and half-finished conversations. Yet, what should be wisdom is error, for like the editor of *Castle Rackrent,* Lady Delacour is frequently misled by her own conceit, bias, and self-interest. Consequently, although the perfidy of a former close friend, Harriot Freke, should have taught her a lesson, she continues to misread people, misinterpret situations, and mishandle her life.

The social problems of the public Lady Delacour are mirrored in her most intimate personal problems. Publicly, she is most vulnerable when she is confronted either by her chief social rival, Mrs. Luttridge, or by the woman who has become Mrs. Luttridge's social agent, the false and manipulative Harriot Freke. Privately, her vulnerability concerns a diseased and disfigured breast that she herself has diagnosed as cancerous and that she has taken extraordinary care to conceal. The fatal cancer, as she calls it, is the result of an injury to her breast, suffered when the gun she fired in a duel with Mrs. Luttridge recoiled. It will not heal. Certain that if this disfiguration and its inevitable consequence (the painful, lingering death she soon must suffer) are revealed, she would lose her social position and end her days as an object of pity and malicious gossip, she has refused to consult a reputable physician but has relied for temporary relief on drug-dispensing quacks. Meanwhile, unaware of Lady Delacour's terrible secret until halfway through the book (when it turns out that Lady Delacour has misjudged her injury as she has misjudged so much else), Belinda is bewildered by her bitterness, her cynicism, her unhappiness. If a lady who has everything—money, beauty, social position, a husband, a child, admirers—is perpetually dissatisfied, what hope is there for herself? Is it really worse to remain single than to marry?

Such questions, improperly raised by a proper young heroine of a domestic novel, were not new to the writings of Maria Edgeworth in 1801. In "Letters of Julia and Caroline" (Letters for Literary Ladies), two well-educated women, Edgeworthian antecedents of Belinda and Lady Delacour, debate how best to respond to the limitations placed on female behavior by law, by marriage, and by social convention. In this fictional correspondence published six years before Belinda appeared, Caroline is the Belinda figure who speaks for prudence and warns of the consequences that may be expected if womanly virtues are abandoned; Julia is the Lady Delacour figure who is brought to grief by her insistence on challenging social realities. A major difference between Caroline and Belinda is that Caroline, like Lady Delacour, regards marriage, happy or unhappy, as the only possible choice of a prudent woman; a major difference between Julia and Lady Delacour is that Julia, like Belinda, is unwilling to accept marriage unless it promises happiness. Despite superficial correspondences to the author's own experiences that give these figures the coloring of everyday life (Butler 172–73; Luria 5–9), none is autobiographical; all are conceptual.

The fact is that ideas were what fascinated Maria Edgeworth. For evidence, there is the succession of novels and tales, from "Angelina" to Helen, in which she experimented with other combinations of the same attitudes, values, and social position to produce different results, and the two other pieces printed in Letters to Literary Ladies: "Letter from a Gentleman to his Friend upon the Birth of a Daughter, with the Answer" and "Essay on the Noble Science of Self-Justification." Both of these reveal thematic incidents and intentional ironies echoed in Belinda. The latter anticipates the advice of Mrs. Stanhope, the philosophy of Lady Delacour, and the cynicism they share. The former, an epistolary exchange identified by Marilyn Butler as a parodic treatment of the actual correspondence between Thomas Day and Richard Lovell Edgeworth on the subject of Maria's proposed publication of Mme. de Genlis's *Adèle et Théodore* (149), is surely indebted also to seventeenth- and eighteenth-century treatises against either educating women or publishing their writings (cf. Coleman) and to Mary Wollstonecraft's previously mentioned *Thoughts on the Education of Daughters*.

Also woven into the text of *Belinda* are quotations from and allusions to a broad selection of well-known works from French and English literature and to English and Continental music and art. Within the fictional story, these are artfully employed to reinforce theme, tone, description, and character development and to establish setting—a fictional fashionable world synthesized in part from literary antecedents, in part from observations of real life. Thus, Edgeworth's ladies and gentlemen (subtle caricatures of ideals promoted by a fashionable education) hum snatches of French opera, are costumed for portraits in which they are sentimentally portrayed as storied figures, and chat easily among themselves about the lives and writings of such celebrated authors as Madame de Sevigné, Jean-Jacques Rousseau, and Bernardin de St. Pierre. The same allusions provide a clue to Edgeworth's anticipated audience, for to retain the interest of readers, she of course had to be sure that allusive references would be meaningful to them, too.

These ingredients of Edgeworth's fiction *qua* fiction have been appreciated and accepted with little question. It is with regard to her plots that fidelity to life becomes an issue on which critics challenge her ability as a novelist. Seeking an art that imitates life—that is, the art they expect from a novel of manners— they reject her sequencing of events as clumsy and contrived and denounce even those episodes for which Marilyn Butler has provided evidence of anecdotal real-life sources (29, 54, 243, 247, 248, 259) as too improbable to be credible. What they miss is the fact that Edgeworth's ironic use of literary models extends to plot: for Edgeworth as for George Bernard Shaw, ironic purpose is best served not when art imitates life but when art imitates art, with the possible exception of such incidents as Butler reports from the life of Sir Francis Delaval, Richard Lovell Edgeworth's rakish friend, when the improbability of life exceeds that of art.

In *Belinda*, for example, as previously noted, plot follows the simple outline of the medieval romance: the young woman of the title is the knight of the tale; she has reached the appropriate age to don her womanly armor and set out on her quest for a marriage proposal; before her are social adventures in which again and again she will be required to prove her strength, her virtue, and her tenacity of purpose. Twin narratives—one focused on herself, one on her antithesis—structure her story, which carries her forward along a winding path beset by dangers, temptations, and follies that serve the double purpose of testing her and entertaining readers (cf. book I of Spenser's *Faerie Queene,* especially the dichotomy between Una and Duessa). Stock episodes that amuse, titillate, startle, arouse curiosity, elicit sympathy, set the scene for numerous costume changes, and otherwise delay the too-immediate satisfaction of reader expectations have a long pedigree (cf. Erich Auerbach) in fiction, drama, and musical compositions that involve plot, character, and narrative.

Familiar to all readers of the literary "canon," for example, are such set pieces found in *Belinda* as the conversation overheard at the masquerade ball; the search for the long lost relative with only an old and faded miniature as clue; and complications that arise from mistaken identity, from situations in which men disguise themselves as women and women disguise themselves as men, from bungled attempts to keep or uncover secrets, from comic contrasts between the upstairs world of ladies and gentlemen and the downstairs world of domestic servants, and from traffic with quacks and charlatans. Specific and topical sources of stock episodes familiar to sophisticated readers of Edgeworth's novel would have included the *intermezzi* of Italian opera, the continental *opéra comique* and *opera buffa,* the plays of Richard Brinsley Sheridan, and the extravagantly costumed musical spectacles long favored by fashionable Londoners. Nor did her readers have to have access to theaters, opera houses, and music halls to recognize these: attractions staged in such centers of cultural and intellectual activity as Paris, London, and even Dublin were fully reported in graphic detail in fashionable reviews of the period; visitors abroad vied with professional writers in recording their impressions and judgments in diaries and journals read by friends and family at home; the mark of an educated woman or man of 1801 was a voluminous personal correspondence in which matters of fashion, taste, and critical perception related to the contemporary cultural scene were expressed. Among the literary celebrities of the preceding century often cited in public print and personal writing was Jean-Jacques Rousseau, whose theories of education had for a considerable time captured the imagination of Richard Lovell Edgeworth. Rousseau had written what often is called the first French comic opera, *Le Devin du village* (1752). It had been parodied by Mozart, who favored the form of the *opera buffa,* in his *Bastien and Bastienne* (1768). Rousseau was also, of course, the author of *La nouvelle Héloise.* The experiences of his Julie provide at least in part a model for those of Edgeworth's Belinda.

From 1801 to 1834, Maria Edgeworth continued to structure her fiction in accordance with public taste and the conventions of the novel of manners. Drawing on her skill as a teller of tales, she created cameo roles within predictable narratives enlivened by comic or dramatic or emblematic episodes; she challenged surface realities with subtle irony, bitonality, and contrasting parallel texts. Central to each individual work was an idea, an abstraction that, although unrelated to the narrative imitations of life and art that were the vehicles of her fiction, was yet manifest through them.

Of Edgeworth's short novels published in 1809 and 1812 under a general title, *Tales of Fashionable Life, The Absentee* (1812) has received particular attention as a novel of manners. Related to its predecessors, it combines the political and historical concerns of *Castle Rackrent* with the social pressures of *Belinda* in a setting divided between England and Ireland. In a technical departure from nineteenth-century convention, it starts with no sense of a beginning and ends with no assurance of a conclusion.

The first page of the opening chapter of *The Absentee* appears modern to twentieth-century readers. Without a page of preface or narrative preparation to suggest what the reader can expect to find between its covers—indeed, with no indication that the narrative persona even recognizes the existence of an audience—it picks up its story *in medias res,* just after the end of a performance of the opera, while a cluster of people engaged in small talk are waiting for their carriages. The exact relationship of those involved in the conversation and their role in the novel are not fully revealed for several pages, by which time the tensions of the narrative have been dramatically rather than narratively introduced.

The technique of *The Absentee* and the striking verisimilitude of its dialogue may derive, as some critics have suggested, from the fact that it originally was sketched as a play rather than a novel (Butler 276–77). However, Maria Edgeworth's ability to re-create the quality of informal speech always has been noted as one of the strengths of her art: it may be that she experimented with dramatic form because it suited her talent. The same may be said of the skill with which she marshals her characters for rhetorical rather than realistic effect. In *Castle Rackrent* and *Belinda,* the strategy she adopted stresses parallelism and polar opposition. In *The Absentee,* characters belong instead to concentric and overlapping circles. One small and elite circle in fashionable London is limited to such dignitaries as the Duchess of Torcaster and those eligible by virtue of rank, birth, or marriage to gather around her. A second and larger circle encompasses others who have gained the favor of or hold in obligation one or more members of the innermost circle. The largest circle, in which the Duchess retains her position in absentia (for she will not attend functions at which such people are present), admits social climbers, the nouveau riche, absentees, and the poorer and more distant kin of members of the inner circles. Some English ladies of the inner circle fulfill what they regard as their duty to protect the Duchess from social exposure to the Irish. Among the Irish are some who deny their background and try unsuccessfully to pass for English. Tension between those who guard access to the inner circles and those who bully, bribe, and contrive in order to achieve a position on the inside looking out provides opportunities for ironic contrast, for among the ladies most eager for recognition in London are those who in Ireland try to hold the line against upstart commoners from the rising Irish middle class.

Absentee landlords and their wives from both countries pose a problem at home and abroad. Too intent on being admitted to fashionable London circles to be concerned with their ethical and economic managerial responsibilities, they leave large estates in the hands of unscrupulous agents, requiring only that enough money be squeezed from the land and its tenants for them to live extravagantly close to the seat of social power. When bankruptcy threatens, reckless parents seek to recoup their lost fortunes by marrying their daughters or sons to heirs or heiresses. Some are foiled by their own foolishness and greed; some by the wisdom of their quarry; some by the honesty and integrity of their adult children.

The characters of *The Absentee* are neatly arranged in types or pairs. There are Irish and English absentee landlords; extravagant and social-climbing Irish and English women; virtuous young Irish and English gentlemen and ladies; honest Irish agents and English tradesmen; dishonest Irish agents and English tradesmen; and trusted and conniving servants of both countries. The movements of this entire army of *Absentee* characters are strategically controlled by the author, as if they were pieces on a board game. The board on which the game is played is the landscape of England and Ireland.

Although almost as simple in outline as *Castle Rackrent* and *Belinda*, the linear plot of *The Absentee* is actually more complicated and complex, for it involves financial maneuvering to avoid court judgments, a question of legitimate birth, a search for a long-lost document, and a race against time from village to village in remote areas of the English countryside to outwit greedy collateral heirs. The focus of the novel, however, is not the foregrounded game-like narrative but—paradoxically—the background, the Ireland through which Lord Colambre passes on his return to his native country after having grown up in England, where his parents, absentee landlords, have made their home. The problems of Ireland engage him as if in passing, while what purport to be far greater personal problems—his love for Grace Nugent that he must not declare, his suspicion that the foolishness of his social-climbing mother has brought his parents close to financial disaster—occupy his thoughts. Gradually, the subordinate characters he meets take over the text as their poetic speech and sincerity win his heart and their struggles against villainy engage his sympathy. Grace Nugent does not disappear: she and others continue to move across the game board in a series of moves with enough surprises to sustain attention. Too artificial to be taken seriously, her story at the same time involves too much intrigue and gamesmanship as it moves toward the finish line to be ignored. Everything comes together at the end—but not quite. In what is again a technique more familiar to twentieth-century than to nineteenth-century readers, the last word is never spoken; the penultimate word is left to Larry Brady, driver of a hired coach in Clonbrony. Writing to his brother Pat (who had been forced by a dishonest agent to emigrate and who now works for a London carriage-maker), Larry urges that he come home now that the landlords have returned. *Soon*, the Big House will be fixed up again, he says. *Soon*, he believes, Lord Colambre will marry Grace Nugent. *Soon*, it will not be fashionable anymore for anyone to be an absentee. Recalling the assurances of the editor of *Castle Rackrent*, writing in 1800, that "the race of the Rackrents has long since been extinct in Ireland; and the drunken Sir Patrick, the litigious Sir Murtagh, the fighting Sir Kit, and the slovenly Sir Condy . . . could no more be met with . . . in Ireland, than Squire Western or Parson Trulliber in England" (vi), can Larry, writing purportedly twelve years later, be believed? (Cf. Hurst 36–38.)

Helen (1834), Maria Edgeworth's last novel, seems at first to be a reworking of *Belinda* with just enough changes in character, situation, and event to present a new story, for like Belinda, Helen is an orphan of modest means whom fortune has placed in a fashionable social circle with an experienced tutor who can provide the social contacts and guidance she requires to make a good match. Her place in the Clarendon household has not been arranged for this purpose, however: she and Lady Cecelia, although as different as two young women can be, have been friends since childhood; following the death of her uncle and guardian, she has been persuaded by Lady Davenant, Lady Cecelia's mother, to join them in the palatial home of Cecelia's husband, General Clarendon, for a visit of indefinite duration.

The reason behind what seems to be a generous and compassionate invitation is that knowing Helen to be more virtuous than her daughter, Lady Davenant wishes her to be on hand as a moderating influence on Cecelia's behavior while she and her husband are abroad. Lady Davenant is uncertain whether Cecelia's amorality is inborn or the result of her not having been given proper guidance as a child—an uncertainty that causes her pain, for she chides herself for having ignored her responsibilities during Cecelia's formative years, relegating child care to others whom she did not properly supervise, while attempting to build for herself a political career on the model of Mme. de Stael. What she does not admit, however, to herself or anyone else (and what the author commendably does not point out in conventional nineteenth-century fashion but implies artistically through action, dialogue, dramatic contrast, and juxtaposition) is that the manipulation and deceit that Cecelia practices for purely selfish purposes are very like the manipulation and deceit she herself had practiced in the service of what she now looks back on as a mistaken yet higher goal. Attempting to compensate for past mistakes, Lady Davenant repeats them by depending on the young and inexperienced Helen to exercise what is still, as conscience tells her, her own parental responsibility.

An eminently eligible bachelor arrives on the scene, and the same pattern of attraction/repulsion that characterizes the early relationship of Belinda and Clarence Hervey is repeated between Helen and Granville Beauclerc until at last they acknowledge their mutual affection. A subtle parallel to the Lady

Davenant–Cecelia relationship is set up in the revelation that General Clarendon is guardian to the young and impetuous Beauclerc. Unable to use his money as he wishes or to marry without Clarendon's approval, Beauclerc chafes under Clarendon's control. Yet, Clarendon insists on discharging his responsibilities in the manner he believes to be best for his ward. Meanwhile, in contrast, Lady Davenant has gone abroad with her husband. During her absence, the hapless Helen, although clearly more virtuous than either Cecelia or her mother, proves neither so resolute nor so resistant to the lure of fashionable society as Belinda. At first, the consequences are minor. She is tempted by petty vanities; she allows herself to be drawn into petty intrigues. But the worst occurs when the self-centered Cecelia implicates Helen in order to extricate herself from a lie that is certain to destroy her husband's trust in her. Poor Helen, deficient in moral judgment, unable to distinguish between duty and loyalty, puts everyone's happiness at risk.

Fortunately for everyone, Lady Davenant returns to England sooner than expected. Quickly perceiving the facts of the situation, she extracts a confession from Cecelia and insists that justice be done, even if it must be accomplished at the expense of the Clarendon marriage (although she does hope that the General will have sufficient compassion to forgive Cecelia's transgressions). The form of the novel of manners is preserved: although complications and diversions are many, in the end both couples are at least reconciled if not happy. Just one nagging question remains: convinced of her daughter's moral weakness, is Lady Davenant ever aware of her own?

The principal women characters of *Helen* bear distinct resemblances to many of their predecessors in Edgeworth's canon. More human and less naïve than her predecessors, Helen evokes, for example, recollections of Caroline (of *Letters for Literary Ladies*), Belinda (of *Belinda*), and Grace Nugent (of *The Absentee*); Lady Davenant and Cecelia have in different respects much of the nature of *Belinda*'s Lady Delacour. In this last novel, however, Edgeworth concentrates on what one critic describes as "unfolding the discrepancies and inconsistencies of human behavior" through "a cross-section in points of view." Characters thus reveal a more "complicated interplay of motives" than is evident in Edgeworth's earlier fiction (Harden 213, 214, 215). Cecelia's slow and conscienceless progression from venial sin to complete loss of integrity; Helen's moral dilemma exacerbated by her guilty awareness that when she first betrayed herself she allowed herself to be betrayed; Lady Davenant's dissociation from her daughter's faithlessness even as she confesses to Helen that she herself has been faithless in the past: these are fascinating psychological portraits, artfully drawn. Such a summary does not do justice to the novel, for also artfully repeated in *Helen* are the mirrors held up to society and the individual in Edgeworth's earlier work. It does, however, suggest the extent to which, through nearly a half century of authorship, Maria Edgeworth had steadily sharpened her skillful use of the conventions of the novel of manners to create fictional situations and portraits that expressed what to her always was primary: the idea.

Figure 3. Gari Melchers (1860–1932), *In My Garden*, 1900
*(Collection of the Butler Institute of American Art,
Youngstown, Ohio)*

4

Men, Women, and Manners in *Wives and Daughters*

Maureen T. Reddy

Six months before coining the term *novel of manners* in a review of *Felix Holt*, Henry James described Elizabeth Gaskell's *Wives and Daughters* as "one of the very best novels of its kind" ("Mrs. Gaskell" 153). But what "kind" is that? Although James's comment begs this question, the elements of *Wives and Daughters* that he singles out for particular praise are strikingly similar to those he later identifies as placing George Eliot's *Felix Holt* within the tradition of the novel of manners. For instance, James comments extensively on Gaskell's skillful use of many "modest domestic facts," asserting that these details are essential to her art: her heroine Molly Gibson is "a product, to a certain extent, of clean frocks and French lessons" and of all the other "modest domestic facts" Gaskell presents (156). Here, James seems to suggest that Molly's character is largely determined by her environment, and that if we wish to understand Molly—or any other character in *Wives and Daughters*—we must first understand the social forces that help shape her. Implicit in this view is a definition of the novel of manners as a genre in which the social world and the individual character are equally important and mutually dependent, a definition James would later employ in his review of *Felix Holt*.

In this later review, James suggests that the novel of manners is the "natural" province of the woman novelist, for reasons Richard Faber states more directly over a century later; of the Victorians, Faber notes, "the women novelists are, within the limits of their experience, the most reliable guides to the Victorian social labyrinth" (14). Disguised as a compliment, this remark is actually damning, for it denies the art of women novelists, implying that they are mere "observers," not creators or shapers of their fiction. And what are the "limits" to which Faber refers? He does not define them, but we can infer from the context that the limits are those of the domestic world, the underlying assumption being that the domestic world is always smaller, less important than the political world, missing the truth that the domestic is itself political, always and everywhere.

Later critics have tended to treat *Felix Holt* as a social problem novel, with affinities to Charlotte Brontë's *Shirley* and to Gaskell's *Mary Barton* and *North and South*, a position that accords well with the often-made but seldom-articulated assumption that the social-problem novel and the novel of manners are two distinct, mutually exclusive categories.[1] I would argue, however, that novels of manners very often are social-problem novels, and that *Wives and Daughters*, like *Felix Holt, Shirley, Mary Barton*, and *North and South*, is both. Granted that *Wives and Daughters* has no single, obvious social issue at its heart that would correspond to the "arguments" of Gaskell's so-called social-problem novels—nothing so clearly defined as the plight of the industrial working classes in *Mary Barton* and *North and South*, or the sexual double standard in *Ruth*—I nevertheless believe it is more useful to think of it in relation to this group of novels than to treat it as more directly comparable to *Cranford* or to *Cousin Phillis*.[2] In *Wives and Daughters*, the social problem is actually the entire society itself, which Gaskell explores in terms of manners. The central question is this: How is the individual, especially the individual woman, to find a way to live in a society that seems hostile to individual desires, and in which members even of the *same* class cannot agree upon the proper relation of the individual to society, much less upon how one expresses that relationship in one's daily conduct? The society Gaskell examines is characterized by often subtle but nevertheless substantial conflict and disorder,.

As Lionel Trilling points out in "Manners, Morals, and the Novel," the focus of the novel of manners is the problem of reality, explored through close observation of the shifts and conflicts of social classes, as expressed in their manners, what Trilling calls a culture's "hum and buzz of implication" (200). Setting *Wives and Daughters* back forty years, during the period of her own childhood and adolescence, in fact, enabled Gaskell to comment explicitly on manners that were old-fashioned even at the time of writing, and also to comment implicitly on the present.[3] Gaskell wrote *Wives and Daughters* during 1864–65, a time when there was much debate about further parliamentary reform; the early 1860s seem to have been close in spirit to the mid-to-late 1820s, the time in which the novel is set. In the 1820s and very early 1830s, there had been considerable talk of parliamentary reform, and a number of other reforms had actually been enacted. By the mid 1830s, the middle classes not only were the source of political power in England but also had established themselves as the nation's moral conscience and the guardians of its manners, with parliamentary reform quickly followed by other reforms important to the urban community of Dissenters within which Gaskell made her adult life: the end of colonial slavery, the factory act, the municipal corporations act, and so on. Although Gaskell does not comment directly on these events in *Wives and Daughters*, they form the background of the novel: in addition to the coming election, there are rumors of a railroad branch for Hollingford (with all that such an event implies), and Gaskell relies on her audience's awareness of political changes to provide a context for her story. The awareness of social change that Gaskell here demonstrates acquires its depth and resonance from a lively engagement with the social and political changes of the two parallel periods with which she works. *Wives and Daughters* presents a society desperately seeking order in the midst of perceived chaos—some members of that society clinging to old and inadequate ways of understanding the world, others actively seeking a new order, and still others responding with confusion and withdrawal.

Tracing the maturation of one young woman, Molly Gibson, *Wives and Daughters* takes as its subject the enormous changes disturbing English society. Molly is likable but unremarkable; her ordinariness, her utter normality, is an important part of Gaskell's strategy: it prevents the reader from explaining away Molly's dissatisfaction and confusion as the predictable result of an extraordinary woman's equally predictable conflict with the conventional mores of her society. Molly's dilemma—determining how to live the best life within a cruelly limiting society—is shared by *all* women, Gaskell suggests.

Many critics agree that *Wives and Daughters* falls somewhere within the tradition of the novel of manners,[4] but there is disagreement concerning just where within that tradition the novel belongs. Some say that *Wives and Daughters* establishes Gaskell as the Victorian heir to Jane Austen through its description of a world made stable by the general acceptance of social standards and of class distinctions (Wright 209–17), with individuals knowing how they are expected to behave and learning to fulfill social expectations (Pollard 227), whereas others see a stronger connection between Gaskell and Henry James, noting the irremediable tensions between the individuals and their society in *Wives and Daughters* (Craik 207–8 and Duthie 42). I would argue that the novel is far more ambiguous than either of these positions fully acknowledges: some elements of the society Gaskell describes are indeed orderly and stable, and some characters do uphold traditional class distinctions and social standards, but other elements of the society are in disorder—many characters are confused by the cultural changes they observe, some find themselves in conflict with established social standards, and several entirely reject old notions of rank. Most importantly, the spirit with which the heroine apparently—and it is only *apparently*—comes into accord with her society differs radically from that of the typical Austen heroine.

Placing *Wives and Daughters* within the tradition of the novel of manners of course assumes that there *is* such a tradition, an assumption Henry James made when he gave the tradition a name in 1866 and one that critics still make today, without seeming to realize that the genre, if indeed it is one, has never been fully defined (and perhaps never can be), as Barbara Brothers and Bege

Bowers point out in the introductory chapter of this volume. The fifth edition of the *Oxford Companion to English Literature* recognizes "epistolary novel," "fashionable novel," "historical novel," "memoir-novel," "oriental novel," and "sentiment, novel of," but has no entry for the novel of manners. This oversight is repeated by some literary handbooks, suggesting either that various handbook editors believe there is no such thing as the novel of manners or that the novel of manners is so well understood that it requires no definition (the latter possibility seems right for the *Oxford Companion,* which also excludes "novel," offering instead "novel, rise of the"). Nevertheless, critics speak of the "tradition" of the genre, as if that tradition were not a matter of dispute. In this essay, I use *novel of manners* to describe those fictional narratives that explore the shaping of individual character by social forces, the self expressing itself in some relation to the values of the society as embodied in its conventions, including but not limited to conversation, dress, and gesture. Gaskell's particular perspective on the extent to which social forces shape the self varies according to the subject's gender, with female characters generally experiencing more extreme dissonance with their society than do similarly placed male characters and therefore resorting to more varied and complex strategies for reconciling felt needs with social demands.

There are two distinct movements in *Wives and Daughters:* one that emphasizes the new possibilities opening for men as the result of shifts in the balance of power, and a second, or counter, movement that emphasizes the continuing restrictions on, the lack of possibilities for, women. The men that Gaskell depicts are to some extent able to shape their own lives, whereas the women must all learn to accommodate themselves to the shapes their lives are given by their relationships with men. Even though Gaskell did not invent the novel's title, the way it draws attention to women's relationships underscores the difficulties awaiting any young woman who hopes for autonomy and self-fulfillment. The contrast between the meanings of adulthood for men and for women is pointed: men are expected to move into the world as self-sufficient individuals, but women may move only from dependence on fathers to what is frequently a still more onerous dependence on husbands. The novel's title appears to define the only socially acceptable roles available to women (Lansbury 109), but the role the novel shows to be most important is the missing term of the title: "mothers," as Stoneman also notes (173). This absence is emblematic both of the absence of mothering that Molly experiences and of the erasure of the mother in the society Gaskell explores, absences that are of crucial significance to the novel's concern with manners.

I want to go back now to look more closely at Gaskell's focus on manners and at the values those manners reflect—the "hum and buzz of implication" of the complex culture Gaskell describes. Trilling says that the novel is born in reaction to snobbery, in an attempt to expose the truth hidden behind a society's carefully constructed illusion of appearances (203). In *Wives and Daughters,* more so than in any of her earlier novels, Gaskell is careful to draw attention to the gap between appearances and reality through dialogue that incorporates explicit commentary on shifting relationships between classes and on individual struggles either to identify with a particular class or to reject the values of the class to which the world assigns one. The longest speeches in the novel concern manners, in the sense of outward behavior, and they are made by the male characters and by the most intellectually limited female characters (Mrs. Gibson and the Misses Browning), all of whom advocate female submission to established social standards, adhering to the ideology of the "pleasing female" (Stoneman 173). Because the novel does contrast men's and women's lives, I want to separate the two here as well, speaking first about the significance of social changes for the male characters and then about their relative lack of significance for the female characters.

One movement of the novel traces the rise of the middle classes and the decline of the aristocracy, a development important mostly for men. By novel's end, the aristocracy's influence has waned considerably, with only the most limited characters—all of them women—caring much about their doings. Osborne Hamley's fall from grace and eventual death are part of this thematic pattern. The eldest son of the local squire, Osborne in appearance and in tastes suggests a move upward from the squirearchy to the aristocracy, a move Gaskell portrays also as a feminization; he is interested in the land only as a source of wealth and of social position, finds dealing directly with the Hamley tenants distasteful, writes sentimental poetry, is "delicate" and fine in appearance and fastidious in his tastes (106). Osborne seems bred for idleness; when his allowance is cut and he is faced with the prospect of having to earn his own living, Osborne cannot think of a single skill that would earn him adequate money, a predicament that parallels the difficulties of women. Significantly, Osborne dies of an unspecified wasting disease—as does his mother, who shares his appearance and tastes—which seems a strain of that "idle women's illness" so common in Victorian novels.

Although Squire Hamley is irritated by Osborne and admits being unable to understand him, just as he cannot understand his own wife, whom Osborne greatly resembles, the Squire also stands slightly in awe of his son, primarily because of the younger man's refinement and social ease. The squire himself feels uneasy with his social peers because he has no education. Nevertheless, he rigidly refuses to acknowledge social changes and stubbornly insists that the world acknowledge his inherent superiority by virtue of his birth into an ancient family. He says he is a "Hamley of Hamley, straight in descent from nobody knows where—the Heptarchy, they say" (106), and that this line of descent should be enough. He places all hope for the future on Osborne, who is expected to excel at university, marry into a wealthy, aristocratic family, and restore

Hamley Hall to the glory of bygone years with the infusion of capital his marriage should bring. Osborne, however, does poorly at Cambridge, falls into debt, marries well beneath his hereditary rank, and dies young, before he has mustered the courage to confess his marriage to his father. The Squire's rigidity is a major cause of the rift between father and son, which in turn hastens the son's death. The Squire's younger son, Roger, on the other hand—a "red-brown, big-boned, clumsy chap" who is thought to be rather slow (106)—makes a great success at Cambridge and is sought after by all ranks, including the new breed of aristocrat represented by the scientific Lord Hollingford, heir to the Cumnor estates. It is Roger who will restore the family estate, not by the traditional route of *marrying* money, but by *earning* money as a naturalist. Lord Hollingford himself seems less an aristocrat than a middle-class professional man, in manner and in tastes like Roger Hamley and Mr. Gibson, Molly's father. Hollingford even looks like Roger: he is a "tall ungainly man . . . shy, and slow at making commonplace speeches . . . his scientific acquirements considerable enough to entitle him to much reputation in the European republic of learned men" (68). He commands respect not by his birth but by his accomplishments.

The Squire, the most traditional man in the novel, changes a great deal by story's end. He accepts Osborne's widow—a French, Roman Catholic nursery maid—because he dotes on his grandson, and ends up hoping that his remaining son will marry exactly the woman he had previously insisted "[i]t would never do" for a Hamley of Hamley to love (88), a member of the "prohibited ranks" (445). The Squire learns the value of flexibility only through hard experience—and without fully understanding why the world has changed so much—but he *does* learn it. Making Osborne's wife French, Roman Catholic, and a servant affords Gaskell the opportunity of stressing the great distance between appearance and reality. Aimée represents all that men of the Squire's class most fear: she arouses all manner of prejudices, including anti-Jacobism (at a time when England was just beginning to get over the war with France), anti-Catholicism (at a time when Catholic Emancipation was a major political issue), and both gender and class hostilities. In reality, though, she is meek, mild, even quite reassuringly genteel. The Squire is certain that Aimée tricked Osborne into marriage via the infamous wiles of French women—also, incidentally, attributed to Molly's stepsister Cynthia, who was educated in France—until he gets to know her and sees that she is entirely innocent, more child than woman.

In the end, the story the novel tells of men's lives shows the wisdom of inclusion: the boundaries between classes shift and are blurrily redrawn to include previously excluded elements that end up strengthening, not weakening, the genteel classes. For instance, delicate Osborne Hamley's French wife produces a sturdy male child to carry on the Hamley name. I think we need to read all this as an expression of Gaskell's uneasy conservatism: the threat of revolution can only be overcome, she suggests, by incorporating as many people as possible into the ruling classes, without fundamentally redefining the ideas of class or of rule. Considering Gaskell's audience—the middle-class readers of the *Cornhill Magazine*—and the fact that, as Terry Eagleton observes, the small size of the electorate before 1867 made it likely that any important novel would reach a large segment of the ruling classes (*The Function of Criticism* 47), it seems clear that this novel is in some ways a plea for change and for tolerance of change, offering reassurance that the basic character of English society will not weaken but actually will strengthen if class relationships shift. *Wives and Daughters* shows such change to be inevitable, the only uncertainty being what the response to change will be. The time when the boundaries between classes were clearly defined and evident to all, when, as Lady Cumnor wistfully observes, "every class had a sort of costume of its own—and servants did not ape tradespeople, nor tradespeople professional men, and so on" (590), is long past even as the novel begins, and more substantial differences among classes are fast disappearing. The novel's three most admirable men—Roger Hamley, Mr. Gibson, and Lord Hollingford—are equals, members of that European *republic* of learned men. All the men are adapting the manners of the middle classes, presumably an expression of their adoption of the values of those same classes— the "democratic tendencies" Mrs. Gibson bemoans in her husband—and the novel examines both the increased freedom and the continued repression this shift implies.

There is evidence in Gaskell's letters that she originally intended Squire Hamley to be a yeoman (no. 550), but she changed her mind, thereby altering the structure of the work, and made him a squire who is, nonetheless, yeoman-like in his love of the land, his lack of education, his total distrust of the city, and his insistence that the ancient order is the best, indeed the only entirely imaginable structure for society. Gaskell's decision to change the class of this character is revealing, as the shift enabled her to limit her attention to representatives of the different segments of those classes that ruled England both before the first Reform Act and after it. Squire Hamley reminds us of the traditional basis of power and status, the land, and his worsening economic situation and increasing confusion stand in direct contrast to the ascendancy and confidence of the new man, Robert Gibson, a propertyless professional representative of the class that became the source of political power after the Reform Act.

Of course, it is men only who are directly involved in these shifts of power: women remain disenfranchised, excluded from the public arena. This gender-based distinction makes women of the middle and upper classes especially suitable subjects for novels of manners, which generally investigate the domestic sphere, the domain of women. *Wives and Daughters* sharply contrasts the very different social roles of men and of women. Subtitled "An Every-Day Story," the novel gives a great deal of careful attention to what one does in everyday life, to how one fills one's days. The men of the novel, with the important exception of Osborne Hamley, are busy with useful work of some type, but the women are a different story; freed from domestic work by virtue of their privileged class (even the comparatively poor Brownings have a servant), prohibited by the mores of that same class from working for pay, the women have trouble finding anything to do, and therefore devote much of their time to analyzing behavior and speculating about feeling.[5] The story the novel tells of women's lives is far more radical than is the story woven from the men's lives, for the former encodes a social critique so far-reaching as to challenge the basis of the society Gaskell dissects. I think those critics who describe *Wives and Daughters* as more conservative and "less ideologically questioning" than Gaskell's earlier novels—who see Gaskell in her final book accepting "social creeds and institutions," to quote Shirley Foster's representative remark (176)— miss the significance of the doubled plot and theme, the clear separation of the sexes.

Much of the novel concerns the relationship of manners to class and the ways in which social class affects the individual life. Three characters—Hyacinth Gibson, Squire Hamley, and Lady Harriet Cumnor—say quite a lot about issues of class. Interestingly, these three people, with their widely divergent views, share a single audience: Molly Gibson, who is herself nearly classless because of her peculiar position as the motherless daughter of a country general practitioner. That Gaskell chose to make her central character the daughter of a general practitioner and planned to marry her to the scientific Roger Hamley draws our attention to the theme of professional accomplishments determining men's status in the new order to come. The medical man who preceded Gibson as the local g.p. was treated as an inferior by the county families, usually sent to eat in the kitchen with the servants when attending the Cumnors at the Towers, and generally ignored socially. When Gibson first arrives in Hollingford, it seems that he, too, will be relegated to a servant's role, but he is not; instead, he is frequently invited to dine at the Towers and treated as an equal by Lord Hollingford. The main reason for this treatment is that Gibson is a "man of science," to use Gaskell's term, not merely a medical hired hand, and Lord Hollingford has a great interest in science—in fact, one of his dinner parties is described as a gathering of the "freemasonry" of science.

Another reason, unmentioned by Gaskell but certainly contributing to her characterization of Gibson, is the shift in medical men's status still working itself out in the first half of the nineteenth century. Until midcentury, medical men were not uniformly true professionals, because of the lack of widely shared standards, and they tended to fall into one of three main groups: surgeons who practiced obstetrics, frequently considered lower class because they worked with their hands; "consultants" who held appointments at London hospitals, made a great deal of money, and were certainly gentlemen by birth and education; and, in the middle, general practitioners, country physicians who often performed surgery and served as midwives as part of their practices. During the debates that carried over to midcentury, consultants several times tried to exclude general practitioners from the profession. There was considerable confusion about the social class of the country doctor: did he take his standing from his birth? His competence? His own achievements and education? On the whole, his social standing was ambiguous.

Molly, the daughter of a general practitioner whose origins are unknown but who has considerable personal polish and an admirable intellect, is unplaceable. Socially, she is clearly superior to the Misses Browning, the spinsters who represent the old middle classes, yet inferior to the Cumnors and even to the Hamleys; she and her father form their own class. Molly is invited to visit at Hamley Hall and at the Towers, in both cases first because the families like Mr. Gibson and then because they grow to care for Molly herself. Molly associates with, but is not of, the various classes described in the novel; she is permanently outside all such placing. Molly's ambiguous class standing is central to the novel's plot because an important part of her education is her observation, and either acceptance or rejection, of the differing codes of conduct of several classes. Feeling instinctively that Molly is not really one of them enables people to speak more openly to her than they might to one of their peers or to someone clearly superior or inferior in class. Also contributing to Molly's suitability as an audience are her youth and the sense that she might end up fitting in anywhere at all. Lady Harriet, for instance, seems to forget that Molly might consider herself a member of the same class as the Brownings, rudely discoursing on "that sort of person" to Molly. By novel's end, Molly sees clearly the multiple ways in which each established vantage point on the world serves to stifle the individual and to limit—artificially—possibilities for happiness. Molly is the character who most intensely experiences the disorder of the transitional period in which she lives. However, unlike Roger, who can go off to Africa and thereby escape the restrictions of social class, Molly has no options for escape except, briefly, an illness that threatens to end her life entirely.

As the novel opens, Molly is a girl of twelve, on the cusp of adolescence. Although she is happiest when climbing trees or riding with her father, she is about to be introduced to the requirements of young ladyhood, an introduction that proves to be deeply painful, in large measure because Molly is motherless and is therefore deprived of the natural guide for what turns out to be the fairly hazardous business of learning the social code—the manners—of her society. Early in the novel, Molly's motherlessness seems nearly incidental; we are told on the second page of the book that there have thus far been no events in Molly's life: "Poor child! it is true that she had lost her mother, which was a jar to the whole tenour of her life . . . [but] she had been too young to be conscious of it at the time" (36). Since she is now old enough to be intensely conscious of this loss, the absence of the mother becomes a felt presence as the novel unfolds. Various people comment on Molly's motherlessness, noting that her life would have been better had her mother survived, and Molly herself comes to feel the want of a mother and to go in search of one, a pattern familiar from Gaskell's short stories and other novels.

Gaskell herself was motherless; her letters reflect the enormous importance she attached to the mother in a girl's life. In her fiction, motherlessness is both actual and symbolic: Gaskell often seems to be exploring the ways in which her culture itself is motherless, with the knowledge that is prized and preserved being the father's, while the experience of the mother is lost or sent underground, passed on in whispers from mother to daughter. The erasure of female experience in official culture symbolized by the absence of the mother may also be an enactment of anger at the mother, who must seem like an enemy of freedom to the girl-child when mother teaches daughter to shrink into the requirements of society. There are no truly effective mothers in *Wives and Daughters,* except perhaps Lady Cuxhaven, of whom we are given but a few glimpses. Lady Cumnor left the rearing of her daughters to various unsuitable governesses, all like the second Mrs. Gibson in their failings; Molly's stepmother herself fails to mother Cynthia, preferring to send her off to boarding school to leave the field free for herself, and she later fails with Molly, a failure symbolized on their first meeting by the older woman's taking the food meant for the girl and then allowing others to believe Molly has eaten it all; Mrs. Hamley's daughter died young, but Mrs. Hamley seems always to have preferred her elder son Osborne to all others, refusing to see his flaws.

Molly first turns to the Gibsons' servant Betty as a mother substitute, but Betty's ability to serve Molly in this capacity is severely limited, both by her own immaturity (which we can discern in her squabbles with Miss Eyre for Molly's affection) and by her lower social class; Betty does not know the subtleties of the rules of the class in which Molly must move. Then, Molly's father decides that Molly needs a mother, and determines to procure one for her by marrying again. Significantly, Gibson sees the mother's function strictly in terms of enforcing patriarchal imperatives: he wants someone to protect Molly from inappropriate (by his standards) male romantic desire. It is Molly herself who must find a mother, and this quest constitutes a central, albeit largely covert, theme of the novel.

Seeing Gibson's earlier care of Molly as excellent "mothering," some of the many critics who note the importance of mother-surrogates in the novel blame him for failing to recognize his own ability to function as a mother,[6] but this critical assessment is true only in a very limited way. Gibson most wants to keep Molly ignorant, believing that women have no use for reading and writing and convinced that education in anything other than domestic arts only destroys female innocence, which he prizes. He has actually given Molly a course in repression and suppression, a teaching role taken up later by Roger, who meets Molly's misery over her father's marriage plans with some unhelpful sermonizing that concludes with "One has always to try to think more of others than of oneself" (152), traditional advice for girls and women. Roger asserts, echoing Gibson's own thoughts on the matter, "It seems as if there might be cases where . . . it must be almost a duty to find some one to be a substitute for the mother" (150). The "duty" Roger mentions, like Gibson's attempts to "mother" Molly himself, involves the portion of the mother's role devoted to patriarchal codes, with the mother seen strictly as the person who molds the child to participate in patriarchal culture. What Molly also needs, though, is the kind of mothering that stands in opposition to patriarchal power, mothering that combines what Sara Ruddick calls "attentive love" with recognition of social demands, mediating between the two in the best interests of the child (359). In fact, though, Molly finds no real mother, no one who can both nurture her and help her to move into her society.

Moving among four family groups, which also represent four gradations of social class—the Gibsons, the Hamleys, the Cumnors, and the Brownings— Molly finds a possible mother in each, but no one fully able to take a mother's place. Molly loves the Misses Browning, her dead mother's old friends, but discovers their limitations quite early in her adolescence; although well-intentioned, neither sister is capable of understanding subtleties of attitude or of behavior. Further, Molly's developing attachment to Mrs. Hamley shows her that the Brownings are rather vulgar. Molly tries to banish such thoughts and to cling loyally to these women, but "she could not help having a sense of refinement, which had made her appreciate the whole manner of being at [Hamley] Hall. By her dear old friends the Miss Brownings she was petted and caressed so much that she became ashamed of noticing the coarser and louder tones in which they spoke, the provincialism of their pronunciation, the absence of interest in things, and their greediness of details about persons" (182–83). Mrs. Hamley herself proves to be an inadequate substitute mother, in part because her invalidism and isolation render her far less helpful than she wishes to be, but also because of her faulty judgment, which leads her to overvalue one son and undervalue the other, and because of her too thorough dedication to the ideal of female submission. On her father's urging, Molly tries to consider her stepmother a real mother, but Hyacinth Gibson's falseness, her flimsy character, her egoism, her devotion to appearances over reality, and her belief that the mother's main duty is to find husbands for her daughters repel Molly and disqualify the stepmother as guide. Lady Harriet Cumnor tries to "adopt" Molly, speaking often of taking Molly under her wing, but she, too, has serious limitations, some of which stem from the inadequate mothering she received from Lady Cumnor and the governesses. Although Lady Harriet provides an important service to Molly, rescuing her from social shunning, it is Molly who instructs Lady Harriet in proper behavior by ignoring their differences of rank and age in order to voice her disapproval of Lady Harriet's habit of making fun of the Misses Browning. Despite her finally taking two men—her father and Roger Hamley—as her standards for both manners and morals, Molly must usually be her own guide, especially since each man fails her at a crucial juncture, Mr. Gibson when he deludedly imagines that Hyacinth would be a good mother to Molly, and Roger when he values Cynthia's physical beauty over Molly's more enduring qualities.

Three of the four family groups presented in the novel also offer Molly examples of marriage, while the fourth, the Misses Browning, shows what it means to be female and unmarried when one is neither young nor wealthy, a situation that seems even more constricting than marriage. In every case, marriage more significantly affects the female character than it does the male, who has outside interests in which to immerse himself; in fact, Mr. Gibson's marriage more deeply affects his daughter than it does himself, for he can contrive to stay away from home much of each day. The Hamleys love each other, but the Squire neither shares his wife's interests nor understands her emotional needs; Mrs. Hamley's response is to give up her interests, sacrificing herself for her husband and her sons. Like Mrs. Hamley, Lady Cumnor is married to a man greatly inferior to her in intelligence, but loving and decent. Also like Mrs. Hamley, Lady Cumnor is intensely lonely. Instead of sacrificing herself, though, Lady Cumnor sacrifices everyone else, ceaselessly meddling in other people's lives. Both Lady Cumnor and Mrs. Hamley fall ill of wasting diseases, but Lady Cumnor recovers whereas Mrs. Hamley dies, fates suggesting that Lady Cumnor's strategy for dealing with life—asserting her will instead of submitting, as Mrs. Hamley does—is the healthier option for women. The other marriage Molly observes is her father's to Hyacinth, which is basically a business transaction—Mr. Gibson gets a guardian for his daughter; Mrs. Gibson, financial security—giving no real happiness and causing tremendous discomfort for both.[7]

Many readers of *Wives and Daughters* find Molly's stepmother both the most amusing and the most exasperating character in the novel. She is silly, offensive, dishonest, wholly without self-knowledge, and, of course, snobbish; she is also the novel's shrewdest observer of manners. Mrs. Gibson understands manners strictly in the sense of social etiquette, not realizing that systems of social codes ought to be based upon deeper values.[8] For Mrs. Gibson, the world *is* merely appearance, and appearances are all that count: to appear genteel is to be genteel, in her way of thinking. She quite literally devotes her adult life to creating the appearance of gentility. Despite striving mightily to impress the Cumnors, for instance, Mrs. Gibson does not really want a friendship with them; what she does want is a display of friendship presented to the rest of the town.

She accepts all casual, even nearly insulting, invitations to the Towers with alacrity, even though these visits consist of long periods of solitude or service for the Countess, followed by brief periods of attention from Lady Cumnor, during which the Countess lectures the doctor's wife as if the latter were a not very bright or good child. Mrs. Gibson will not admit her true relationship with the Countess even to herself. Similarly, she believes it her duty as a stepmother to maintain the *appearance* of impartiality, which results in her frequently making Molly miserable by forcing her stepdaughter to have exactly the same things her own daughter has, despite enormous differences of taste between Molly and Cynthia.

When we first meet Mrs. Gibson, she is still Mrs. Kirkpatrick, the ex-governess of the Cumnors (who persist in calling her by her maiden name, "Clare," throughout two marriages), now a widow trying (badly) to run a small school. She is eager to marry again because, as she puts it to herself, marriage is "the natural thing; then the husband has all that kind of dirty work to do [what she calls "toiling and moiling for money"], and his wife sits in the drawing-room like a lady" (131). When Mr. Gibson proposes marriage, she bursts into hysterical tears, caused by its being "such a wonderful relief to feel that she need not struggle any more for a livelihood" (140). Gaskell does criticize Mrs. Gibson for her devotion to appearances, but the widow's practical conception of marriage is not harshly criticized and is, in fact, a truer description of what marriage means to an impoverished woman than are the romantic notions we might find more attractive: it *is* hard for a woman to earn her own way in a society that believes marriage to be "the natural thing" for all women and that effectively closes off other possibilities. Although a man may gain status through his work, a woman can only lose.

Mrs. Gibson's basic flaw is her lack of a moral center, which Gaskell illustrates by detailing the myriad ways in which Mrs. Gibson's manners are entirely separate from moral standards of any sort. This essential emptiness can also be seen in Mrs. Gibson's mutable identity, symbolized by her many names: "Clare" to the Cumnors, "Hyacinth" to her husband (who hates the silly, affected, not-English name), "Mrs. Kirkpatrick" to her pupils, "Mrs. Gibson" to the Hamleys and to the townspeople, and, most jarring of all, "Mama" to Cynthia and Molly, who feel no daughterly affection for her. Interestingly, Mrs. Gibson lies repeatedly without really noticing she is lying; indeed, she once tells Lady Harriet that if she *had* ever lied, which of course she denies doing, "I should have died of self-reproach. . . . But then I have so much that is unbending in my nature, and in our sphere of life there are so few temptations, if we are humble we are also simple, and unshackled by etiquette" (404). Like so many of Mrs. Gibson's speeches, this one is unintentionally self-revealing: in just two sentences, she suggests that etiquette requires one to lie; that only the lack of temptation prevents people from lying; that honesty is a virtue for the humble only, not to be expected of those in a higher sphere; and that manners are "shackles" worn only by those in higher classes.

Not surprisingly, Mrs. Gibson's daughter Cynthia has no enduring moral standards either; unfortunately for her peace of mind, however, Cynthia is intelligent enough to realize that she is missing an essential element of character, and she tries unsuccessfully to live up to the standards she perceives to be held by Molly and Mr. Gibson. In other words, she adopts the Gibsons' manners as far as she can, thinking that outward conformity will lead to inner comprehension of values. An important component of Cynthia's universal attractiveness is actually closely connected to her lack of moral standards: she is able to be all things to all people because she has no inner core and so is infinitely adaptable. Above all, Cynthia wants to be liked; yet, as a result of her early deprivation of love, she is unable to like herself or to love anyone else. Cynthia's chameleon-like self is nicely represented by her nearly magical ability to transform clothing. Molly marvels at one point that "the pale lilac muslin gown [Cynthia] wore this evening had been worn many times before, and had looked unfit to wear again till Cynthia put it on. Then the limpness became softness, and the very creases took the lines of beauty" (277). A moment later, Molly notices that Cynthia has "put on her armour of magic that evening—involuntarily as she always did; but, on the other side, she could not help trying her power on strangers" (277).

In this novel, Gaskell uses women's clothing and their sense of style to symbolize the relation of self and society. The men all dress similarly, with the exception of the dandyish Osborne, and therefore cannot be "placed," morally or socially, by their dress; women's clothing, however, continues to be the sort of "costume" Lady Cumnor imagines to have vanished from the world. The issue of clothing is closely connected to the ways in which characters see themselves, whether from the inside only, from the outside only, or through some combination of both; that is, a character's mode of dress serves as a reflection of the extent to which the real self is identified with social pose. Only Osborne among the male characters exhibits any dissonance between the public and the private self, his social pose—the sophisticated man about town, bantering with Mrs. Gibson and Cynthia—carefully constructed to hide his actual feelings, his real self. Molly, who knows Osborne's secret, sometimes wonders if she dreamed the whole story of his marriage, puzzling over this "fact which seemed so all-important to Osborne, yet which made so little difference in his way of life—either in speech or action" (272). Osborne, as we have seen, is "feminized" in other ways as well.

Only Cynthia and Lady Harriet can see themselves simultaneously from the inside and the outside, each woman manipulating appearances at will but always recognizing her inner self as separable from others' views of her. Lady Harriet goes about in twice-worn, rumpled muslin gowns, little caring what others think of her, because she is secure in self-knowledge and in her lofty social position; however, she never falls into the error of imagining that appearances do not matter. When the townspeople are disappointed at the annual charity ball—having hoped to see a "real duchess" arrayed in diamonds, they instead find the duchess "a fat, middle-aged woman . . . dressed almost like a girl—in a sprigged muslin, with natural flowers in her hair, but not a vestige of a jewel or a diamond" (332)—Lady Harriet realizes that this disappointment may translate into lost votes at election time, and she organizes her family into dancing with the folk in compensation. As she tells her baffled brother, who is oblivious to appearances, "it's like having a pantomime with harlequin and columbine in plain clothes" to have a duchess without diamonds at a ball (337).

Cynthia, too, is remarkably adept at separating her social self (the way others see her) from her private self (the way she sees herself), able to manufacture a charming and convincing interest in others even when she is feeling most troubled. As we might expect, Cynthia excels at manipulating appearances through clothing: several times in the novel we see Cynthia creating a beautiful something from "nothing," restyling old clothes or using a bit of cheap ribbon to transform a plain dress into an elegant one. The most striking instance of this skill is Cynthia's remaking the bouquets sent by Osborne and Roger for Molly and Cynthia to take to the ball. Molly, ever sensitive to the feelings of others, urges Cynthia to leave the bouquets as they are, exclaiming, "Don't you see how carefully the colours are arranged—they have taken such pains," but Cynthia insists on making the two bouquets into a "little coronet . . . sewn on black velvet, which will never be seen—just as they do in France" for Molly's hair and a smaller bouquet for herself, explaining to Molly, "I never would allow sentiment to interfere with my choice of colours" (319). Typically, Mrs. Gibson thinks long and hard about her own dress for the ball, wondering how best to impress her neighbors, while Cynthia "was the one who took the affair most lightly" and "Molly looked upon the ceremony of dressing for a first ball as rather a serious ceremony. . . . [She] wanted her appearance to be correct and unnoticed" (320).

Mrs. Gibson, who is able to see herself only from the outside, is puzzled when others try to see beyond appearances, because she believes the world is only appearance. Her attitude toward clothing reflects this view: for Mrs. Gibson, clothes indeed make the woman. When Cynthia leaves Hollingford for a long stay in London, for instance, her mother is more concerned with giving her daughter commissions for fashionable items than she is with Cynthia's welfare. Mrs. Gibson concerns herself with Cynthia's and Molly's dress for the ball, for example, only because she decides that the ball will be the girls' "debut," and will therefore reflect on her: "Aping the manners of the aristocracy as far as she knew them, she intended to 'bring out' Molly and Cynthia on this occasion, which she regarded in something of the light of a presentation at Court" (274). The elder Miss Browning is "half puzzled and half affronted" by this ridiculous conceit, telling Mrs. Gibson that "I don't understand it at all. In my days girls went wherever it pleased people to ask them, without this farce of bursting out in all their new fine clothes at some public place. . . . There was no talk of 'coming out' in those days for any one under the daughter of a Squire" (275). But Mrs. Gibson does not understand this objection; in her view, to mimic the aristocracy is to become the aristocracy.

In direct contrast to Mrs. Gibson, Molly can see herself only from the inside. She likes pretty clothes simply because they are pretty, a childlike view of fashion. She has no sense of the symbolic value of clothing, wishing only that her clothes will let her blend into the group around her. Molly makes the social mistake of thinking appearances unimportant, an error that leads her into trouble several times. While the social code may be changing for men, it remains rigid for women. One area in which women challenge prevailing manners, and then only at the risk of complete social banishment, is that of relationships between unmarried men and women. All such relationships are presumed to be potentially romantic; few people can conceive of a real friendship between a man and a woman. When the secretly married Osborne becomes friendly with Molly, everyone imagines they are romantically involved. Cynthia is severely chastised by Mr. Gibson for encouraging a young man's attentions, yet we know that Cynthia expends precisely the same amount of energy making herself agreeable to men and to women. She wants to be liked and admired by all, but to young men a woman's attention seems always to signal romantic interest. There is some ambiguity here, though, as Cynthia's skill at manipulating appearances through clothing suggests: she uses her body for social ends, clear-sightedly playing the marriage market to her best advantage. She is so used to attracting others that she often seems to forget other behavioral possibilities, almost instinctively flirting with every man, and woman, she meets. Gibson criticizes her, but Gaskell really does not, showing Cynthia's failings to be social, not merely personal, problems.

Innocent Molly is excluded from Hollingford's polite society and actually cut by acquaintances in the street when she is suspected of sexual impropriety after being seen alone with the Cumnors' land-agent, Preston. Her father, who prides himself on caring little for appearances and on doing what he chooses without regard to social strictures, in this case is eager to refute the town's gossip, telling Molly that "everyone makes it their business to cast dirt on a girl's name who has disregarded the commonest rules of modesty and propriety" (568). Later, he makes the same point to Cynthia by saying that she has been a "flirt and a jilt, even to a degree of dragging Molly's name down into the same mire. . . . You cannot tell what evil constructions are put upon actions ever so slightly beyond the bounds of maidenly propriety" (596–97). Gibson is right, of course, in describing the importance of appearances to women in his society, but the issue is fraught with Gaskell's own ambivalence. On the one hand, she is critical of people who make judgments based solely on appearances, as well as the standards of conduct for women that make such judgments so dangerous; on the other, she seems to endorse women's suppression of their feelings and strict adherence to a constraining code of manners. Molly is wrongly accused, but she is never vindicated; instead, Lady Harriet comes to her rescue and essentially forces Molly on the townspeople's notice by creating a situation in which continuing to snub Molly would be to insult Lady Harriet.

The ease with which Lady Harriet restores Molly to her former position emphasizes the great distance between manners and morals. The townspeople accept Lady Harriet's opinion and are ruled by it, allowing it to override their own belief that Molly has committed a grave error, an acceptance suggesting that their interest in appearances, in manners, is far greater than their interest in morality or their concern for the truth. The gap between manners and morals points to the conclusion that the code governing women's behavior needs re-thinking, but Gaskell undercuts this suggestion in the final chapters of the book. Molly, visiting Hamley Hall after the death of Mrs. Hamley, assumes a "digni-fied reserve" toward Roger (686), abandoning all the friendly ease of their long relationship, because she is worried about the construction people will put on her visit to the Hall. One of the women who believed the rumors about Molly and Preston, and who consequently refused to allow her granddaughter to so much as speak to Molly for fear of social contamination, is the person who puts this fear into Molly's head. Even though she believes this person to be a "commonplace, unrefined woman" (682), Molly allows the imputation of pos-sible impropriety to disturb her, causing her to affect indifference to Roger, which in turn causes Roger to think Molly no longer cares for him. The odd thing here is that Gaskell evidently approves of Molly's ridiculous behavior, holding it up as an example of the heroine's delicacy and refinement.[9]

Just as women's position in society remains static, so are women's manners portrayed as unchanging. The "freemasonry of science," with all that it symbol-izes, is not open to women, who cannot hope that people will look beyond their manners in order to judge them on the basis of their achievements, as they would judge a Lord Hollingford, a Roger Hamley, or a Mr. Gibson. Because there are so few avenues of achievement open to them, women remain at the mercy of a stifling, dehumanizing social code. To violate this code, or even to *appear* to violate it, puts a woman outside her society entirely, where she cannot hope to survive. Given women's economic dependence on men, to make oneself ineligi-ble for marriage by becoming the subject of scandal is to commit social and economic suicide if one is female. Gaskell is critical of the sexual double standard but seems unable, or unwilling, to imagine genuine changes.

Gaskell does, however, see clearly that the society in which Molly lives encourages dishonesty in women by reckoning their manners more important than their morals. In this way, Mrs. Gibson's basic flaw—her lack of a moral center, of a real self—is one that reflects the social training offered women of all classes. As Patsy Stoneman shrewdly points out, Mrs. Gibson's moral bankruptcy is the logical result of her dedication to the notion of the "pleasing female," an ideology into which she, like other women, has been carefully socialized (173–74). The surprise is not that Mrs. Gibson worships appearances but that some other women somehow manage to escape superficiality and to maintain inner selves. Whatever else we might say about her, Mrs. Gibson grasps the basic facts of the society that made her.

Molly, too, comes to understand these facts, although she refuses to be entirely the product of her society. In Molly's case, knowledge is symbolized by a wasting illness. She becomes progressively weaker, having fallen ill while visiting Hamley Hall after Mrs. Hamley's death, a visit marked by the strain of keeping up a false reserve toward Roger for the sake of appearances, and her father seems to doubt that she will survive the illness. Her illness, after which she is acknowledged to be a woman, no longer a girl, can be read as a response to her recognition of the severe limitations imposed on women, just as her earlier identification with men can be seen as an attempt to circumvent those as yet only half-perceived limits. We may also think of the illness as a process of infantile regression, signifying Molly's desire both for a reunion with her dead mother and for an escape from the rules that regulate adult womanhood. Her recovery, which is incomplete at the end of the book, suggests an acceptance of the limitations and a willingness to try for whatever measure of happiness may be possible; it suggests also a turning away from the dead mother toward her more acceptable adult substitute: the man that Molly loves, Roger Hamley.

The fact that the novel is unfinished—Gaskell wrote *Wives and Daughters* as a serial for the monthly *Cornhill Magazine* and died before completing the final installment—is peculiarly appropriate. Gaskell's text breaks off with Roger's setting off to complete his research in Africa, hoping to return to ask Molly to marry him; at this point, however, no understanding has been reached between them, and Molly does not know Roger loves her. Although her editor, Frederick Greenwood, wrote a conclusion for *Wives and Daughters* in which he told how Gaskell planned to end the novel, using her letters and conversations as a guide and making it clear that Gaskell intended for Molly and Roger to marry, the lack of closure is more consistent with the rest of this novel than any formal closure would be. We feel certain that the men of the novel will evolve new and useful ways of dealing with their society, and will come into harmony with it because that society will be of their own creation. Women, however, will remain enclosed by the one social institution that most directly affects them—marriage—and will have no power to change its public meaning.

Continuing conflict with their society can only destroy those women who engage in it, but complete acceptance of that society has the same result: three of the women who fully accept social conventions—Mrs. Gibson, Mrs. Hamley, and Lady Cumnor—suffer wasting but unspecified illnesses much like the one from which Molly is recuperating when the novel breaks off. There seems to be no way for women to achieve actual happiness within the confines of their society, and this social problem seems insoluble.

Notes

1. See, for example, Millett, 341–42, cited in the introductory chapter of this volume.

2. Patsy Stoneman alone among critics writing on Gaskell offers a model for reading her novels as part of an integrated whole; most critics divide Gaskell's works into social problem or "lady novelist" categories.

3. Angus Easson makes a similar point, 187.

4. See Craik (211) and Pollard (225).

5. Spacks also notes this, 88–89.

6. See, for example, Berke and Berke, 98–101. Stoneman considers Mr. Gibson, who silences Molly by disallowing discussion of emotions, to be "only the most attractive of a long line of fallible fathers [in Gaskell's novels] . . . from whom their daughters must fight free" (177). Among critics who remark on Molly's motherlessness and her search for mother surrogates, Stoneman offers the fullest analysis and the one closest to my own, albeit without my focus on manners. In chapter 10 of *Elizabeth Gaskell,* Stoneman argues that *Wives and Daughters* demonstrates Gaskell's awareness that women's effectiveness as mothers is limited by their inadequate educations and lack of autonomy, with social restrictions making it nearly impossible for mothers truly to take care of their daughters. Margaret Homans, in *Bearing the Word,* also sees Molly's motherlessness as thematically significant, but Homans's approach is quite different from mine, as she is primarily concerned with issues of language and therefore focuses on Molly's split "between her dead and her living mothers' languages, between the literal and the symbolic order" (272).

7. Spacks makes similar points, 88–94.

8. Easson, 192, makes the same point, as do most critics writing on *Wives and Daughters.*

9. Patricia Beer also comments on this, 170–71.

Figure 4. Louis Charles Moeller (1855–1930), *A Political Discussion*
(*Collection of the Butler Institute of American Art,
Youngstown, Ohio*)

5

Anthony Trollope and the Unmannerly Novel

James R. Kincaid

The novel of manners, insofar as there is such a thing, is a menacing genre. Because it has a great deal to protect, it is given to threatening gestures, sometimes in disguised form but often not. It offers rewards, of course, to those with good manners—and often even to those whose manners are not so good; but it will not tolerate those who raise questions about the very basis for a particular system of manners. Malvolio need only be embarrassed, but Falstaff threatens to give the game away and must be banished. Closer to home, Mrs. Proudie is a raucous upsetter of applecarts but can be uneasily accepted all the same; the Stanhope family makes jokes about the apples themselves, about the orchard and the greengrocers, about the entire system—and must be shipped back to Italy. The novel of manners is often liberal and kindly, welcoming the diversifying of its codes, softening the inflexible, including in its sweep nearly everyone. But not quite everyone. The loafer, the fool, the loudmouth, and the incompetent can all be tolerated; but not the incendiary, the woman from Mars, the anarchist: the one who questions the rules.

Actually, this "novel of manners" I have been discussing scarcely exists for us in any realized form. Where is the novel without these alien questioners—the Mary Crawford, the Wilkins Micawber, the Lady Mabel Grex—who do more than break the rules: they expose the rules for what they are—artificial, often ridiculous means for maintaining an ideology. I know of no novel of manners that cannot be constructed as an anti- or meta-novel of manners, no novel, that is, that does not expose and often subvert the codes of behavior, the habitual practice of the communities with which it deals, and the individuals who populate those communities. The expulsion or defeat of the alien voices may, I suppose, be construed as a means of protecting the ideology of the prevailing manners, but it may also be construed as a device for exposing the raw power, the snarling brute force underlying that ideology.

Ideologies function in these novels to convert manners into the appearance of nature. On the one hand, this sleight of hand, this presto-chango of mere form into substantial habit, is done very subtly, by means of a whole network of implicit assumptions; on the other hand, the grin, like that of the Cheshire Cat, must expose some fangs. After all, we need no one come from the grave to point out that our own manners—codes of dress, modes of making contact with one another, ways of doing business, or religion, or even seduction—are ridiculously hollow, stylized, unnatural. We all, I suppose, wish "nice days" to those whose hideous deaths would trouble us not at all, sign ourselves "sincerely" to manifest hypocrisy, wear, as the case may be, uncomfortable and unflattering bits of cloth about our necks or skirts whose length is indicated not by the attractiveness or otherwise of skin and bone beneath but by the profit motive of "designers." We are, as Trollope is fond of pointing out, not fundamentally different from those who paint their bodies blue and wail at the moon. The ideological pressure exerted by manners, however, is aimed directly at the very few who, like Trollope, are inclined to blow the whistle on it.

Even the word *manners* has a slippery way of hiding beneath its bland descriptive surface a fierce guard assigned to police the borders. A walk through the *Oxford English Dictionary* entry reveals how the liberally empirical definition—"Customary mode of acting or behaviour, whether of an individual or of a community; habitual practice; usage, custom, fashion"—quickly glides toward the schoolmasterly prescriptive: "*good* manners." Those customary modes of acting or behavior are, it turns out, not random or accidental, and they are enforced by customs officials. The word carries the shadow of "in due measure or moderation" (from the old French *manière:* moderation, measure), suggesting not only the existence of rules for the measurement but a kind of Bureau of Standards that sets the rules. And the rules depend on "moderation," a cozy and conservative term that, by guarding against excess, maintains a rumpus-free middle course. So long as everyone runs this middle course, more or less, no one is going to have breath enough to ask who laid out the course, why everyone is running it, or why it might not be more fun to abandon the track and take off through the woods. (Interestingly, any chafing against the restrictions of manners is not allowed to invade the main term but is siphoned off onto related words with slightly negative connotations: *mannered, mannerism, mannerist.*)

All of this is a windy way to suggest that manners—and the novel of manners—do not just happen but are tied to forms of cultural power and control; further, that actual novels of manners tend to allow a pretty fierce criticism of the system upholding any given set of manners. No novels, then, are more relentlessly political and ideological than these presumably domestic and personal works. They resist the dissociation of the personal from the political and see forms of power everywhere—from the codes governing what a woman must say to a man she wants to marry or sleep with (both in a few cases) to those prescribing how one rids oneself of excess nasal mucus. The novel of manners is most interestingly seen as an attack on the novel of manners, centering the subversive Falstaff, not the snug Squire Western.

It must be admitted, though, that critics have a tendency to settle down with the Squire. What, after all, justifies a collection like this one, organized around an unnatural construction and offering thereby an opportunity for a series of conservative exercises in pretending that the construction is natural, even that it exists? That is, we establish a formal category, "the novel of manners," distinguish it with some skill from other categories, equally hallucinatory, and then proceed to imagine that "novels of manners" are as much a natural category as frogs or peonies—both of which are, by the bye, artificial categories as well. We then pack into this "novel of manners" pudding all sorts of features or characteristics that, lo and behold, we proceed to find there. There are no novelists or novels that, given enough ingenuity, might not have been studied in this collection and under this rubric. Nothing needs to be here, nor need anything be left out: one could as easily see *The Last of the Mohicans* as a novels of manners as *Emma*.

So why am I writing here and why on Trollope, since the whole category is a pious fraud and since Trollope has no more place in this bogus tradition than anyone else who ever wrote something that might be construed as a fiction? Perhaps because such a traditional focus does allow one to expose both the artificiality of the focus and the way in which novels may be made to squirm away from categories. Trollope is wonderfully handy here because he can so easily be made into a Houdini, escaping in a matter of seconds from tight generic bonds. Terry Eagleton suggests that all resolutely formal commentary amounts to "the protection of private property," securing meanings, intentions, generic properties once and for all in the words of the critic (*Literary Theory* 68). Perhaps there is a way not to padlock and install alarm systems for meanings, intentions, and generic properties but to give them away or, if no one wants them, throw them into the void. The model for the critic, then, is not the keeper of the vault but David Copperfield's friend Mr. Dick, who attaches his most solemn words to a kite and offers them to the wind.

Any defense of the instinctive behavior of a culture, any defense of "manners," is bound also to be an exposure of the artificial situatedness of that behavior and of the interested power motives that uphold it. Manners can operate efficiently only when they are not seen as manners, not, in fact, seen at all. One might be able to convince one's students that they should attach purple ribbons to their noses if one could just assume that such behavior were somehow natural, proper, and, most of all, traditional. The traditional can so easily be made to seem the natural. But one had better not launch into a passionate defense of the cogency of such a system, precisely because it would then be revealed as a system.

And that's just what Trollope does: expose the system as a system, tied to values, historical situations, the protection of position and power. And the system he attacks-by-defending we might as well call the novel of manners, so long as we explain what we have in mind by that term and explore some of its ideological implications. Trollope has long been associated with what convention (i.e., commentators searching for handles) has designated "the comedy of manners."[1] Bradford Booth, who for a very long time was the only commentator writing substantial criticism about Trollope, admitted that his favorite author "rarely attempts more than the comedy of manners."[2] It is a little tough to see why, even if this is somehow so, it should be matter for sadness or apology. More to our point, though, is to reconstruct what it may mean: How can we locate Trollope within this tradition? What does such locating say about Trollope and about the tradition? What does it say about our own processes of reconstruction? Later, I will examine one novel, *The Duke's Children,* in some detail; but for now I would like to see what might come of situating a construction of an averaged-out Trollope novel (or a consistent "tendency" of Trollope) within a tradition (constructed itself, of course) of the novel of manners. It probably goes without saying that such a tradition, like all traditions, is ideologically conservative—or at least seems as though it should be: it serves the interests of the powers that be. Again, however, the novels themselves are ideologically ambiguous, very unstable, Figaro sorts of servants. They tend to make explicit what should be implicit. They talk too much.

Let's begin by assuming that the novel of manners takes somehow for granted a large system of moral and social codings, codings that manifest themselves in enlightened and highly sophisticated behavior. Such enlightenment, however, is directed, as it were, from *within;* it is presumably "instinctive," developed not in reference to theories or elaborated rationalizations as to what civilization is or should be but through inheritance and practice. These purported instincts are highly traditional, but they exist necessarily without much historical sense; they do not look to the past consciously; they just *are.* Such instinctive behavior, never conscious of its base and certainly never justifying or even articulating itself, is, again presumably, a reflex of a generally supported cultural norm. Gentlemanly behavior, to take one example, is, in Trollope, always social behavior, activity within the culture. Though very seldom public in the explicitly political sense, it is always public (and political) in its assumption that such behavior will be echoed back, that the gentleman is a universal standard.

In Trollope, however, such a system is forced into speech, forced out of hiding and thus, to a large extent, forced out of power. For one thing, there are so few gentlemen around, and there are so many liars, so many swindlers, so many who are selfish, greedy, even lustful or homicidal, so many who are loud, so many who don't know how to go in to dinner or ride to the hounds, so many

Americans! Trollope's novels often give the sense that the morality and grounds for behavior are traditional enough but that the tradition is alive only in the narrator and in a few isolated characters; it is now about to become extinct along with the grand old class of gentlemen. Because the world no longer seems to support the assumptions held by gentlemen and because those assumptions are implicitly social and communal, gentlemen often appear alien, even ludicrous. Who supports the gentlemen? Who even understands what on earth they are saying or doing?

Worse, even gentlemen sometimes distrust the basis of their gentleman-liness, giving ground that actually lies right under their feet. When Phineas Finn (in *Phineas Redux*) finds himself on trial for a murder he did not commit, he also finds himself without any support from the gentlemanly society whose instincts should tell them that he is innocent. Despite the warmhearted support of a large group of women (who seem, ironically, to be the only ones true to the gentlemanly code), Phineas must learn to live in a world where even the staunchest of traditionalists, the Duke of St. Bungay, accommodates himself easily to a relativistic, substanceless vision: he "had learned at last that all loyalty must be built on a basis of self-advantage" (40; vol. 1, ch. 5). The innocent Phineas is put through a trial that judges not the man, his innocence or guilt, but the quality of the "evidence," quite a different and impersonal thing—a thing no gentleman should attend to. And his friends do not perhaps attend much to the evidence. It's not that the world has become rational and impersonal; it has become decentered and chaotic, without any governing code whatever. Mr. Monk explains to Phineas that he never lost "confidence" in his friend but that such confidence could not justify "conviction" (250; vol. 2, ch. 68). Why not? A community that cannot translate confidence into conviction is one that has lost hold on the power of its instincts, one in which the dominant ideology has crumbled. The novel of manners, in other words, circles back on itself when manners become the reflex of nothing whatever.

Similarly, the faith in "civilization" as an independent force that can be trusted to take care of itself suffers when no one holds the faith or feels the force. The novel of manners, one might say, holds to a deep-seated irrational-ism, mocking rationalists, reformers, and systematic thinking of any kind, and holding up in their place instinctive behavior, the force of "experience" (which might unkindly be called habituation), and, when pressed, the importance of "blood." In the novel of manners, the emphasis is on gradual understanding and acceptance, not on radical transformation. Such gradual understanding is tied to certain theories of education, but the pedagogical model advanced is the opposite of Gradgrindian. One "grows," "soaks in," "comes to understand" simply by being around and not pushing too hard. Youth should, in fact, be mute, satisfied with adding a certain mild liveliness to the proceedings without presuming to direct or even to play a large part in them: age, grumbled Trollope, is so much superior to youth, "that it may be doubted whether youth is justified in making public its work by any other consideration than that of the doubt whether maturity may come."[3]

This early-retirement-in-reverse policy is, I think, so extreme as to function to give the game away, to show the desperation of those who would sustain a world now lost. Still, Trollope's irrationalist faith in this power of mature and civilized manners can take milder forms: "The simple teaching of religion has never brought large numbers of Natives to live in European habits; but I have no doubt that European habits will bring about religion" (*South Africa* 2:188). The subtle habits of a civilization, its manners, are equivalent to its spiritual life, a mystery that cannot be taught but which, all the same, must be trusted, accepted, and gradually absorbed. But where *is* this religion? Its temples—drawing rooms and the like—are full of heathens, and the faithful are a dwindling band. Trollope's smug trust in the power of European manners to create "religion" among those living in ill-mannered darkness is countered by a recognition that this civilization can spread only by baring its teeth: it is very difficult, he sarcastically comments, to make "a wretched savage understand that you intend to do good to him, when he clearly does perceive that you intend to take away from him everything that he calls his own" (*Tireless Traveller* 133).

The values associated with tradition, with the sort of manners the novels appear to admire, are never just *there* in Trollope. If they survive at all, they must be formulated anew and somehow, however shakily, established. In the process, too much is made explicit; too much is shown to be manufactured for ideological purposes in these learned "instincts." This subversive stripping away of the trappings of the habitual becomes clearest in Trollope's contradictory defenses of the "gentleman" and of "blood," defenses of the irrational on what masquerade as rational grounds. Though we are told countless times that the way to define a gentleman is to "be one and then you'll know"—surely an appropriately irrational and circular definition—such mystery-cult hinting is often supplemented by fatal particulars: a powerful unselfishness, a distrust for show, an unconscious yearning for and ability to exercise power over others, an aversion to such vulgar pursuits as gambling (taking money out of another person's pocket), a desire to make others comfortable (arguably a subtle form of the exercise of power), and, most of all, a disgust with lying so deep that it would never occur to a gentleman to lie or to suspect others of doing so. This last is especially disastrous, since it is often made central, and since it is so palpably ineffective as a *rule*. The finest gentlemen are often surrounded by liars whom they are very ready to know as liars; what's more, they often lie themselves when delicacy or even convenience demands it. The principle of truthtelling, in other words, is too ridiculously absolute to stand in such a subtle world, where so many conflicting codes make so many different demands. One can search for stability in a relativistic world, but by doing so one risks being a fool. The actual gentlemen in the novels often seem quite fluid, adaptable to shifting conditions and willing enough to apply what Ruth apRoberts calls Trollope's "situation ethics" *(Moral Trollope)*, but the general discussions of "the gentleman" posit a kind of essentialism that comes close to mocking or undermining the concept that is being defended. At the very most, the concept, however abstractly beautiful, is shown to be hardly functional.

So one turns to subtlety itself as a principle, a principle that constitutes one of the strongest weapons in this ideological armory. We are asked to believe that the truly expressive speech is always indirect, that the plain speakers are rude, ill-mannered people who, like the American senator, do not ever understand what is going on. According to this code, indirect speech, sly ironic asides, gestures, raised eyebrows, even silence speak loudest and most to the point. The less talk there is, the more one expresses confidence in the mutual understanding, unstated but complete, that underlies the social code. Silence, then, is more than golden; it is brick and mortar. Lots of words lead to confusion, danger, anarchy—and there's lots of talk in a Trollope novel. Those who go by the single phrase, the effective gesture, are likely to be ineffective, to be ignored.

To be fair, though, it's not just the amount of talk but its quality or mode that matters. Talk that slithers around the corner rather than advancing head-on expresses an assurance in what is around the corner: not a mugger or a tiger on the loose, but someone who shares such a wide field of understanding and assumptions that the field need only be touched, not cultivated. Trollope writes to his brother, for instance, on hearing that a child is expected: "The pleasures of paternity have been considerably abridged, since the good old Roman privilege of slaying their offspring at pleasure, has been taken from fathers. But the delights of flagellation, though less keen, are more enduring. One can kill but once; but one may flog daily" *(Letters* 1:31–32). But such cozy writing demands an audience, an entire social group or culture that in the novels is, more often than not, absent. Mr. Harding's appeals to the gentlemanly code as an explanation for his behavior fall on the double-deaf ears of the Archdeacon and are mistaken as cowardice; Lizzie Eustace's criminal schemings seem natural enough to most, apart from her inability to turn them to her own advantage; and even the presumably traditional Silverbridge and Isabel Boncassen are forced into blunt "down-rightness" to make themselves understood. As the plain speakers gain authority, the novel of manners loses potency. And such plain speakers, even the boorish Senator Gotobed, seem to speak more and more clearly from the heart of the novels as Trollope's career progresses.

In the novel of manners as we have constructed it, the conservative bias means that any rejection of illusion, any movement toward clarification, is figured as a relaxation into "things as they are." In Trollope, such an education into ease can indeed be accomplished, but not always: there are many who are ineducable or who remain, like Roger Carbury, isolated by their own gentleman-liness. Even worse, Trollope's novels characteristically raise uncomfortable questions about "things as they are." Just how are things? Very often quite awful, which in turn makes it difficult to see how or why a good man or woman can possibly adjust to, be educated into the worlds of *Is He Popenjoy?, The Way We Live Now,* or *Mr. Scarborough's Family.* "Things are very far from being perfect. Things are always very far from being perfect," says Trollope in a lecture on the "Higher Education of Women" (*Four Lectures* 77). This notion of an untransformed and untransformable world is all very well so long as one does not pay too great a price for accepting things as they are. Many women in Trollope's initial audience may well have felt that things as they are did not offer them much, in the way of higher education or in anything else. Very many of the women in Trollope's own novels feel this way, certainly, and find that the answers to the blunt and repeated question, "What is a woman to do with her life?", are very limited—limited, in fact, to the often dreary, sometimes pan-icked question of whether or not to marry. Men sometimes fare little better: "It is sad to say it, and sad to think of it, but failure is the ordinary lot of man" (*Clergymen* 74).

The casting away of illusions may land one in bleak territory, with few protections and very few rewards. An intelligent physician in *He Knew He Was Right* says about a dangerous disease, "The truth is . . . a doctor doesn't know so very much more about these things than other people" (477). This candor puts us all in the same boat, but it is not so much a cruise ship as a leaky life raft. The doctor is not a pompous fool to be deflated but an honest man who reveals that the slogan of *Barchester Towers*—"we are all of us men"—may be a lovely, unbuttoned attitude to take toward clergymen (or to have clergymen takes toward themselves) but not much of a protection against failing health. Nor, when we think of it, is the comic devaluation of clergymen all that comfort-ing. Reducing clergymen to the level of civil servants and the like cuts away any pretensions they may have to social prominence, but it also, however much Trollope may protest to the contrary, removes their ties to the divine. A clergy-man who cannot stand up to Mrs. Proudie or to the narrator's ridicule surely would cut a poor figure before the Almighty. As a result, as Lady Chiltern says, the doctrine of the afterlife becomes "so cold and comfortless in the theory that we do not relish the prospect even for our children" (*Phineas Redux* 21; vol. 1, ch. 2). So, instead of a conservative affirmation of the harmonious beauty of things as they are, Trollope can leave us with the ironic possibility that these things as they are are simply all we have, comfortless and disheartening as that may be.

These anomalies in Trollope, his subversive use of the novel of manners, can be smoothed over by a fairly simple maneuver: simply assert that the emptiness, ironic nihilism, and so forth reside in the public arena and that the true virtues and the true joys are private.[4] If one constructs such a sharp distinction between the public, institutionally or socially defined being and the private one, certain ambiguous twists and turns become straight lines. Money, for instance, and the getting of it can be both applauded and despised, approved in reference to the comfort and freedom it can allow, disgusting in its tendency to corrupt the social and political order at large. The problem with such a unifying device is that it concurs so readily with the ideology (and the ideological contradiction) it is trying to explain. Naturally, it works, since it comes out of the same warehouse. One must act as if money appeared from nowhere, as if it were nice to have, even essential, but not an active agent in determining one's behavior. One of the marks of the gentleman is the ease with which he gives away, loses, is cheated of his money. One should certainly marry for love and love alone. At the same time, many (most?) are in circumstances in which they would be idiots not to look to the financial situations of their prospective mates.

While money clearly invades, even controls, all areas of life, one must operate as if it did not. Those who really do so operate, who fully internalize these manners, do so, of course, at their own considerable peril. Those who get by keep the code of manners outside, a matter of behavior only, and sometimes not of behavior. The seasoning of Silverbridge and Gerald in *The Duke's Children* is all very sweet and moving, but it is, very emphatically, accomplished by the payment of enormous sums of money: huge racetrack losses on Silverbridge's part, card-table debts for Gerald. We can construe all this ironically pretty easily: the proper seasoning can be acquired, and one can adjust happily to the status quo—as long as one has the equivalent of several million dollars to dump without missing it. Money, then, cannot be so easily accommodated to the tradition, nor can excuses for it be easily made on the basis of this division between the public and private being.

Ideologies are not so divided and, if anything, operate more powerfully and more insidiously in the unconscious private life than in public. Mr. Slope is a grasping, rude man in the pulpit and on the sofa making love: he cannot hide his uninitiated status, his ignorance of the rules, his lower-middle-class origins. Similarly, Mr. Crawley is a tragic hero everywhere he goes, not least when he enters the bosom of his family. Marriage and love are for men and, especially, for women so patently affairs of class, politics, and cash that it seems preposterous to think of any private realm that is safe from these forces and thus free for the exercise of decency.

Finally, there is a parallel tendency in reading the novel of manners, even Trollope's slippery version of it, to see something in the *process,* the experience of a thing that belies the form in which it appears.[5] Dynamic experience, one might suppose, is what counts, not the abstract structure that lies behind it. Work, we say, was what counted to Trollope, work for its own sake, and not the product of that work. Same with politics, where those who believe there must be some*thing* to be done are ridiculed, contrasted with the true statesmen, who are in politics for the work itself, knowing that *things* will come to be done, if at all, by themselves, like spring showers. One does not initiate or plan; one carries through what is initiated, presumably, by itself. Same with marriage and love: "The beauty of it all was not so much in the thing loved, as in the loving" (*He Knew He Was Right* 237). Same, most importantly, with fox-hunting, where the enormous joy of the riding seems to have no relation to whether or not a fox is killed or even found, much less to abstract notions about the idiotic cruelty of the whole endeavor.

But how can a distinction between the doing and the form in which the thing is done be maintained? It's all very well to say that the old bedesmen at Hiram's Hospital are as happy as larks, even if they are being cheated, or that farmers really welcome hunters trampling down their crops. The point is that such arguments reveal their own premises all too baldly. And this is the way the novel puts the arguments: by saying that the form of the thing is irrelevant to the activity, they reveal how the form makes possible and controls the activity. Form can be distinguished from the activities it allows only by a sleight of hand, exactly the sleight of hand mastered by the novel of manners. It's not that Trollope doesn't use the full array of tricks; it's just that he has a disarming way of showing us what's up his—and the tradition's—sleeve. I would like to demonstrate a little of this in reference to one novel, *The Duke's Children.*

Here is a formula for the novel of manners, one that Trollope seems often to have adopted: take a character about whom we are made to care and whose values and integrity we are, at least in some measure, made to respect; then put him (or her, of course, though in Trollope it is quite often a him) in a situation where he is, for one reason or another, severely isolated from the social group and culture he thought was supporting him. Through this isolation and the problems it causes, raise questions about the values, the behavior, the manners not only of the individual but also of the culture as a whole. Then, dispel the questions or, rather, resolve them in favor of a set of traditional assumptions made more flexible and lively through a comfortable resolution for all but the scoundrels and the reformers. *The Duke's Children,* the last of the Palliser series,[6] can be construed as fitting this formula in an especially compelling way. It can also be construed as exposing the formula *as a formula* and thus subverting the assumptions that prop up the code of manners apparently being supported. It is this last construction that interests me here.

As I see it, the novel concerns the Duke's struggle to reconcile himself to what he perceives as a new and alien world. The radical estrangement is initiated by the sudden death of his wife, Glencora, announced at the novel's beginning; and the sense of having dropped in from Pluto continues as his children resolutely act in ways the Duke cannot fathom, cannot fit into the codes he has always felt govern the lives of all people—or at least of all gentlemen, or at least of all the aristocracy, or at least of all politically liberal aristocrats who are not debauched or otherwise selfishly immoral. His daughter, Lady Mary, declares her unalterable love for one Frank Tregear, the second son of a country squire and possessed neither of a profession nor of money. The Duke's eldest son, Lord Silverbridge, gets himself sent down from Oxford for a juvenile prank, declares that he is, by nature it seems, a Tory, spends most of his time at a rag-tag gentlemen's club and the track, where he manages to bet and lose upwards of £100,000. Worst of all, he forms a kind of half-baked engagement to Lady Mabel Grex and tells his father about it, which suits the father fine but which does not, in the long run, at all suit Silverbridge, who finds Lady Mabel a good bit too intelligent and mature for comfort and pins his affections instead on Isabel Boncassen, an American nearly as ludicrously ineligible in the Duke's eyes as is Tregear. The second son, Gerald, is a sweet-hearted, fairly stupid hobbledehoy like his brother but too young as yet to have run the whole course of Silverbridge's follies. To be sure, Gerald is sent down, from Cambridge in this case, and he loses money disreputably, at the card table; but he hasn't come to the point of thinking about politics or marriage. In time, one is led to believe, he will scandalize and hurt the Duke just as much as his elder brother has.

These are the problems, the conditions that act to isolate the Duke and the tradition he holds to. From one point of view, all turns out well. Mary and Tregear, Silverbridge and Isabel are joined, more or less with the Duke's blessing; Silverbridge even switches his parliamentary allegiance back to the old Palliser liberalism, declaring that one's party affiliation doesn't really matter much and that the current leader of the Conservatives is, after all, "a beast." Major Tifto and Lady Mabel are cast aside rather brutally, it is true; but all comic rituals, we might say, contain these little purification gestures, these clarifying acts of identifying and expelling the unfit. There is no doubt that the novel can be read or reported on as a pleasant fable in which everyone, almost, wins; the Duke and all his children do, anyhow, and they represent everything that counts. Even the tendency to psychologize the novel,[7] to treat it as a subtle recording of the Duke's psychic turmoil, suggests that all that is needed is a little therapy. Nothing is seriously out of joint except for the Duke, and he needs simply, as Trollope would say, to retrick his beams.

The first sentence of the novel, announcing the Duke's terrible loneliness, can be read as anticipating his cure: "No one, probably, ever felt himself to be more alone in the world than our old friend, the Duke of Omnium, when the Duchess died" (1). The Duke, we may suppose, *feels* himself to be alone but really isn't—or won't be for long. The opening goes on with an elaboration on his desolation that hints at a therapeutic educational course before him: "He did not know how to look out into the world" (but he will learn); "there was no one of whom he could ask a question" (but there will be). The mythic structure controlling the novel seems to rest on the mild and comic conflict between generations, here between fathers and sons: "Fathers never do quite understand the changes which are manifest to their sons" (489). But fathers have a way finally of understanding these changes or adjusting to them and, in the end, of giving the younger generation their blessings.

The odd thing about *The Duke's Children* is that the Duke never does understand the changes, never reconciles himself to them, never is able to see whether his children are too headstrong and stupid to see the importance of the permanent values he espouses or whether, in fact, those values are gone, the world transformed into a madhouse. The focus throughout is not on any real change in the Duke, any graceful reconciliation, but on his increasingly lonely steadfastness and his bitterness. The Duke's essential isolation increases as the novel proceeds; he does not see the light but is bludgeoned into accepting the darkness. He never loses the pain that comes from the certainty of having been abandoned, even when all is settled: "My opinion is to go for nothing,—in anything!" he cries to Silverbridge (563), and again to Silverbridge, "Gerald, I suppose, will bring me some kitchen-maid for his wife" (586). The celebration parties and dinners he gamely arranges for the young lovers are spoiled by his grim hilarity: "it was the Duke who made the greatest efforts, and with the least success" (588). Even at the altar-steps, "he was reminding himself of all that he had suffered" (633), and the last words of the novel are given to his grumbling about Tregear's arrogance and about a world where the unspeakable has become the colloquial: "I do not know that one ought to be surprised at anything" (633).

Manners, then, simply are not coordinated, and the Duke is not so dishonest as to pretend that they are. One can, of course, blame all this on the Duke, on his inadequate recovery, on his stubbornness, on his archetypal role as a refuser of festivity. It seems to me more interesting, however, to attend to the way in which his stubborn holdout against the allures of the novel of manners manages to expose the somewhat violent ideology of that genre. The Duke suggests, for instance, that the notion of a smooth modification of manners from one generation to the next may mask considerable coercion, that change may really be disruption rather than flexible continuity, that loneliness may not be curable, that manners may die, that catastrophic models of destruction and disappearance may be as apt as linear models of adjustment. The liberal Duke, that is, ironically exposes the deeply conservative ideology of the novel of manners, its belief in compromise, small-scale fiddlings with the system, universal human tendencies, and the like. The traditional Duke suggests a cultural relativism and a radical historicism that are potentially anarchic or revolutionary. By being unable to pretend that his world and his beliefs have survived, the Duke questions the ideological base on which continuity and the survival of the past are enforced.

The Duke, the tradition of the novel of manners, or we as readers might, of course, escape this dilemma by doing what all ingenious sorts do when they find themselves cornered: make a distinction. Proposing once again that the public life is sharply divided from the private, we can then protect the stability and continuity of the novel of manners tradition by claiming a sanctity for a centered character or hero and heroine, whatever may be the case with the world at large. Jane Austen is very often read in this way: the "world" may be chaotic, ruled by gross materialism and selfishness, individualism run amuck, vulgar ignorance of traditional values and their reflection in manners; but an enclave is established with Elizabeth and Darcy, Emma and Mr. Knightley, even Anne and Wentworth, where the delicate life of manners is known and endures. Such a distinction, one might say, is characteristic of bourgeois idealism; it depoliticizes and elevates the "personal," allowing "the world" to go its way. Such liberal gestures account for the pervasive readings of "romantic love," "the inward turn of the novel," "the rise of complex characterization," and the like. All are impositions of an ideological distinction, one that claims, among other things, a realm of personal loyalties, love, virtue, and dignity, untouched by the sordid issues of power.

The Duke's Children brings these distinctions into the foreground so blatantly that the invitation to accept them ought to strike us as a little suspicious. We are told at once that the Duke has lost in his wife the "link between him and the world." His "loving and his liking" had been confined to one or two, and those feelings had been "exclusively political"; "he had so habituated himself to devote his mind and his heart to the service of his country, that he had almost risen above or sunk below humanity" (3). We read these comments, very likely, as indicating that the Duke had used his wife to make up for personal deficiencies, principally an habitual aloofness and impersonality born of shyness. But what really is "political loving"? And to what "world" was his wife a link?

We probably think, roughly, that the Duke, who was, after all, Prime Minister, has done very well with the world but was lacking personally; but the passage seems to tell us just the opposite and generally sets up very confusing signals as to what constitutes the world, the personal, and the "humanity" that the Duke is either above or below but not "in." The passage, in other words, invites us to separate the private and public but then muddles or deconstructs the basis on which such a distinction might rest. Similarly, the Duke of St. Bungay, in an extraordinarily cagey letter urging the Duke to return to public life, uses this same distinction in arguing that the Duke should consider public duty ahead of any private concerns, that a man so competent and so needed "cannot be justified in even remembering that he has a self" (171). This puts the ideological position in its purest and most revealing form: a person's true self or only self is private, not operated on by power in any form, certainly not politicized or publicized. Clearly, however, the Duke's motives for resisting his old friend's appeals are deeply personal. Just as personal are his reasons, announced very late in the novel, for returning to the public duty he loves—his eagerness for power and his feeling that he is nothing if he is not engaged in hard work: "But it is the grind that makes the happiness. . . . For myself I can conceive no other" (196). The Duke returns to politics for that most personal of all reasons, the pursuit of happiness. By doing so, he suggests an integration, a disavowal of the distinction that seems to be holding the novel together.

Still, he tries to inculcate in his sons the very separation of public and private that he believes sustains both his politics and his personality. As an aristocratic liberal, the Duke is committed to a gradual easing of the barriers between classes, by which he means a way of squeezing together the vertical spectrum without giving up at all the lines that distinguish the levels of society. The Duke proposes not to see the rainbow as a continuum but to preserve even more rigorously the illusion that colors are divided and discrete. He simply wants a thinner rainbow in which red and yellow fraternize more under certain circumstances without producing orange. The way this is to be managed is to see that public life—politics, say—is one thing and private life—marriage, say—another: "I should not turn up my nose at the House of Commons because some constituency might send them an illiterate shoemaker; but I might probably find the illiterate shoemaker an *unprofitable* companion for my private hours" (204; emphasis added). After the Duke meets the pathetically uncouth Major Tifto, he rebukes his son for associating with a man for "profit," adding that he does not see how Silverbridge can "gain" anything by such a companionship (213–14). Why does the Duke use such importations from the public world of commerce to explain the intricacies of the sanctity of the private life? Partly, one supposes, because the Duke cannot, in his austerity, associate the private life with anything so hedonistic as pleasure or self-indulgence. He is caught, then, one way or another, in defending the private life with a language and ideology drawn from public morality and duty, again betraying the split he needs to maintain.

What arguments can the Duke use with his children? Perhaps he is successful as regards Tifto: Silverbridge does dump him—after waiting to see what will happen in a couple of big races. But Tifto is a minor matter, and one might wonder whether Silverbridge's obedience is a signal of his coalescence with the Duke or the result of Tifto's role in a public scandal and his utter failure to hand over to Silverbridge a single winner. The real tests come with the mates selected by his children, prospective partners who violate everything the Duke holds dear: "Such drawing-nearer of the classes was the object to which all this man's political action tended. And yet it was a dreadful thing to him that his own daughter should desire to marry a man so much beneath her own rank and fortune" (175).

The distance is so great that it threatens a merging, and a very dangerous one. Plus, there is the vulgar issue of money: Tregear has none, and Mary will have carloads of it. Deeply in love with Lady Mabel Grex at one time, Tregear has been persuaded by her that he and Mabel do not have money enough between them to live in the manner to which they would like to become accustomed. They part, Mabel with such pain and reluctance that she can never forget it, Frank with what we might gather is a temporary twinge that slows him down only for a step or two before he is able to get back into the race. We are told right at the beginning and then many more times by the narrator and by Frank himself that he had not sought Mary out because she was an heiress, because of her ethereal rank, or because of the alluring combination: Frank "was certainly not the man to pursue a girl simply because of her fortune; nor was he weak enough to be attracted simply by the glitter of rank; but ..." (22). But what? Surely Frank's reasons for loving Mary, for wanting to marry her, should not be at all connected to wealth and rank. No! "[B]ut he was wise enough with worldly wisdom to understand thoroughly the comforts of a good income, and he was sufficiently attached to high position to feel the advantage of marrying a daughter of the Duke of Omnium." We know, in fact, that, as with Lady Mabel, all the love in the world would not induce Frank to engage himself to Mary were she not oozing with cash.

Where does this leave us? Frank loves her purely, for her very self, and simply finds it pleasant that she comes equipped with these external attractions? Hardly; that would be a little like the short-handed building contractor finding it merely pleasant that the woman he loves is the best bricklayer in the Western world. All this is not to suggest that a cynical reading of Frank gets us very far; it's just that the issue of money and love, though foregrounded in about every other chapter, is never settled. Further, this insistent equivocation blurs the public-private distinction awfully. We would much prefer to have it all as clear as a bell: love is one thing, worldly position and money another. The Duke would rather have it this way, too: even after he has officially given in, he frets over his own failure to sort out the appropriate roles of men and women, of love and power:

> "A gentleman should not look to live on means brought to him by a wife. You say that he did not."
>
> "He did not think of it."
>
> "A gentleman should do more than not think of it. He should think that it shall not be so. A man should own his means or should earn them." (585)

The Duke makes it all lucid. But what he describes is not what Tregear does, and the Duke cannot clarify the world in this way.

The most damaging possibility introduced here in the Duke's outline of proper conduct is that Tregear is not a gentleman. A gentleman is . . . well, something ineffable, but something quite certain. What is at stake is not so much the existence of a class to be known as "gentlemen" as the ability to recognize them. It is the mode of perception—irrational, unempirical, hence not to be questioned or subject to change—that is crucial. And certainly the best gentleman-spotter in the novel should be the Duke. But, when his daughter protests that her chosen is, after all, a gentleman, the Duke responds:

> "So is my private secretary. There is not a clerk in one of our public offices who does not consider himself to be a gentleman. The curate of the parish is a gentleman, and the medical man who comes here from Bradstock. The word is too vague to carry with it any meaning that ought to be serviceable to you in thinking of such a matter."
> "I do not know any other way of dividing people," said she. . . .
> "You are not called upon to divide people. That division requires so much experience that you are bound in this matter to rely upon those to whom your obedience is due." (67)

Although the Duke tries to rescue himself at the last, arguing that the dividing of people is not to be explained in words but absorbed through the skin with "experience" (a splendid and standard irrationalist dodge), he has already thrown in the sponge: "The word is too vague." Mere clerks or curates may or may not be gentlemen. The Duke suggests that he knows who is a gentleman, but does he? If he knows, it is on the basis of some internal wisdom that has come to him with age and blood. And if he has the wisdom, why is the application of it "vague"? And what kind of wisdom does he possess? Is Tregear a gentleman, or is he not—or does it even matter? Late in the novel, the Duke admits that there is no reason Mr. Boncassen should respect his view of things, even though Mr. Boncassen doubtless respects him: "That which to me is deep wisdom is to him an empty prejudice" (563), a near-cynicism the Duke regards as natural enough. Gone is the universal intuition that can uphold the private sensation that maintains the external world of rank, class, and wealth. Mere cultural relativism that mixes public and private has crept up and taken over.

Even more overtly, the Duke is forced to use public and political arguments—duty, position, noblesse oblige—to address his children at all. He must abandon the distinction between public and private, abandon the tradition that supports both him and the novel of manners. When the Duke speaks, he speaks always with the intense feeling of a public man, especially when he is being most intensely personal. He believes, above all, in calling things by their proper names, and for much of the novel he nurtures the belief that he can train his children linguistically and all will be well. The Duke's language is thus insistently ideological, but it makes no contact with the world and words of his sons. Much of the comedy of the book arises from the enormous gap between the Duke's abstract vocabulary and beautiful long periods and his sons' colloquial and concrete speech. Even when the father strives for crisp directness, the results are no better:

> "Do you ever think what money is?"
> The Duke paused so long, collecting his own thoughts and thinking of his own words, that Gerald found himself obliged to answer. "Cheques, and sovereigns, and bank-notes," he replied with much hesitation.
> "Money is the reward of labour," said the Duke. (517)

Ironically, the Duke sees no connection between experience and the explanation of experience; he can use abstract terms only because he is trying to believe that there is a community out there somewhere which will provide solidity, a form of general "reality," to abstraction. The Duke, in other words, speaks from and with a series of assumptions that make no sense to the new generation. Issues are resolved, but only when speech is downright, often brutal: Silverbridge to Tifto, Silverbridge to Lady Mabel and vice versa, Isabel to Dolly and even to Silverbridge.

Silverbridge is, we assume, finally "seasoned," but to serve what menu? Tifto is ruined and pathetic; Lady Mabel is not pathetic, perhaps, but only because her strong bitterness upholds her: "Time is but a poor consoler for a young woman who has to be married" (582). Silverbridge could not enter the old world of his father, even if he wanted to and were equipped to do so. There is no real reconciliation of the sort we had imagined, precisely because the reading habits, the tradition we had assumed, cannot be maintained. The private realm is riddled through with political forces; it always has been, only now it is riddled through much more obviously. What *The Duke's Children* does is to expose the political underpinnings of the attempt to construct an unpoliticized personal realm. It deconstructs its own governing genre, making available to us not so much the weakness of the Duke's assumptions as the weakness of our own. We are shown the ideological base of this "novel of manners," that is, of our own need for such a construction. It is not, finally, the Duke who is caught in the ludicrous position of being a liberal aristocrat, a man of the people with deep-seated prejudices in favor of a very small group of people, a political leveler and equalizer committed to the status quo. It is us.

Notes

1. The editors of this volume argue against a confusion of the comedy of manners with the novel of manners, quite justly, since the first term restricts the range they wish to explore. With Trollope, however, the associations with the dramatic comedy of manners and even the implied constraints of "comedy" seem to accord with many readers' perceptions of the books.

2. *Anthony Trollope: Aspects of His Life and Art*, 24. Booth adds that this adherence to the comedy of manners explains why Trollope's novels "do not move us profoundly" (43). Many now would

certainly dispute this estimate of Trollope's or the tradition's power. Many also would find Trollope's range much wider than Booth allows, reading the novels in political, sociological, or even formal terms quite alien to Booth's model. They might also cite the very large number of novels written in other modes: *La Vendée* (historical romance), *An Eye for an Eye* (melodrama), *The Fixed Period* (science fiction), *The Way We Live Now* (satire), *The Landleaguers* and other Irish novels (tragedies or sociological fictions), *The Three Clerks* and *The Struggles of Brown, Jones, and Robinson* (Dickensian romps).

3. "To Alfred Austin," 2 May 1870, in *The Letters of Anthony Trollope*, 1:515–16, hereafter cited as *Letters*.

4. Alas, I have been guilty myself of manufacturing just such an argument: *The Novels of Anthony Trollope*, 57–59.

5. Alas again: *The Novels of Anthony Trollope*, 59–61.

6. Though there is some controversy as to whether this is or was intended to be a series, it is ordinarily taken as such. The earlier novels, in the usual order, are *Can You Forgive Her?*, *Phineas Finn*, *The Eustace Diamonds*, *Phineas Redux*, and *The Prime Minister*.

7. The most influential study along these lines has been John H. Hagan's "*The Duke's Children:* Trollope's Psychological Masterpiece."

6

George Eliot's *Middlemarch* and the "Text" of the Novel of Manners

Bege K. Bowers

"[T]he social moulds civilization fits us into have no more relation to our actual shapes than the conventional shapes of the constellations have to the real star-patterns."
Sue Bridehead Phillotson in Thomas Hardy, *Jude the Obscure*

Of all George Eliot's novels, *Middlemarch* seems most to defy classification: it "will run into any mould, but [it] won't keep shape" (70; ch. 8). If at times we feel transplanted into a world of nineteenth-century manners and drawing-room wit, at others we feel displaced into a world of romantic rebellion, Dickensian chance, or Hardyesque fate. The more we try to set the "boundaries" of Eliot's text, the more the boundaries shift; the novel refuses to be contained. But this is particularly appropriate since *Middlemarch* itself is a "study" of "shifting boundaries" and elusive "texts"—and since both of these concepts play significant roles in Eliot's treatment of the equally elusive term we are considering here: *manners*.

From the beginning of her career, George Eliot depicted "commonplace characters" grappling with the unsettling problems of everyday life ("Amos Barton" 42; ch. 5). When her publisher, John Blackwood, complained in June 1857 that portions of "Janet's Repentance" could have been "pleasanter" and that her "sketch of English County Town life" was "rather harsh" (*Letters* 2: 344), Eliot adamantly refused to soften either the central characters or the spiteful and hypocritical society in which they lived. "I undertake to exhibit nothing as it should be," she wrote Blackwood; "I only try to exhibit some things as they have been or are, seen through such a medium as my own nature gives me" (2:362).

This "realism," tempered through the medium of artistic imagination, permeates the later works as well. Critics such as Raymond Williams have pointed out that although Eliot was often "defensive and self-conscious" about presenting "unfashionable" characters or scenes from "low-life," she extended "the socially selective landscape" of the English novel nonetheless (77–82). We see this extended landscape quite fully in *Middlemarch*, with its uneasy combination of "country gentry," businesspeople, laborers, and "interlopers" (720; ch. 74)— a social backdrop indicative of what Eliot calls the "shifting . . . boundaries of social intercourse" at the time just preceding the first Reform Bill (95; ch. 11) but also indicative of those "nice distinctions of rank" (226; ch. 23) and gender whereby the Chettams look down on the Vincys, the Vincys look down on the Garths, and any self-respecting woman sits home and drinks tea.

What reader of *Middlemarch* is not struck by such pictorial representations[1] of this class- and gender-conscious society as Eliot's bird's-eye view of the Featherstone funeral, a scene presented through the eyes of Mrs. Cadwallader, the Chettams, and the Brookes (country gentry) as these guardians of the old class structure look down (both literally, from an upstairs window, and metaphorically, from their "stations up the mountain") upon the "wonderfully mixed set" below (316–17; ch. 34)? Or the sweeping panorama of Mr. Brooke's dinner party, from which the manufacturing *women* are noticeably absent—"for Mr. Brooke, always objecting to go too far, would not have chosen that his nieces should meet the daughter of a Middlemarch manufacturer unless it were on a public occasion" (89; ch. 10). Little wonder, in a society in which middle-class women have as yet met so little acceptance, that Mrs. Cadwallader and Sir James, peering down with "imperfect discrimination" upon the funeral party below, can identify only the *men* in the crowd!

The social "mixture" is tenuous, to say the least. In fact, the more slippery the boundaries become, the "nicer" the distinctions of rank and gender and the greater the emphasis on observable "manners," for how else can one member or segment of society preserve the *illusion* of so-called superiority once the time-honored reality is gone? How else can individuals show that they have crossed over the boundaries except by mimicking the manners of those who were already inside? And how else can one set oneself apart from a particular stratum of society except by openly defying the manners that distinguish it from another? Thus, even when the particulars of nineteenth-century Reform slip into the not-too-distant "background" of Eliot's fictional landscape, her emphasis on manners remains strong.

But what about the "mould" itself—the novel of manners "tradition"? To what extent does *Middlemarch* conform to the tradition, if indeed we can isolate such a tradition at all, and to what extent does it break away? Certainly, there is no one formula for a novel of manners, as the essays in this collection make clear. Nevertheless, if we define the tradition, or its origins, in terms of such authors as Burney and Austen, we come to expect a certain progression: Early on (call it point A), the author introduces and elicits our sympathy for a young woman who is as yet inexperienced in and untainted by the artifice of society-at-large; in the course of the novel, the young woman "goes out" into society and meets a variety of young men, most of whom pretend or profess to be "gentle-men," socially speaking, and one of whom really is or is capable of being, in the deeper, moral sense; the two central characters (the young woman and the man who is different) overcome their individual "pride and prejudice," plus whatever social differences keep them apart; and finally (point Z), the two marry and take their place in the very society whose affected manners and general superficiality they have served to expose.

If we limit ourselves more or less to points A and Z, *Middlemarch* seems the most "mannerly" of all George Eliot's novels. The story begins auspiciously when the narrator introduces Dorothea Brooke, a young woman ready to "go into society," with the prototypical (if tongue-in-cheek) question, "And how should [she] not marry . . . ?" (11; ch. 1). And it ends eighty-some chapters later with the only possible answer in an "imperfect social state": she should, and she does. Only when we look at the points in between—the bulk of the novel—do we perceive the potential problems: Dorothea is married quite *early* in the novel, to a man who is *not* young; the marriage is stifling and ill-fated; the man dies, but not, unfortunately, before appending to his will a codicil designed to keep her from marrying a particular young "rival"; Dorothea disappears from the story for chapters at a time, during which the focus shifts to other groups of characters and *their* struggles with self and society; and eventually, she gets married *again*, to the forbidden rival, a character whose presence in the novel has been sporadic at best. Add the further anomalies—that much of the novel centers on males in professional life and there isn't a ball to be found—and what do we have? Not quite the *traditional* novel of manners, as Eliot inherited it, but this, I think, is the point. Neither courtship and marriage nor Dorothea herself can be viewed apart from the larger "web" that has so often been identified as a dominant image in *Middlemarch*—a web that traps individuals in social conventions as surely as it draws them together.

We know from Eliot's journal and Jerome Beaty's study of her "creative method" that she had originally conceived and attempted to write two separate works, one a novel of provincial life, the other a short story about a "marriage-able" young woman at odds with the values of society, before combining the two in 1871 to create the first chapters of the novel as they now stand. The narrator makes the importance of manners explicit early and repeatedly in these chapters, most notably perhaps in Sir James's blindness to the fact that Dorothea does not consider him a "match." Prone to interpret the outward behavior of others "in the way most gratifying to himself" (31; ch. 3), he thinks "it probable that Miss Brooke like[s] him, and manners must be very marked indeed," the narrator notes, "before they cease to be interpreted by preconceptions either confident or distrustful" (23; ch. 2).

The "preconceptions" through which individuals interpret the manners of others may be idiosyncratic, like Dorothea's ironic, idealistic belief that marriage to a scholarly "sort of father" (13; ch. 1) will free her from the "labyrinth of petty courses," the "walled-in maze of small paths that [lead] no whither" for women in patriarchal society (30; ch. 3), or more widely held, like those of Sir James and Edward Casaubon, both of whom suppose at first that Dorothea will conform to society's ideas of the "proper" lady and wife. But in either case, the notion of manners as "signs" to be interpreted, and inevitably therefore *misinterpreted*, extends throughout the novel, long after Dorothea has married Casaubon and the honeymoon is over—in other words, long after the prospective husband, the so-called "object in life" (Forsyth 334–35) of mothers and daughters in the novel of manners, has been "hunted" and, of course, "caught."

Thus conceived, as "clusters of signs" (140; ch. 15), manners take their place alongside other systems of signs, or "texts" (Peter Featherstone's funeral script, the codicil forbidding Dorothea to keep Casaubon's property if she marries Will Ladislaw, the misplaced letter bearing Bulstrode's signature), that wield their power in *Middlemarch*. J. Hillis Miller, among others, has stressed the fact that for Eliot and her characters, "seeing is never simply a matter of identifying correctly what is seen"; it "is always interpretation" (143). Can the "distinguished-looking" man with a "great soul" and the sallow old geezer with white moles, who scrapes his spoon and blinks before he speaks, be one in the same? Yes, Eliot avows, for while societies and individuals may indeed "reveal" themselves "from the outside in" (to use Elizabeth Locke's definition of *manners*, iii–iv), what is inferred will be different for every reader of the text. Hence, Dorothea finds Casaubon's "manners . . . dignified" (18; ch. 2) though her sister Celia finds them repulsive. "Signs are small, measurable things," according to the narrator, "but interpretations are illimitable, and in girls of sweet, ardent nature, every sign is apt to conjure up wonder, hope, belief" (27; ch. 3).

In openly equating manners with signs and thus with texts, and then following each of several "texts" through to its predefined conclusion, Eliot writes not merely a novel of manners per se but a "meta-novel of manners," a commentary *on* the novel of manners, in its traditional sense, and a novel *about* manners in a much-expanded sense: a "philosophy" of manners, if you will. The problem is not—as Lydgate supposes—that Dorothea fails to "look at things from the proper feminine angle" (95; ch. 11), nor—as her sister supposes—that she "never see[s] what is quite plain" (38; ch. 4). When it comes to interpretation, nothing is ever "plain." She reads as we *all* do: making inferences beyond and between the lines when she should also look at the words on the page; looking only at the words on the page when she should read between the lines.

(Mis)taking both Casaubon's formal written marriage proposal and the "frigid rhetoric" of his "wooing" for professions of love, Dorothea creates her own version of the "text," "suppl[ying] all that [his] words seemed to leave unsaid" (51; ch. 5). Throughout the courtship, "His efforts at exact courtesy and formal tenderness [pose] no defect for her. She fill[s] up all blanks with unmanifested perfections, interpreting him as she interpret[s] the works of Providence and accounting for seeming discords by her own deafness to the higher harmonies" (74; ch. 9).

This propensity to order the world and interpret the manners of others according to her own ideals and misconceptions is all the more ironic since Dorothea (like such predecessors in the novel of manners as Elizabeth Bennet and Emma Woodhouse) is so determined *not* to fall prey to what she perceives as the weaknesses of other young women of "marriageable age." To be sure, "her manner and expression" show no "search[ing] after mere effect" (88; ch. 10)—or at least not the *typical* effects; she "dares" to defy "provincial fashion" with her "plain garments," "bare . . . style" (9; ch. 1), and flat braids. But though she may never wear her late mother's jewels, or stoop to the "artificialities" of traditional courtship, or "correspond to [Sir James's] pattern of a lady" ("Every lady ought . . . "), her tendency to misinterpret, the narrator suggests, is no different from that of anyone else:

> Dorothea's inferences may seem large; but really life could never have gone on at any period but for this liberal allowance of conclusions, which has facilitated marriage under the difficulties of civilization. Has anyone ever pinched into its pilulous smallness the cobweb of pre-matrimonial acquaintanceship? (24; ch. 2)

Like Sir James, like Emma Woodhouse interpreting Mr. Elton's charade ("courtship," but of what sort and of whom?), and like so many of Eliot's readers, Dorothea "take[s] up the idea . . . and ma[kes] every thing bend to it" (*Emma* 134; vol. 1, ch. 16); she re-creates the text in her mind's image.

Thus, it comes as no surprise to the reader that Dorothea's marriage fails to live up to her high expectations, that instead of "the large vistas and wide fresh air . . . she had dreamed of finding in her husband's mind," she awakens to the nightmare of "anterooms and winding passages which [seem] to lead nowhither" (193; ch. 20).[2] I say "thus" because the gradual wearing down of illusions is a common motif in the novel of manners—but perhaps I should say "ironically" as well. After all, novels of manners are supposed to end comically, with marriage-as-resolution, not begin tragically, with such a marriage as this. Can it be that Eliot, too, "re-creates the text [of the novel of manners] in her mind's image"?

Even if Casaubon's "blood" is not "all semicolons and parentheses" (71;

ch. 8), to use one of Mrs. Cadwallader's more apt expressions, he certainly conducts his marriage, like all other aspects of his life, "in a measured, official tone" (194; ch. 20). Never in the course of the marriage is he able to let down his carefully constructed persona, his "manners," and meet Dorothea's or his own deepest feelings head-on. Repeatedly, Eliot uses references to propriety and honor—that is, to Casaubon's conception of "good manners"—plus references to the customs, tones, and gestures that make up manners in the broader sense, to suggest that this "marriage," though recognized by law, is really no marriage at all. To Dorothea's open expressions of feeling, Casaubon offers no

> other sign of acceptance than pronouncing her, with his unfailing propriety, to be of a most affectionate and truly feminine nature, indicating at the same time by politely reaching a chair for her that he regard[s] these manifestations as rather crude and startling. Having made his clerical toilette with due care in the morning, he [is] prepared only for those amenities of life which [are] suited to the well-adjusted stiff cravat of the period and to a mind weighted with unpublished matter. (195; ch. 20)

Granted, the restraint that marks the first and one of the few "outbursts" in their relationship, a "discussion" of the "usefulness" of Casaubon's research, may keep them from coming to blows, but it also prevents their reaching an understanding. An emotional "mummy" (58; ch. 6), his "irritation reined in by propriety," Casaubon is unable to examine either the truth of Dorothea's "accusation" or the depths of his own "self-doubt" and fears. Their "anger," though "betrayed," is hardly resolved (198–99; ch. 20).

In "most of our social ties," Martin Price explains in an article on "Manners, Morals, and Jane Austen," it is perfectly normal for manners to serve as a sort of public "code," a vehicle for "formalizing conduct and distancing feeling":

> [W]e do not feel the less for giving that feeling an accepted form, which allows us to control its expression in shared rituals. . . . To the extent that manners allow us to negotiate our claims with others, they become a system of behavior that restrains force and turns aggression into wit or some other gamelike form of combat. (266–67)

They have their place. It is *not* normal, however, nor is it desirable, always to hoist the manners of public social intercourse as a defense against our *own* innermost feelings or the feelings of those we love. The mannerly aggression with which Casaubon reaches out and strangles Dorothea's emotions, though combative, is neither witty nor gamelike nor productive, his "politeness" notwithstanding.

However much the narrator may ask us to "pity" Casaubon, however much Eliot may have pitied him herself (*Letters* 5:322), it is difficult to like this character who "always sa[ys] 'my love' when his manner [is] the coldest" (221;

ch. 22). On the one hand, Dorothea's misery is a product of her sex and era—the "stifling oppression of that gentlewoman's world, where everything [is] done for her and none [ask] for her aid" (268; ch. 28). She is made to feel useless by a society that offers few outlets for a woman's creative energy, just as Casaubon himself is a victim of the socially "sanctioned" belief that a "man of good position" must take as a wife "a blooming young lady—the younger the better, because more educable and submissive—of a rank equal to his own, of religious principles, virtuous disposition, and good understanding." When, the narrator proposes facetiously, did society ever make "the preposterous demand that a man should think as much about his own qualifications for making a charming girl happy as he thinks of hers for making himself happy" (272; ch. 29)?

On the other hand, and equally important, Casaubon is simply too "mannerly" for his own or Dorothea's good. If only, for once, he could be so *un*mannerly as to pour forth his rage at his own frustration and sense of lost purpose, perhaps, for once, he might meet her feelings as they deserve to be met: openly and "unrehearsed" (198; ch. 20). Having internalized the values of society and been disappointed by a woman who doesn't entirely fit the bill, he resolves not to look *inward* to the source of his unhappiness (as Dorothea's criticism has suggested he might) but instead to fulfill the *outward* "requirements" of marriage "unimpeachably." And this he professes to do until his miserable end—"a man of honour according to the code; . . . unimpeachable by any recognized opinion" (273; ch. 29).

Characteristically, Casaubon cloaks his altering of the will ("his last injurious assertion of his power" [479; ch. 50]) and his jealousy of Will Ladislaw in terms of "social fitnesses and proprieties," for his "sense of rectitude and an honourable pride in satisfying the requirements of honour . . . [compel] him to find other reasons for his conduct than those of jealousy and vindictiveness." It is his "duty," he feels, to "hinder to the utmost the fulfilment" of those "designs" he imagines on the part of Will (409–10; ch. 42), just as it is his right of "possession" to demand that Dorothea promise not to cross him after he dies. What more appropriate way to signal the death of a marriage that never truly existed, a marriage in which feelings—though seething beneath the surface—have been "distanced" almost into nonexpression, than the mannerly, oblique terms Eliot chooses?: "Dorothea never gave her answer[;] . . . the silence in her husband's ear was never more to be broken" (468; ch. 48).

It is in terms of Dorothea's idealism and gradual disillusionment that critics have most often linked the Dorothea-Casaubon strain of the novel to the other dominant strain, the story of Lydgate and Rosamond. Lydgate, too, exhibits the propensity to order the world according to his own ideals and preconceptions, and like Dorothea, he also tries—unsuccessfully—to set himself apart from the social "medium" in which he lives. In focusing so much of our attention on this new addition to Middlemarch society, this "cluster of signs [ripe] for his neighbours' false suppositions" (140; ch. 15), Eliot suggests once again that men as well as women may constitute a proper study of manners.

We know the story: As a fledgling doctor, Lydgate resolves to rise above "petty" concerns and make great "discoveries," unfettered by "worldly" allegiances or the ties of marriage. Yet, almost immediately, he is drawn into two equally destructive forms of power play, the "politics" of professional life and the crippling blows of a manner-ridden marriage. Having set out to "shape" the world in his own image, to be a "unit" who would "tell appreciably upon the averages," he himself is unwittingly "shape[d] after the average and fit to be packed by the gross"—or to use another of Eliot's metaphors, "swallowed" and "assimilated" by the very society he had set out to change (143–44; ch. 15). And if, like Dorothea, Lydgate is "disposed" to blame this assimilation on "the intolerable narrowness and the purblind conscience of the society around [him]" (38; ch. 4), the narrator is quick to point out that Lydgate is largely responsible for his own fate, precisely because he *shares* so many of the manners and underlying values of those he scorns.

In fact, the narrator notes, Lydgate is "no radical in relation to anything but medical reform. . . . In the rest of practical life he walk[s] by *hereditary habit*, half from . . . personal *pride* and unreflecting egoism . . . and half from that naïveté which belong[s] to preoccupation with favourite ideas" (339; ch. 36, emphasis added). His "spots of commonness" lie "in the complexion of his prejudices, which, in spite of noble intention and sympathy, [are] half of them such as are found in ordinary men of the world." Unfortunately, the "distinction of mind" that sets Lydgate apart intellectually fails to "penetrate his feeling and judgement about furniture or women or the desirability of its being known (without his telling) that he was better born than other country surgeons" (148–49; ch. 15). Thinking of his own family origins, he is "irritated" that he must "mingle" with the likes of the Vincys (340; ch. 36); believing that his own "manners" come naturally, he sneers at the artificiality of theirs (261; ch. 27). But having based his attitudes toward marriage and women on fictional heroines and on "that traditional wisdom which is handed down in the genial conversation of men," he falls for the "flower" of "female accomplishment"—herself a Vincy—and *writes himself* into the text of her "preconceived romance" (162–64; ch. 16).

Granted, Rosamond's "social romance" is a rather unlikely hybrid. Granted, it requires a "stranger" of good birth, and Lydgate just happens to "correspond . . . to [Rosamond's] ideal, being altogether foreign to Middlemarch, carrying a certain air of distinction congruous with good family, and possessing connexions which [offer] vistas of that middle-class heaven, rank."

And granted, a young doctor may "be especially delightful to enslave" (118; ch. 12). The problem, however, is not simply that Rosamond's hybrid is unmanageable or that *her* text clashes with *his* but rather that Lydgate himself is simultaneously weaving *two* contradictory texts, one of which corresponds very closely to hers.

On the one hand, this young doctor will be no one's "captive"; he "fores[ees] that science and his profession [are] the objects he should alone pursue enthusiastically" (Text 1). On the other, "he [can]not imagine himself pursuing them in such a home as Wrench ha[s]—the doors all open, the oil-cloth worn, the children in soiled pinafores, and lunch lingering in the form of bones, black-handled knives, and willow-pattern" (Text 2). Like Rosamond, Lydgate feels that their marriage will raise her above the "vulgar" of Middlemarch, and like her, he feels that if they are going to marry, they must acquire all the "requisite things"—"perfect dress," a fine home, and all the expensive "trappings" (345, 338; ch. 36). If Rosamond can flaunt her newly acquired "connexions" by "appropriating" the "finished manners" of the relatives at Quallingham (118; ch. 12), the proper accoutrements, Lydgate feels, may camouflage the fact that he himself is "*descending* a little in relation to [*her*] family" (340; ch. 36, emphasis added).

And thus the ill-conceived marriage of Lydgate and Rosamond proceeds on the course we might expect, socially "determined" in "much . . . the same way" as the "tie" of a "cravat" (143; ch. 15). Although Lydgate once found the "subservience of conduct to the gaining of small sums thoroughly hateful" and "ungentlemanly" (176; ch. 18), he plunges further and further into debt, "degraded" (627; ch. 64) by the necessity of raising money not only to support Rosamond's costly and "controlled self-consciousness of manner" (419; ch. 43) but also, at first, to support his own desire to keep up appearances, and later, to keep from "fracturing" altogether the "delicate crystal" of an all-too-fragile marriage (631; ch. 64). If Lydgate's earnings are inadequate to achieve the "social effects" he and Rosamond once imagined, they are also inadequate to support the two separate "texts" he once envisioned. How can he remain "independent," or maintain his enthusiasm for professional ideals, when every day he is drawn deeper and deeper "into the absorbing, soul-wasting struggle with worldly annoyances" (716; ch. 73)? Lydgate dies "defeated" at age 50 not because he is "unsuccessful" in the world's eyes but because Text 2 (long since beyond his control) has overwritten Text 1; he hasn't "done what he once meant to do" (808; finale).

Whether we call it "moral imprisonment" (268; ch. 28) or "creeping paralysis" (568; ch. 58), what we see in both the dominant strains of *Middlemarch* is manners run amuck. Once set in motion, the "texts" with the most power—those corresponding to years of tradition and accepted social "code"—take on a life of their own, not only eating away at personal aspirations but also limiting and eventually destroying the capacity for moral choice.

Despite the perception of at least one contemporary reviewer that *Middlemarch* might be too much a portrait of nineteenth-century England to be meaningful for "posterity" (Colvin 648–52), it is Eliot's depiction of the general nature of manners, rather than her picture of pre-Reform England, that constitutes her most telling contribution to the novel of manners. And a sobering depiction it is. Compare the following passages, one of which we have already examined in relation to Casaubon's marriage, the others Lydgate's "uneasy" rationalizations of his failure to launch an investigation into Raffles's suspicious death at Stone Court:

> Mr. Casaubon had many *scruples*: he was capable of a severe self-restraint, he was resolute in being a man of *honour* according to the *code*; he would be *unimpeachable by any recognized opinion*. (273; ch. 29)

> As it was, [Lydgate] had rested in the consideration that disobedience to his orders, however it might have arisen, could not be considered a crime, that in the *dominant opinion* obedience to his orders was just as likely to be fatal, and that the affair was simply one of *etiquette*. (717; ch. 73)

> And he told [Dorothea] everything . . . [,] entering fully into the fact that his treatment of the patient was opposed to the *dominant practice*, into his doubts at the last, his ideal of medical duty, and his uneasy consciousness that the acceptance of the money [a loan from Bulstrode] had made some difference in his private inclination and professional behaviour, though not in his *fulfilment of any publicly recognized obligation*. (740; ch. 76, all emphases added)

What are manners, codes of socially acceptable behavior, and codes of professional ethics but interrelated, prewritten systems, or "texts," that "determine the angle at which most people view" things (228; ch. 23)?

Do we call Casaubon's restraint "scruples," or mental cruelty? Is the codicil to his will merely "ungentlemanly" (470; ch. 49), as Sir James suggests, or is it blatantly immoral? Is Lydgate's failure to question the circumstances of Raffles's death justified on the grounds that professional "etiquette" has been doubly honored (he *prescribed* what he considered the "best" treatment/Raffles *received* the "accepted" treatment), or is he just as much an accessory-after-the-fact as Bulstrode himself? These, Eliot suggests, are matters of interpretation, matters of "naming" and "defining" as arbitrary and socially-conditioned as the systems on which they are based: "when a youthful nobleman steals jewellery [*sic*] we call the act kleptomania" (230, 228; ch. 23).[3] Lydgate is not forced to confront the moral issues head-on, because once again, Text 1—his individual morality and spirit of medical reform—has capitulated to the more powerful, self-sustaining text of "publicly recognized opinion." Who, in such a position, would have the strength to act otherwise?

Once we get beyond Henry James and others like him who have dismissed Will Ladislaw as a weak and feminine character, Will and Dorothea are the critics' most frequent responses to the question of who would do otherwise. For James, the question of marriage between these two characters was "relatively trivial," an unnecessary extension of the plot past its appropriate conclusion (*Literary Criticism: Essays* 961); for us, however, it is crucial. Defining Will as Eliot's attempt to "pull free" from convention, Raymond Williams notes that "Ladislaw is a free man in the way the others [Casaubon and Lydgate] are not; a free mind with free emotions; a man who is wholly responsive":

> He is not tied by property, which he can reject in a principled way. He's not of 'good birth' and doesn't try to depend on it. . . . [And] since unlike Lydgate he can accept poverty, he is not frustrated, is not corrupted, does not become resigned. . . . [T]his is George Eliot thinking beyond, feeling beyond, the restrictions and the limitations she has so finely recorded; thinking into mobility not as dislocating but as liberating; . . . following a thread to the future, as she tried in *Daniel Deronda*; a single thread that has come loose from the web, but that she insists is there, running beyond Middlemarch as she herself ran beyond it: a responsiveness and a courage to live in new ways, under the weight, the defining weight, of a limited and frustrating world. (93–94)

Similarly, Susan Gubar and Sandra Gilbert describe Dorothea's marriage to Will as "the most subversive act available to her within the context defined by the author, since it is the only act prohibited by the stipulations of the dead man, and by her family and friends" (530).

Such assessments are right—as far as they go. At times, Will is, indeed, a "sort of gypsy" who "enjoy[s] the sense of belonging to no class" (447; ch. 46), and Dorothea herself feels "daringly defiant" not only for receiving him in the library, "where her husband's prohibition seem[s] to dwell" (782; ch. 83), but for marrying him as well: a double violation of proscriptive texts. Nevertheless, I must ultimately part ways with Williams, with Gubar and Gilbert, and with Joseph Wiesenfarth, who argues in *Gothic Manners and the Classic English Novel* that the marriage of Dorothea and Will represents a "new way of rendering . . . the novel of manners"—that through it, Eliot "frees Dorothea to be herself—to be the alien wife of an alien Will" (112). As I read *Middlemarch*, freedom and defiance are only part of the story. Just as significant, particularly in the context of the novel of manners, is the *other* side of the story.

Surely, it is no accident that Eliot so often presents Will in the same terms we come to associate with Lydgate: "Genius, [Will] held, is necessarily intolerant of fetters" (82; ch. 10); "There are characters which are continually creating collisions and nodes for themselves in dramas which nobody is prepared to act with them" (189; ch. 19); "Will . . . could not bear the thought of any flaw appearing in his crystal" (455; ch. 47). Perhaps his secret passion is metaphorically "like the inheritance of a fortune" (455; ch. 47), but at the same time, his day-to-day relationship with Dorothea is very much hampered by the literal fortune he lacks. Even before he knows about the codicil, Will perceives the "chasm" that separates him from the object of his desires: the "imputation," even on her part, that he may be "trying to win the favour of a rich woman" (483; ch. 51). Eventually, he goes away to seek his fortune as a barrister because "poverty may be as bad as leprosy if it divides us from what we most care for" (527; ch. 54), and ultimately, he returns to Middlemarch willing to accept a settlement from Bulstrode, if necessary, in order to make his way in the world. Where is the spirited young man who once swore by his "unblemished honour" to refuse gifts of money that had been "dishonourably" and nefariously won (606; ch. 61)? If Will is "not corrupted," as Williams argues, surely he is at least "frustrated" and "resigned"—leveled and "shaped" like so many others whose manners and values he disdains.

Ultimately, too, Eliot herself seems forced to submit to the shaping influence of society's codes. Early in the novel, when Lydgate feels obliged to vote against his conscience in an election that offers no healthy alternatives, we see the effects of frustration and compromise. "How could a man be satisfied with a decision between such alternatives and under such circumstances?" the narrator asks; "[n]o more than he can be satisfied with his hat, which he has chosen from among such shapes as the resources of the age offer him, wearing it at best with a resignation which is chiefly supported by comparison" (184; ch. 18). But who in any age is so free as to discard the "hat"—the mold of custom and tradition—altogether? Not Dorothea and Will, certainly, nor Eliot either. One contemporary reviewer worried that

> if our young ladies, repelled by the faint and "neutral" virtues of Celia on the one hand, and the powerfully drawn worldly Rosamond on the other, take to be Dorotheas, with a vow to dress differently from other women, and to regulate their own conduct on the system of a general disapproval of the state of things into which they are born, the world will be a less comfortable world without being a better one. (Review of *Middlemarch* 646)

The reviewer need not have worried about the "world." Eliot strongly suggests that Dorothea and Will, try as they might, cannot separate themselves from "the state of things into which they were born." Whose actions, in a world like that of *Middlemarch* or even our own, are *not* limited by the shape of things as they are?

In the first place, Dorothea must marry and be "absorbed into the life of another" as wife and mother, for "no one," including Eliot, knows "exactly what else that was in her power she ought rather to have done" (809; finale); there *is* nothing else in her power in an "imperfect social state." In the second place, the marriage between Dorothea and Will is possible only because Dorothea has her own private inheritance, apart from Casaubon's property, and *she* can provide the fortune Will lacks. Not even Eliot or Dorothea's Uncle Brooke would suggest that these two defiers of tradition might go so far as to marry if she did *not* have resources of her own. Mary Poovey, in her analysis of the "proper lady" and women writers, notes that "as long as an individual's self-definition—the terms in which he or she conceptualizes and evaluates behavior—is derived primarily from the values implicit in the culture he or she wishes to change, the solutions the imagination generates will be governed, on some level, by these values" (xvi). Such, clearly, is the message inherent in the marriage of Dorothea and Will.

With *Middlemarch*, Eliot set out to show "the gradual action of ordinary causes rather than exceptional" (*Letters* 5:168); she succeeded in writing a novel of extraordinary power. If, in the end, her characters must revise their re-created texts to conform to the stronger text of tradition, so must Eliot herself, and so, as a rule, must we all. This is not life as it "should be," to repeat Eliot's words, but life as it "is," and the *nature* of the novel of manners. Nevertheless, in re-creating the text of the novel of manners to the extent that she did, in pushing the edges of the "mould" to their limits, Eliot lets us imagine what fiction and life *might* be, if ever the mold *is* broken. "Every limit," she writes in the finale, "is a beginning as well as an ending" (805)—and with every beginning, comes hope for a different ending.

Notes

1. Like fellow novelists Thomas Hardy and Henry James, Eliot frequently paints "pictures" in words—descriptive vignettes in which the relative positions of the characters (above, below, beside, behind) are significant. Such pictures, notable for what they exclude as well as what they include, occur often in *Middlemarch*, particularly in the scenes involving Dorothea and Casaubon, Dorothea and Will, and Rosamond and Lydgate.

2. The Gothic metaphors with which Eliot depicts Dorothea's marriage to Casaubon are appropriate, for as Joseph Wiesenfarth explains in *Gothic Manners and the Classic English Novel*, "*Middlemarch* is a novel about the horrors of respectability," a novel in which "[i]mpeccable manners ravish the peccant heart" (105).

3. The kleptomania comment is one of many passages on language that appear in the Fred Vincy-Caleb Garth portions of the novel. Like similar statements in the Bulstrode strand of the story, these passages serve as a sort of marginal gloss or running commentary on the manners of characters in the main plots. At the same time, they serve to redefine such socially conditioned terms as *noble* and *gentleman*.

7

The Portrait of a Lady: Gothic Manners in Europe

Joseph Wiesenfarth

Henry James went to Harvard to read law, but he read Balzac instead, left Cambridge, and became a novelist. The precise details of this episode in James's education escaped Ford Madox Ford, who somehow thought that James had studied law at Geneva, a university that lacked the academic distinction of "Oxford, Bonn, Heidelberg, Jena or even Paris" (Hueffer 101) but that conferred the social distinction of *respectability.* Consequently, Geneva was not James's tender mother; Geneva was James's respectable mother: "I allow myself to discover in Mr. James . . . a trace of—I won't say of affection, for the word would be ill-applied to this University that is *Mater,* not *Alma,* but *Respectiblissima*—a trace of remembrance of the respectability of this haunt of his contemplative youth" (Hueffer 106). This cachet of respectability is important to Ford's James, whose "conscious or unconscious mission . . . was to civilise his people—whom he always loved" (Hueffer 140–41). But Europe failed to provide James the respectability he sought: "He had tried to find his Great Good Place—his earthly Utopia—in Italy, in France, in English literary life. He had failed" (Hueffer 146). James found himself, therefore, "in the same boat with Flaubert, with Zola, with Turgenieff, with Maupassant, and even with Baudelaire" (Hueffer 138).

> From Italy, France and England the dayspring was to have come; but half a century of pilgrimages . . . left [James] with no further message than that—that the soul's immortal, but that most people have not got souls—are in the end just the stuff with which to fill graveyards; that *cela vous donne une fière idée de l'homme; homo homini lupus,* or any other old message of all the old messages of this old and wise world. Bric-à-brac, pallazzi [*sic*], châteaux, haunts of ancient peace—these the pilgrim found in matchless abundance, in scores, in hundreds.

A version of this essay appeared previously in *Gothic Manners and the Classic English Novel* by Joseph Wiesenfarth (Madison: U of Wisconsin P, 1988).

Figure 5. Frederick Frieseke (1874–1939), *Good Morning
(Collection of the Butler Institute of American Art,
Youngstown, Ohio)*

Figure 6. William M. Chase (1849–1916), *Did You Speak to Me?*, 1900
(*Collection of the Butler Institute of American Art,
Youngstown, Ohio*)

Poynton, Matcham, Lackley, Hampton. . . . "The gondola stopped; the old palace was there. How charming! it's grey and pink. . . ." From the first visit to Madonnas of the Louvre, in *The American*, to the last days of the eponymous vessel of *The Golden Bowl*, there is no end to the *articles de vertu*. . . . But as for the duchesses with souls—well, most duchesses haven't got them! (Hueffer 141–42)

It is the James whose duchesses have no souls who wrote *The Portrait of a Lady*. If in *The American* a marquis and a marquise have no souls, in *The Portrait* "the cleverest woman" (176) and "the first gentleman" (430) in Europe have no souls; nor does the Countess Gemini: "The Countess seemed to . . . have no soul; she was like a bright rare shell, with a polished surface and a remarkably pink lip, in which something would rattle when you shook it" (449). James's subjects in *The Portrait* are Americans who go to Europe in search of civilization and find their own savagery. If Conrad uncovered the heart of darkness in the Congo, James uncovered it in cities. The unholy alliance of the Bellegardes, mother and son, in Paris, gives way to the unholy alliance of estranged lovers, Madame Merle and Gilbert Osmond, in Florence and Rome. This is what makes James an ally of Baudelaire. For if Henry James found the "fatality of British decorum" in *Middlemarch* (*Literary Criticism: Essays* 963), we today find the fatality of European decorum in *The Portrait of a Lady*.[1] If Ford made a mistake about James's studying law at Geneva, he made no mistake when he showed James depicting the decay of contemporary manners in the cultural centers of Europe.

When James tagged George Eliot's characterization of Rosamond Vincy as inscribing "the fatality of British decorum," he signaled his awareness of what could be done by driving a wedge of middle-class respectability between manners and morals. Whereas Casaubon is a gentleman in Middlemarch, Osmond is "the first gentleman in Europe." This ominous fact eventually makes the jaded Madame Merle say that "society is all bad" (239). And certainly there is something of Henry James in that remark because he knew from reading Sainte-Beuve that "as soon as you penetrate a little under the veil of society, as in nature, you see nothing but wars, struggles, destructions, and recompositions" (*Literary Criticism: French* 688). The truth of that observation of his own came home dramatically to Henry James in 1914 at the outbreak of World War I: he virtually ceased writing about society and took to reading to wounded soldiers and distributing tobacco in the hospital wards. *The Portrait of a Lady* penetrates Sainte-Beuve's veil of society by showing what it means for an American girl to become a "lady" in European society. This focus requires James to emphasize Isabel Archer's consciousness and sensibility more exclusively than Eliot did Dorothea Brooke's.

Many things make *Middlemarch* an important novel. George Eliot's blending of the elements of Gothic fiction with those of the novel of manners is not least among them. She makes a thoroughly respectable clergyman, Edward Casaubon, by virtue of his starched notions of correct conduct, into a monster who crunches bones in a cavern; she makes a respectable society wife, Rosamond Vincy, by virtue of her ladylike ways, into a basil plant that feeds on a murdered man's brains; she makes a respectable banker, Nicholas Bulstrode, by virtue of his calling as God's instrument, into the Old Nick of the novel. These three prominent characters in *Middlemarch* dramatize the horror of good manners. They expose the bankruptcy of a myth of social concern founded on nothing more than respectability—that "Damocles sword," as Carlyle called it, that hangs "forever over . . . poor English life" (157)—when it confronts a myth of individual freedom founded on a love of justice. *Middlemarch* engages to show how a Gothic tradition that centers on death can become psychologically ghastly when it appropriates a manners tradition that centers on life. For characteristically the novel of manners centers on what Plato defined as the cardinal virtues—prudence, justice, fortitude, and temperance—and the Gothic novel centers on what the Book of Revelation presents as the last things: death, judgment, heaven, and hell.

Henry James learned a variety of things from his reading and study of George Eliot's fiction; and *The Portrait of a Lady* shows that what he learned from *Middlemarch*, especially, was a sense of Gothic manners, a sense of the horror of respectability.[2] He saw how ladies and gentlemen, by their insistence on a total adherence to socially accepted norms of conduct, became horrible human beings. *The Portrait of a Lady* presents a trenchant critique of a culture and civilization that have come to prize formalism over life. As an exposé of Gothic manners, the novel makes its finest lady, Madame Merle, a damned soul, and its finest gentleman, Gilbert Osmond, a devil. In his search for alternatives to such a lady and such a gentleman, James hit upon a man and a woman: he hit upon Ralph Touchett and Isabel Archer. But to tell their story differently from the way Eliot told hers of Ladislaw and Dorothea, James chose to emphasize Isabel's consciousness and sensibility more exclusively than Eliot did Dorothea's. He had, therefore, to focus his attention and ours on a woman in *The Portrait of a Lady*. That choice makes his novel a searching indictment of Gothic manners at the same time that it makes it a telling permutation on the kind of fiction that George Eliot practiced, perhaps even invented, in *Middlemarch*. Although Isabel Archer is far from being a New Woman of the kind that Henrik Ibsen and Bernard Shaw were to make the focus of attention, she shares with the New Woman a desire for a fullness of life beyond that allowed to women of a more conventional stamp.[3] Isabel wants to achieve "the union of great knowledge with great liberty: the knowledge would give one a sense of duty and the liberty a sense of enjoyment" (431). Because such knowledge and liberty are her goals, she turns down proposals of marriage from Lord Warburton and Caspar Goodwood: "She will not submit to the demands of those who would place her in the center of a traditional setting enclosed by a formal frame" (Ward 3). And James presents both Warburton and Goodwood as traditional in the extreme: they appear as modern displacements of medieval figures. Their ideas of woman as wife are feudal compared to Isabel's ideal of woman as knowing and free. In portraying them, James invoked the Victorian addiction to chivalry, giving us a knight-errant in Goodwood and a feudal lord in Warburton. James presents an American businessman who is as "selfish as iron" (332), as a knight-errant. Goodwood is shown as "naturally plated and steeled, armed essentially for aggression" (155). His eyes "shine through the vizard of the helmet" (154). When he fights with Isabel, she penetrates his armor with her sharpness (156–57). When he asks her for a "pledge" (157), she gives him none at all. So he strides about "lean and hungry," keeps "his ground," and dresses his "wounds," determined to watch over her whether she likes it or not (158–59). Isabel is the Queen of Beauty to whom Goodwood vows loyalty and service and from whom he takes as reward a single kiss. But he differs from knights-errant of old in that he mostly battles his lady rather than battling for her. And when Goodwood at last proposes adultery to her, she finds him "mad" (588). Isabel can be neither his wife nor his mistress. If his passion frightens her, his interdiction of her "love of liberty" (162) frightens her even more.[4] Only after Goodwood leaves her is Isabel free: "She had not known where to turn; but she knew now. There was a straight path" (591).

Lord Warburton also offers Isabel an outdated model of what it means to be a woman. He addresses her as a feudal lord would and invites her to be his chatelaine. His sisters, Miss Molyneux and Mildred, illustrate the type of woman Isabel chooses not to be:

> "I suppose [Isabel said] you revere your brother and are rather afraid of him."
>
> "Of course one looks up to one's brother," said Miss Molyneux simply. . . .
>
> "His ability is known," Mildred added; "everyone thinks it's immense."
>
> "Oh, I can see that," said Isabel. "But if I were he I should wish to fight to the death: I mean for the heritage of the past. I should hold it tight."
>
> "I think one ought to be liberal," Mildred argued gently. "We've always been so, even from the earliest times."
>
> "Ah well," said Isabel, "you've made a great success of it; I don't wonder you like it. I see that you're very fond of crewels." (77–78)

In the absence of a critical faculty, being a lady amounts only to a taste in embroidery. Being a gentleman like Warburton is largely a matter of property and power. "He owns fifty thousand acres of the soil of this little island," Mr. Touchett tells Isabel, "and ever so many things besides. He has half a dozen houses to live in. He has a seat in Parliament as I have one at my own dinner table" (74). This hardly seems to qualify him as "liberal," except perhaps in

Mildred's terms. Warburton, according to Ralph, "regards himself as an imposition—as an abuse" (71). But Warburton is not liberal enough to do away with that abuse by disestablishing himself in any way. Ralph finds that Warburton is "the victim of a critical age; he has ceased to believe in himself and he doesn't know what to believe in" (71). A rich, privileged, landed feudal lord, Warburton is not suited to be Isabel's husband. He does not even understand her: "'He thinks I'm a barbarian,' she said, 'and that I've never seen forks and spoons'" (70). Warburton's failure of imagination is even cruder in his pursuit of Pansy Osmond and in his eventual marriage to a woman he does not love. If Goodwood restricts Isabel's freedom, so too does Warburton: she could really never be herself with him and hope to be understood.

To marry, therefore, either the knight-errant or the feudal lord, either Goodwood or Warburton, would be for Isabel to take a step backward into the past rather than a step forward into the future. Both men invite Isabel to choose deliberately to live intellectually and emotionally in the past. If she eventually finds herself in a more horrifying version of a Gothic world with Osmond, it is because she once saw herself finding "great knowledge" and "great liberty" with Osmond. That she was frightfully mistaken in her choice of Osmond does not at all argue that she was mistaken in her dismissal of both Goodwood and Warburton. That she should not have married a Gothic villain does not logically argue that she should have married either a knight-errant or a feudal lord. As a young woman affronting her destiny, Isabel Archer cannot do herself justice by accepting either Goodwood or Warburton. Yet, what she desires above all, once her quest for great knowledge and great freedom begins, is justice.[5]

It is because Isabel is convinced that she is doing herself and Osmond justice that she agrees to marry him. When she passes her life in review in chapter 42, she asks herself a rhetorical question about Osmond: "Hadn't he all the appearance of a man living in the open air of the world, indifferent to small considerations, caring only for truth and knowledge and believing that two intelligent people ought to look for them together and, whether they found them or not, find at least some happiness in the search?" (429). To the Gilbert Osmond of this vision, Isabel is determined to do the justice she feels is denied him by Ralph Touchett. "I can't enter into your idea of Mr. Osmond," she tells Ralph. "I can't do it justice, because I see him in quite another way" (346). When she does come to see Osmond as Ralph sees him—as a "sterile dilettante" (345)—Isabel realizes that her husband's limitations are even greater than Goodwood's or Warburton's. The "aristocratic life" that to Isabel meant "the union of great knowledge with great liberty" is to Osmond "a thing of forms, a conscious, calculated attitude" (431). "There were certain things they must do, a certain posture they must take, certain people they must know and not know. When she saw this rigid system close about her, draped though it was in pictured tapestries," a "sense of darkness and suffocation . . . took possession of her; she had seemed shut up with an odour of mould and decay" (431). With this image of the tomb, so characteristic of Gothic fiction,[6] James gives us a pointed expression of the horror of respectability—of the fatality of European decorum, of the deadly propriety of Gothic manners. It is totally appropriate that the name Osmond should come out of a play by Monk Lewis entitled *Castle Spectre*. The Palazzo Roccanera is hardly more healthy a place: it is "the house of darkness, the house of dumbness, the house of suffocation" (429). In it, Isabel is buried alive.[7] She is no better off there than Claire de Cintré is in *The American,* a Carmelite nun in the Rue de l'Enfer—in a street named after hell itself.

Isabel had not, of course, expected anything like this in marrying Osmond. She had seen vistas opening to her as Osmond's wife that were not in the prospect of a Lady Warburton or a Mrs. Goodwood. But her first public appearance after her marriage presents her as bound in on all sides. The irony of Isabel's appearing as "framed" in a golden doorway is inescapable. Having been collected by Madame Merle, Isabel is framed by Gilbert Osmond. Isabel herself has supplied the gilding on the frame by bringing Osmond her fortune in marriage. The woman who above all wanted to be free—the woman whose fortune, by Ralph's reckoning, was to guarantee her freedom—has been "captured" by Gilbert Osmond's "beautiful mind" (428). The woman who wanted to combine great knowledge with great liberty sees that her "real offence . . . was her having a mind of her own at all" (432). Osmond's "egoism lay hidden like a serpent in a bank of flowers" (430). Isabel, as the image suggests, is the victim of the devil himself. She is now neither to think nor to act outside the boundaries he has set her: "he had expected his wife to feel with him and for him, to enter into his opinions, his ambitions, his preferences" (432). "Osmond's beautiful mind" gave her "neither light nor air; Osmond's beautiful mind indeed seemed to peep down from a small high window and mock at her" (429). Her function is now what Ralph once warned her it would be: "to keep guard over the sensibilities of a sterile dilettante" (345).

What James reveals in the drawing rooms of a man of taste is a degraded principle of life: Osmond pointed out to Isabel

> so much of the baseness and shabbiness of life, opened her eyes so wide to the stupidity, the depravity, the ignorance of mankind, that she had been properly impressed with the infinite vulgarity of things and of the virtue of keeping one's self unspotted by it. But this base, ignoble world, it appeared, was after all what one was to live for; one was to keep it forever in one's eye, in order not to enlighten or convert or redeem it, but to extract from it some recognition of one's own superiority. On the one hand it was despicable, but on the other it afforded a standard. (430)

On this scale of values, the cardinal virtues are redefined and degraded. Prudence is degraded to a concern for worldly regard; justice is degraded to a husband's right to his wife's obedience; fortitude is degraded to her endurance of their miserable marriage; temperance is degraded to her suppression of all firm ideas and strong feelings of her own. The cardinal virtues are no longer the moral foundation of the good life as promoted by civilized manners; they are as corrupted as the manners themselves. Those manners, which should be integral to the civilized intercourse of life, are now only the empty civilities of a horrible life: Isabel sees that she and Osmond "were strangely married, at all events, and it was a horrible life" (433). Manners as dictated by respectability— extracting from the world "recognition of one's own superiority"—variously put Isabel in a dungeon that becomes a tomb and makes her the companion of an egotistical devil. Gilbert Osmond reveals to Isabel Archer what Henry James's novels suggested to Ford Madox Ford: "most people have not got souls—are in the end just the stuff with which to fill graveyards." Here where life turns deadly as manners become horrors, *The Portrait of a Lady* defines itself as a novel of Gothic manners.

One person with a soul who is nevertheless about to fill a grave is Ralph Touchett. Oddly enough—but then again not so oddly in a novel of Gothic manners—the dying Ralph is the most satisfying lover for the vital soul that is buried in Isabel Archer. The most extraordinary love scene in the novel takes place between them at his deathbed. In her intensely passionate last moments with Ralph, Isabel does justice to him and in so doing does justice to herself as well. This scene enacts the climax of the quest for justice involved in the question that *The Portrait of a Lady* asks: How can a woman give up being a girl to become a lady without giving up being her *self?* How can Isabel Archer give up being a naïve American girl to become a sophisticated European lady without giving up what is vitally essential to being herself? Isabel, as a girl, flatters herself that she is "a very just woman" (59). She promises to do Warburton "justice" (109). She shows a "passionate desire to be just" and tells Ralph "I am very just" (342) when they discuss Osmond. In the midst of her unhappy marriage, she prays, "Whatever happens to me let me not be unjust" (404). And as her quest approaches its climax, Isabel finds her "old passion for justice" reasserting itself (537). Seeking justice, then, Isabel makes her life a case; but, at the same time, seeking an understanding of her *self*, she makes it a riddle.[8] The case demands a judgment on whether she has acted justly; the riddle asks how she can be woman and lady, friend and fiancée, sister and wife and still be herself. Isabel's gradual understanding of the full implications of justice and of selfhood informs her relationship with every man in the novel. It also reforms her relationships with Mrs. Touchett, Madame Merle, and Pansy. And, finally, it places Osmond, once her complementary lover, increasingly in tension with Ralph, who becomes ever more completely her affined lover. This telescoping of case (seeking justice) with riddle (seeking selfhood) is the focal point for

James as he paints his portrait of Isabel Archer in his novel. The niceness of the case and the bafflement of the riddle are immediately evident when Gilbert Osmond requires Isabel as his wife to bring her lover, Warburton, to propose marriage to his daughter, Pansy. How in this complex of demanding relationships is Isabel Archer herself to survive? How can she do justice to all the parties involved and to herself as well?

As Osmond's spouse, Isabel manifests a concern for their marriage by limiting her freedom of action and trying to do as her husband wishes: "It seemed to Isabel that if she could make it her duty to bring" Warburton to propose to Pansy "she should play the part of a good wife" (415). But whereas "play[ing] the part" makes her seem "a good wife" by satisfying Osmond's desire that she appear such, it threatens her personal integrity. Isabel has instinctively been opposed to a match between Warburton and Pansy—"at first it had not presented itself in a manner to excite her enthusiasm" (414)—but "the idea of assisting her husband to be pleased" allows her to rationalize the suitability of the proposed match (417). When she decides to help Osmond, she, for a moment, feels good about being a useful spouse. But James's subtle psychological dramatization of Isabel's emotional make-up shows her instinctive life rebelling against her rationalized sense of wifely duty: "After all she couldn't rise to it; something held her and made this impossible" (417). Without fully understanding the reasons for her actions, Isabel begins to play what Osmond later calls "a very deep game" (481). Before she instructs Pansy to obey her father and accept Warburton if he proposes, Isabel prevents Warburton from proposing. Her visit to Pansy becomes, therefore, simply a calculated act of self-justification. Isabel now lives in a world where such acts of casuistry have become a wearisome necessity.

When Madame Merle tells Isabel that she, Madame Merle, is going to ask Pansy what Isabel had to say about Warburton, we know that Pansy will report that Isabel told her to accept Warburton if he proposes marriage. But we also know that Warburton will not ask Pansy to marry him. Isabel has had it both ways. She has done Osmond a legalistic kind of justice by literally following his advice in telling Warburton to send his letter of proposal and in instructing Pansy to obey her father; at the same time, Isabel has done Warburton, Pansy, and herself justice, too, by seeing to it that Warburton does not send the letter and consequently seeing to it that Pansy will not need to obey her father. James puts Isabel through this extraordinary performance to demonstrate what a tight spot she finds herself in; indeed, to demonstrate what it means for a once-carefree girl now to have become a careful lady. The myth of concern that is generated in Isabel by her marriage is at this moment directly at war with the myth of freedom that is the spring of her vitality. James's realistic characterization of Isabel shows her adapting painfully to her surroundings. When James, as Theodora Bosanquet reported, "walked out of the refuge of his study into the world and looked about him, he saw a place of torment, where creatures of prey perpetually thrust their claws into the quivering flesh of the doomed, defenseless children of light" (33). Accommodation is necessary to survival. In Rome, Isabel does as the Romans do: she becomes super subtle. Such are the measures the children of light must take to survive in the "darkened . . . world" (425). *Il faut hurler avec les loups.* That is what it means to be a *lady.*

But Isabel is not quite the Roman wolf that Madame Merle is. She avoids the trap that would make her so. In the chapters treating Pansy's courtship, Isabel has the chance to do for her husband what Madame Merle has already done for him: she has a chance to secure a spouse for an Osmond. Although Madame Merle tries to revivify her life of feeling through Isabel—she has Isabel marry her lover and mother her child—Isabel refuses to give Serena Merle the last satisfaction she craves. Isabel refuses to become the damned creature that Osmond has made of his former mistress. Madame Merle—who tells Osmond, "You've dried up my soul" (522)—tells Isabel that "if we can't have youth within us we can have it outside, and I really think we see it and feel it better that way" (195). When we think about it for a minute, the differences between a Madame Merle and a Miss Havisham are superficial at best, as are the differences between a Compeyson and an Osmond. Both women are caught in the same Lacanian plot of trying to define themselves through others who are fated to act on their own as both Estella and Isabel (and in a small way Pansy too) do. Both Miss Havisham and Madame Merle seek to live the life they lost in younger versions of themselves who disappoint them. Serena Merle—who, according to Ralph, "got herself into perfect training, but had won none of the prizes" (252)—wants to win Warburton with Isabel's help so that she can live vicariously through Pansy. "She has failed so dreadfully," says the Countess Gemini of Madame Merle, "that she's determined her daughter shall make up for it" (547). But Isabel disappoints "the cleverest woman" in Europe turned emotional vampire. Isabel refuses, in the imagery of the novel, to serve the devil and lose her soul.[9] In playing the Roman lady by doing what the Romans do, Isabel finds and holds onto some shreds of her identity and begins to present herself as a woman to be reckoned with—an identity that she arguably possesses even more fully and formidably at the end of the novel when she leaves for Rome following Ralph's funeral.

Isabel's decision to return to Rome is the culmination of a pattern of knowing and choosing that first manifests itself dramatically in her decision to go to the dying Ralph against her husband's wishes. After talking with the Countess Gemini, who reveals to Isabel the past life of Osmond and Madame Merle, Isabel's head is "humming with new knowledge" (548), and she decides to go to Ralph at Gardencourt. This decision is the beginning of what becomes an abbreviated life of greater knowledge and greater liberty, which, until that moment, eluded Isabel during her marriage to Osmond. The structural logic of chapters 50 through 55 is to provide Isabel with more and more knowledge so that she can make a thoroughly enlightened choice at the end of the novel. In chapter 50, Isabel learns from Ned Rosier that he has sold his bibelots for fifty thousand dollars to make himself more acceptable in Osmond's eyes as a suitor to Pansy. In chapter 51, Isabel learns from the Countess that Madame Merle was Osmond's mistress and is the mother of Pansy. In chapter 52, Isabel learns from Madame Merle that Ralph is the architect of her fortune. In chapter 53, Isabel learns from Henrietta that Mr. Bantling and Henrietta will marry and settle in England. In chapter 54, Isabel learns from Mrs. Touchett that Lord Warburton is soon to marry. And in chapter 55, Isabel learns from Goodwood the meaning of passionate love. This new knowledge crowds in upon Isabel and leads her to make a series of judgments: Madame Merle is wicked, Osmond vulgar, Mrs. Touchett dry, Henrietta unoriginal, Warburton dead, and Goodwood mad. Isabel finds all her friends wanting, and, with Ralph in the grave, Isabel consequently finds herself very much alone, "humming with new knowledge" and prepared to make a final choice.

This intensified pattern of knowing and choosing is a late and realistic achievement of Isabel's earlier romantic desire for great knowledge and great liberty. This pattern also rapidly rounds out a compositional structure that has been leisurely built on interior events such as gaining knowledge, formulating judgments, and making choices. And this pattern is likewise James's contribution to the form of the novel that he appropriated from Turgenev, who said of his own work that it lacked architecture (*Portrait* vii). So that finally this pattern allows James to provide a frame for a view of life that he attributed to Turgenev but that was also very much his own:

> Life *is*, in fact, a battle. On this point optimists and pessimists agree. Evil is insolent and strong; beauty enchanting but rare; goodness very apt to be weak; folly very apt to be defiant; wickedness to carry the day; imbeciles to be in great places, people of sense in small, and mankind generally, unhappy. But the world as it stands is no illusion, no phantasm, no evil dream of a night; we wake up to it again and for ever and ever; we can neither forget it nor deny it nor dispense with it. We can welcome experience as it comes, and give it what it demands, in exchange for something which it is idle to pause to call much or little so long as it contributes to swell the volume of consciousness. In this there is mingled pain and delight, but over the mysterious mixture there hovers a visible rule, that bids us learn to will and seek to understand. (*Literary Criticism: French* 998)

The Portrait of a Lady dramatizes Isabel Archer's life as a battle, and it shows her experience of mingled pain and delight swelling the volume of her consciousness and teaching her to learn to will and to seek to understand.

Taking his cue from Turgenev, James attempted to reshape the English novel as it was bequeathed to him by George Eliot: *Middlemarch* "sets a limit" for James "to the development of the old fashioned English novel" (*Literary Criticism: Essays* 965). James thought of *Middlemarch* as both the "strongest" and the "weakest" of English novels, and he identified the weakness with what he saw as its "diffuseness": its unwillingness to center on Dorothea Brooke and its giving nearly equal importance to the stories of Lydgate, Bulstrode, and Mary Garth. For James, then, *Middlemarch* appeared to be "a mere chain of episodes." What he demanded in a novel was "an organized, molded, balanced composition, gratifying the reader with a sense of design and construction" (*Literary Criticism: Essays* 958). To achieve that ideal, James centers his novel on one character and, with that choice, transforms Dorothea Brooke's struggles with duty and respectability into Isabel Archer's passion for justice in a darkened world.

Along with the overall design of *Middlemarch*, James set out to reform its ending, too, in *The Portrait*. The flash of lightning in *Middlemarch,* which leads to a kiss that unites Dorothea and Ladislaw for life, becomes a metaphor in *The Portrait* for a kiss that separates Goodwood from Isabel. James transforms a sign of sentiment into a signal for separation; therefore, what he considered a realistic ending for his novel leaves everything to the reader's imagination:

> But when darkness returned [Isabel] was free. She never looked about her; she only darted from the spot. There were lights in the windows of the house; they shone far across the lawn. In an extraordinarily short time—for the distance was considerable—she had moved through the darkness (for she saw nothing) and reached the door. Here only she paused. She looked all about her; she listened a little; then she put her hand on the latch. She had not known where to turn; but she knew now. There was a very straight path. (591)

This is the second time that Isabel pauses in this doorway. She leaves the novel as she entered it, through "the ample doorway" of Gardencourt (15). In chapter 2, she had stepped into the light of "a splendid summer afternoon," a "tall girl in a black dress" (5), and declared, "I am very fond of my liberty" (21). Between the framed picture of the girl who is fond of her liberty and the framed picture of the woman who is free comes the portrait of a lady: "The years had touched her only to enrich her; the flower of her youth had not faded, it only hung more quietly on its stem. She had lost something of that quick eagerness to which her husband had privately taken exception—she had more the air of being able to wait. Now, at all events, framed in the gilded doorway, she . . . [was] the picture of a gracious lady" (367). The three presentations of Isabel as framed in doorways are three portraits of her at different stages of her existence. The first, Isabel framed in the Gardencourt doorway, shows her as an American girl in love with her freedom. The second, Isabel in the gilded doorway of the Palazzo Roccanera, shows her as the European lady hemmed in by a concern to present herself as Osmond's wife and handmaiden. The third, Isabel barely visible in the dark but once again framed in the Gardencourt doorway, shows her as the woman who has regained some modicum of her freedom. The three portraits represent Isabel in the three phases of her existence. The first shows her as a representative of the myth of freedom; in it the great round world lies before her as brightly and as broadly as the Gardencourt lawns in the summer sunshine. The second shows Isabel as a representative of the myth of concern, Osmond now having reduced her great round world to a tiny circle defined by his own exquisite "taste": "a thing of forms, a conscious, calculated attitude." The third shows Isabel as a representative of an integrated life of freedom and concern, Goodwood's proposal having given the last stroke to her characterization when she rejects his final plea: "We can do absolutely as we please; to whom under the sun do we owe anything? What is it that holds us, what is it that has the smallest right to interfere in such a question as this? . . . The world's all before us—and the world's very big. I know something about that" (590). Goodwood's argument articulates precisely what was once Isabel's sense of the world.

When she stepped out of the ample doorway onto the Gardencourt lawn for the first time, "she had a fixed determination to regard the world as a place of brightness, of free expansion, of irresistible action" (51). Isabel's rebuttal of Goodwood sums up the changes that four years have worked in her: "The world's very small" (590). Isabel's sense of herself is now such that it is only in that smaller world where she has planted the roots of her concern that she can allow her freedom to grow. She needs coherence and continuity in her life to face the facts that finally confront her: Ralph, generously, made her fortune, and Madame Merle, selfishly, made her marriage; Osmond, who once loved her but now hates her, vulgarly, married her for her money; Ralph adored her, but Osmond wanted her to adore him; Ralph's life was beautiful, but others' lives are not; Pansy needs her, and Isabel has promised to help her; Osmond without Madame Merle, who is to leave Rome and even Europe perhaps, is at half-strength at best; and, finally, "the day when she should have to take back something she had solemnly bestown" now rapidly approaches (462). What dominates *The Portrait of a Lady,* as James's analysis of Turgenev's novels suggests, is his heroine's need first to understand her situation and then to choose to do something about it. But as Elsa Nettels argues, the resolution of the novel cannot appropriately be effected by a change in Isabel's "external circumstances, for the rewards of Isabel's experience lie in the inward change, in her deeper knowledge of herself and the other characters" (13). No other character understands as much as she does by the time the novel ends. Isabel knows at last that she cannot be free without having the truths she has discovered become the basis of the last choice she makes.

The advantage that Isabel has over Osmond is that he fears these same truths because they threaten to expose his pose as "first gentleman in Europe." Because Ralph is dying and dying men tell the truth, Osmond objects to Isabel's visiting her cousin: "It's dishonorable; it's indelicate; it's indecent," says Osmond, for Isabel to "travel across Europe alone . . . to sit at the bedside of other men" (536). But Isabel does not finally care how things look; she finally does not care for her own or for Osmond's respectability. Isabel, the narrator says, "lost all shame, all wish to hide things" (575). Her last moments with Ralph, not her final minute with Goodwood,[10] consequently constitute the great love scene in the novel. Isabel, kneeling at Ralph's bedside, holding the dying man in her arms, is "supremely together" with him (575): " 'And remember this . . . that if you've been hated, you've also been loved. Ah but, Isabel, *adored!*' he just audibly and lingeringly breathed. 'Oh my brother!' she cried with a movement of still deeper prostration" (578). This follows on what the narrator calls Isabel's "passionate need to cry out and accuse herself, to let her sorrow possess her" (576). This is unmistakably a love scene of considerable power even though it contains no explicitly erotic event. It takes place in a man's bedroom, the woman has lost all shame, the man is dying in the woman's arms, the lovers are supremely together, and they experience a great moment of ecstasy, followed by exhaustion. James rewrote this passage to emphasize the ecstasy and the exhaustion. What Ralph said to Isabel in the 1881 edition of *The Portrait* was "that if you've been hated, you have also been loved." Nothing more. Isabel's response was, "Ah, my brother!" According to F. O. Matthiessen, the James of the 1908 *Portrait* "felt impelled to a more high-keyed emotional register" (172). This passage shows that feeling clearly. If John Donne once used a vocabulary of knowing and dying to express the power of sexual love,[11] James now uses a vocabulary of sexual love to express the power of knowing and dying. "In the world of Isabel Archer," Stephen Donadio writes, " 'the bribes and lures, the beguilements and prizes,' may be many, but the prize is still 'within' " (81). So Henry James's great love scene is a moment of truth in which Isabel Archer's soul is ravished by the adoration of Ralph Touchett.[12]

Ralph is Isabel's lover in the romantic tradition of affined souls.[13] Isabel's every encounter with Goodwood is a battle: they clash like knights in the lists with the clatter of arms overwhelming words of love. They are anything but lovers who are alike. Ralph, however, begins the novel as Isabel's "cousin," becomes her "best friend" (462), and ends it her "brother." Brothers and sisters are frequently lovers in Gothic novels; and, as Elizabeth MacAndrew reminds us, they exist as "uncorrupted figures in a harsh and wicked world" (67). Ralph is Isabel's affined lover because he is, in Tony Tanner's words, "her true image of what her self wants to be" ("Fearful" 157). Isabel, who wanted to make her life a work of art, now pronounces Ralph's to have been "beautiful" (570). Appropriately, Ralph never allows anyone to use the room that Isabel once used at Gardencourt; Ralph keeps Isabel's room inviolate in the same way that Heathcliff kept Cathy's at Wuthering Heights: "something told Isabel that it had not been slept in since she occupied it" (570). Ralph's serious decline in health begins with Isabel's engagement to Osmond: "He felt cold about the heart; he had never liked anything less" (339). So just as the last years of his life were centered on Isabel—"It was for you that I wanted . . . to live," he tells her (504)—so is his death. In the great tradition of romantic love, Ralph's death is a *Liebestod*.[14] James dramatizes in this love scene between Isabel and Ralph the truth that Hans Castorp nicely articulates to Claudia Cauchat in *The Magic Mountain:* that love (*l'amour*) and death (*la mort*) are so entangled in the body as to be scarcely distinguishable: "Oui, ils sont charnels tous deux, l'amour et la mort, et voilà leur terreur et leur grande magie!" (Mann 342). James makes it difficult for his readers to distinguish between *l'amour* and *la mort* when, by telling each other the truth, Isabel finds love and Ralph death.

Part of the truth they speak anticipates the ending of the novel:

> Then he murmured simply: "You must stay here."
> "I should like to stay—as long as seems right."
> "As seems right—as seems right?" He repeated her words. "Yes, you think a great deal about that."
> "Of course one must." (577)

After Isabel has thought a great deal about what "seems right"—about where justice lies—she starts back to Rome.[15] She goes back as a woman who has seen her lover's ghost. Ralph, "the only true living spirit she has ever known" (Banta 172), once told Isabel that to see such a ghost at Gardencourt was a "privilege" given only to those who "have suffered greatly, have gained some miserable knowledge" (48). "She apparently had fulfilled the necessary condition; for the next morning, in the cold, faint dawn, she knew that a spirit was standing by her bed. . . . She stared a moment; she saw his white face—his kind eyes, then she saw there was nothing. She was not afraid; she was only sure" (578–79). These eight words are Ralph's only legacy to Isabel; he leaves her no other. Having faced the past with Ralph, Isabel now faces the future without him. He has bequeathed her strength and certainty.

Writing of the fate of Louis Trevelyan in Trollope's *He Knew He Was Right,* James—finding Trevelyan "living in a desolate villa on a hilltop near Siena"—sees a conclusion so determinedly real that he judges it worthy of Balzac in its pitilessness: "Here and in several other places Trollope has dared to be thoroughly logical; he has not sacrificed to conventional optimism; he has not been afraid of a misery which should be too much like life" (*Literary Criticism: Essays* 1351). This should be taken as much as a comment on James's own endings as on Trollope's, in the same way that James's analysis of Turgenev's sense of life as a battle is really a comment on James's own sense of life. The ending of *The Portrait of a Lady* avoids easy solutions and the kind of closure that James constantly criticized in George Eliot's novels, not excluding *Middlemarch*.[16] The open ending of *The Portrait* is meant to stimulate the reader's moral imagination: reading the novel is meant to provide the reader with "great knowledge," which, in itself, ensures the reader "great liberty" in supplying a meaning for the conclusion of Isabel's story.[17] The novel is written to allow the reader to emulate life insofar as life bids us all to "learn to will and seek to understand." Among the many ways of understanding the ending, two seem to represent opposite poles of the range of choice: one reading follows Jacques Lacan and pushes *The Portrait* more deeply into a world of Gothic manners; the other follows Mikhail Bakhtin and suggests a gradual emergence from the world of Gothic manners; both readings require a theory of the *Other*.

When Henrietta tells Goodwood that Isabel has left for Rome, she is saying that Isabel—somehow, some way—is going to confront Osmond. Gilbert Osmond constitutes the principal Other for Isabel. For Lacan, the Other is definitive of the self. The Other is the inescapable mirror-image through which the subject acquires a self that is always inadequate because "to know oneself through an external image is to be defined through self-alienation" (Silverman 158). Osmond is perhaps the best example of a person whose own identity has been and continues to be defined by lack. Neither Osmond's first wife nor Madame Merle nor Isabel has brought him fulfillment; in the delusive hope that Pansy may, he has imprisoned her in a convent until she agrees not to marry Ned Rosier and comes round to marrying a man he selects for her. As a collector not only of women but also of art objects and public adulation, Osmond is a classic Lacanian example of someone after an object (Lacan calls it *objet petit a[utre]*) "that derives its value from its identification with some missing component of the subject's self, whether the loss is seen as primordial, as the result of a bodily organization, or as the consequence of some other division" (Silverman 156). In the world of hopeless cases, Gilbert Osmond is the most hopeless: "He has a genius for upholstery" (385). For Isabel to return to Osmond further allows him to attempt to define himself through her as Other. Since he cannot do that by love, he must do it by mastery: as her "appointed and inscribed master" (462). Osmond's first wife died mysteriously; his estranged mistress accused him of drying up her soul; his present wife knows he hates her. Even if Isabel returns to Osmond under the impulse of being true to "the most serious act—the single sacred act—of her life" (463), the best she can hope for is the worst because such idealism on Isabel's part would only be an indication of some lack in her; it would derive its value, just as in Osmond's case, from an identification with something missing in herself. Indeed, it would be Isabel's acquiescence to the cultural values that have been defined for women by men, "values which define male subjectivity within patriarchal society" (Silverman 183). These values, having established an outpost in her mind by her treating them as ideals, would be seen to overthrow her in her weakness, which, delusively and ironically, presents itself to her as her strength, her virtue. In this Lacanian reading of the meaning of the ending of *The Portrait,* respectability would be preserved— Isabel would appear "as solemn . . . as a Cimabue Madonna" (210)[18]—and, in the soil of that respectability, the manners that sustain its horrors would flourish.

Bakhtin's reading of the process of self-realization is the opposite of Lacan's. If for Lacan there is an inevitable dismemberment of a total self, for Bakhtin there is a continual movement toward a self that is never total but always capable of further realization: "The Bakhtinian self is never whole, since it can exist only dialogically" (Clark and Holquist 65). Lacan looks back to what it is impossible to recover; Bakhtin looks forward to what it is possible to become. For Bakhtin, there is no self without the Other: there is no subjectivity without intersubjectivity; "Bakhtin conceives of otherness as the ground of all existence and of dialogue as the primal structure of any particular existence, representing a constant exchange between what is already and what is not yet" (Clark and Holquist 65). The ineluctable facts of Osmond's presence and of Isabel's having to deal with him constantly present her with the Other against whom she must define herself. Isabel has yet to do herself and Pansy complete justice. She has further to understand her obligations to the single sacred act of her life—"marriage meant that a woman should cleave to the man with whom, uttering tremendous vows, she had stood at the altar" (540)—by a revaluation of her marriage under the changed conditions of her knowing about Osmond's past, her experiencing Goodwood's passion, and her accepting Ralph's love. Isabel, having faced and routed Madame Merle, has demonstrated that she is capable of dealing with Osmond, whom Madame Merle represents: "that Madame Merle had lost her pluck and saw before her the phantom of exposure— this in itself was a revenge, this in itself was almost the promise of a brighter day" (552). The heterological nature of discourse that Bakhtin exposes and espouses has led Isabel to victory in this confrontation. She has learned from the world of gossip and infidelity that characterizes the Countess Gemini. She confronts the discourse of brilliant "deviltry" and "vile[ness]" that characterizes Madame Merle (522), "a woman who had long been mistress of the art of conversation" (551). Isabel intuits the discourse of her husband's heartless cruelty—"Osmond wished it to be known that he shrank from nothing" (553)—in Pansy's convent: "a well-appointed prison" (549) that Osmond calls "a school for good manners" (532). Isabel is deeply touched by the discourse of young love and tells Pansy, "I won't desert you" (557); "I'll come back" (558). In these scenes with Madame Merle and Pansy, Isabel grows in a strength and tenderness that carry over to her dismissal of Goodwood's passion and her acceptance of Ralph's love. In short, the closing chapters of *The Portrait of a Lady* may be read as showing Isabel Archer immersed in a world of heterological discourse and becoming more aware and assured of herself in the process: "She was not afraid; she was only sure."

Reading the end of the novel from the perspective of Bakhtin does not guarantee Isabel's triumph over Osmond or Pansy's marriage to Ned Rosier, nor does it shut down the moral imagination that James sought to stimulate in his readers. It suggests, simply, that Isabel is better prepared to enter into dialogue with the Other and that Osmond's world of Gothic manners now has less a purchase on her because she better understands his "blasphemous sophistry" (537) as well as the complexities and commitments of justice and love. In other words, a Bakhtinian perspective makes sense of what Irene Santos identifies as "the central irony" of *The Portrait of a Lady:* "that in the cold and selfish Osmond Isabel finds the person who of all the characters can best bring to maturity her potential strength and nobility" (577).[19]

Notes

1. James reworks some very specific new Gothic elements of *Middlemarch* in *The Portrait.* Casaubon haunts his library, drawing imaginary lines of connection between antique myths; Osmond sits in his study "drawing . . . an antique coin." James called Casaubon an "arid pedant" in his review of *Middlemarch;* Ralph calls Osmond a "sterile dilettante." These unproductive husbands despise their young wives' worlds and demand obedience to their own judgments. They darken their wives' worlds and make them miserable. "Dorothea, shrouded in darkness," finds her life a "nightmare" in which "every energy" is "arrested by dread"; Isabel, sleepless in a darkened world, is "assailed by visions." Their husbands' ever-narrowing minds imprison the women in suffering. Casaubon's dark mind is projected in Lowick and Osmond's in Roccanera, each house suitably named for its darkness. These houses contain dungeons in which Dorothea and Isabel suffer: Dorothea longs for a "lunette [to be] opened in the wall of her prison, giving a glimpse of the sunny air"; Isabel sees Osmond's beautiful mind "peep[ing] down from a small high window [to] mock at her." Dorothea is a "virgin sacrifice[d]" to Casaubon, who grows "grey crunching bones in a cavern"; Osmond grinds Isabel "in the very mill of the conventional." The irony of the horror is that Casaubon and Osmond are monstrous and devilish because they are, impeccably, gentlemen. The one is "a man of honour according to the code"; the other is "convention itself." Nonetheless, Casaubon is "a dragon"; Osmond is worse, "the deadliest of fiends." If Dorothea, "shut . . . in prison," has a purgatorial life, Isabel has a "hellish" life, "her soul . . . haunted with terrors."

2. "The novel of manners assimilates the myth of concern, the case, the cardinal virtues, and complementary lovers into its structure as a matter of course. Manners require a stable society which the cardinal virtues promote. The virtues are in turn promoted by a myth of concern for their coherence in the present and their continuity in the future. Difficult cases are judged in the context of this myth. Such cases most frequently involve differences between a man and a woman who resolve them and eventually marry" (Wiesenfarth, *Gothic Manners* 15). For fuller discussion of these elements of the novel of manners, see *Gothic Manners,* 3–22.

3. Birute Ciplijauskaite discusses James and Ibsen as well as the convention of marriage in *La mujer insatisfecha* 123–44. Ibsen, it should also be noted, invented the drama of Gothic manners. And *Ghosts* is clearly the most striking example of the genre when fidelity to her marriage vows requires Mrs. Alving to deal with syphilis, insanity, and incest.

4. Robert White argues that by the time Isabel meets Goodwood this one last time, she has enough sexual experience, especially from the first passionate year of her marriage, not to be frightened by Goodwood's sexuality: "Isabel desires to surrender to Goodwood. Her cries—'I beseech you to go away!' and 'As you love me, as you pity me, leave me alone!'—spring not from a timid fear of passion but from Isabel's recognition, finally, of the power of the passion that has all but engulfed them" (69).

5. A more positive view of Goodwood and Warburton in terms of their manly sexuality has recently been made by both Leon Edel and Robert White.

6. Ann B. Tracy notes that the "obsession with putrefaction, though not exclusive to the Gothic novel, does suggest an interest in death as something more than a lurid plot device." She continues: "The point of all this wormy circumstance is that death is a peculiar, even distinguishing, characteristic of the fallen world" (5).

7. Martha Banta gives a detailed account of James's indebtedness to the Gothic tradition in *Henry James and the Occult*, 169–78.

8. *Case* and *riddle* are literary categories that André Jolles discusses in *Einfache Formen* (137–58), and that I associate, respectively, with the novel of manners and the Gothic novel. The case evolves as a literary form from law, courtly love, and theology; it emphasizes the mind's ability to propose solutions to difficult problems and solve them so as to allow life to continue within an orderly society. Whereas the case admits of more than one approach and resolution, the riddle does not. The riddle evolves from magic and religion, is seemingly insoluble, and punishes failure to produce the one right answer to it (frequently enough with death, as in the Sphinx's riddle). The form of the riddle is like that of an examination in which only one answer is acceptable.

9. Robert Emmet Long works out this imagery in detail in *The Great Succession*, 110–16.

10. The sexual aspect of the Goodwood scene has been reemphasized by Dennis L. O'Connor. Whereas I do not wish to deny the sexual significance of the Goodwood scene—Isabel does feel "she has never been loved before" (589)—I want to suggest that Isabel's last moments with Ralph are more subtly erotic than anything else in the novel; whereas she does not love Goodwood, she does love Ralph. To experience one man's passion for her and to give her own love to another man are clearly distinct events for Isabel.

11. Donne writes, for example, "Women are like the Arts, /. . . unpriz'd if unknowne" ("Change," lines 5–6); "Then since I may knowe, / As liberally as to a midwife showe / Thy selfe; cast all, yea this white linen hence" ("To His Mistress Going to Bed," 43–45); "Call us what you will, wee'are made such by love; / Call her one, mee another flye, / We'are Tapers too, and at our owne cost die" ("The Canonization," 19–21).

12. Robert White has very effectively demonstrated the subtlety of James's use of the language of sexuality elsewhere in the text of *Portrait*, and his analysis of Isabel's last encounter with Goodwood, in terms of this language, is particularly astute.

13. Lovers who die for love are almost invariably affined lovers who have similar natures, dispositions, and tastes. They are so much like one another that they define themselves as one heart and soul. Such affined lovers differ from complementary lovers who bring distinctly different qualities of mind and heart to a marriage that welds their differences into a bond that does not sacrifice their individuality. Affined love is frequently found in Gothic romances; complementary love, in novels of manners.

14. MacAndrew points to the Sentimental tradition to discover the pattern and value of such a love-death: "Mackenzie's Harley goes into a 'decline' and dies. His Julia de Rubigné is poisoned. Virginia is drowned. Werther shoots himself. Such chronic failure, however, does not detract from the ideal itself [of "complete spiritual union with one like themselves"]. These novels affirm the Sentimental concept of virtue by showing that to know oneself virtuous, to develop one's sensibilities to the full, is more important than worldly 'success' and even than life" (67–68). Boone also discusses *Liebestod* lucidly and succinctly (38–39).

15. By what "seems right," Isabel does not mean what "looks right"; she means, as far as she can determine, what is the best thing to do. Irene Santos catches this substantive sense of "seems right" when she writes of Isabel, "As she confides to Ralph right before he dies, her final decision will be dictated by what 'seems right' (577). To ratify retroactively [by her decision to return to Rome] her initial choice of fate [to marry Osmond] had meant to choose her destiny again, to redefine her marriage as freedom fulfilled, to assume her identity as Mrs. Osmond, without which she would now be lost" (514). For Isabel "to redefine her marriage" is what "seems right" to Santos.

16. James complains about George Eliot's endings of novel after novel: "Her conclusions have been signally weak, as the reader will admit who recalls Hetty's reprieve in 'Adam Bede,' the inundation of the Floss, and, worse than either, the comfortable reconciliation of Romola and Tessa. The plot of 'Felix Holt' is essentially made up, and its development is forced. . . . The termination is hasty, inconsiderate, and unsatisfactory—is, in fact, almost an anti-climax" (*Literary Criticism: Essays* 907). James also finds the treatment of Dorothea's movement toward Ladislaw in the last two books of *Middlemarch* "almost ludicrously excessive" (961).

17. Patricia McKee reaches the same conclusion in her reading of James's *The Golden Bowl* (270–346).

18. *The Cimabue Madonna,* an 1855 painting by Frederic Leighton, was famous in its time and known to James, who used Leighton as a model for Lord Mellefont in "The Private Life" (1892). As an art critic, James noted in Leighton's depiction of women a lack of animation: "his texture is too often that of the glaze on the lid of a prune-box; his drawing too often that of the figures that smile at us from the covers of these receptacles" (*Painter's Eye* 214–15). Leighton's canvases were well known for the waxy complexions and masculine features of his female figures. As president of the Royal Academy, he refused to allow women to be voting members. Joseph A. Kestner has pointed to the misogynistic character of Leighton's political attitudes and of his paintings in *Mythology and Misogyny*. If James is thinking of Leighton when he mentions the *Cimabue Madonna* in *The Portrait,* given all the implications of Leighton's misogyny, it is certainly an unhappy and forbidding analogue for Isabel Archer.

19. Elizabeth Sabiston writes in a vein similar to Santos's:

> Every reader of *The Portrait of a Lady* has his [or her] own theory as to why Isabel returns to Osmond in Rome after rebelling for long enough to hasten to Ralph's deathbed at Gardencourt. Whatever the reasons that can be adduced for Isabel's return—existential commitment, flight from Caspar Goodwood, fidelity to the marriage bond, and the protection of Pansy, the belief that Isabel, like Strether in *The Ambassadors,* must gain nothing for herself—it remains evident that she is spiritually free and launched on a life of fine perception. What is not so often remarked is that she chooses, of her own free will, to remain in the visibly fallen world of continental Europe, while it is Madame Merle who must return to America—perhaps for a refresher course in innocence! (42)

Figure 7. Nicholas R. Brewer (1857–d?), *Rebecca Campbell and Her Daughters, Nancy and Carol*, 1920 (*Collection of the Butler Institute of American Art, Youngstown, Ohio*)

8

"'I' Rejected; 'We' Substituted": Self and Society in *Between the Acts*

Mark Hussey

From the standpoint of world-history, the individual subject is indeed unimportant; but then it must be remembered that the world-historical is an extraneous addition. Ethically, the individual subject is infinitely important.

Søren Kierkegaard

What more natural, then, with this insight into their profundity, than that Jane Austen should have chosen to write of the trivialities of day-to-day existence, of parties, picnics, and country-dances?

Virginia Woolf, *The Common Reader*

Late in 1940, Virginia Woolf was scolded by the village police officer for showing lights during the blackout. The Second World War was under way, and German bombers flew every night over the Sussex Downs on their way to London. In her diary, Woolf noted that the officer seemed to enjoy bullying her, taking the opportunity "to give a lady a bit of his mind." The "working man male," when not being "respectful," she wrote, had "no 'manners' to fall back on" (*Diary* 3 November 1940). Living in Rodmell village in the early days of the war, drawn reluctantly into participation in the local Women's Institute (a body that exemplified for Leonard Woolf "the English genius for unofficial organisation"), and suffering the ire of "[t]he village cabal against us" as she resisted "the threat of the Sewage Pump" (*Diary* 22 August 1938), Virginia Woolf gave considerable thought to "manners." She toyed with the idea of writing "supports & additions for my old TLS articles; a good deal about manners, & our class" (*Diary* 22 October 1940). She took mental notes as the village officer dressed her down, finding "useful this breach in the bank of class manners" (*Diary* 3 November 1940).

Bored by the Women's Institute's efforts at putting on plays, she resented the way the "simple" sucked at hers and Leonard's intellects: "Anyone with 500 a year & education, is at once sucked by the leeches. . . . Last night L.'s lecture attracted Suckers. . . . From this to manners:—a thought to keep for my book" (*Diary* 29 November 1940). Like her character Mrs. Manresa in *Between the Acts,* Woolf seemed to think, "It's all my eye about democracy. . . . The people looked to them. They led; the rest followed" (*BTA* 102–3).

In the memoir she had begun in 1939 at her sister Vanessa's suggestion— "A Sketch of the Past"—Woolf recalled their early "tea-table training." She remembered how she and her sister had learned to be "young ladies possessed of a certain manner":

> We both still possess that manner. We learnt it partly from remembering mother's manner; Stella's manner, and it was partly imposed upon us by the visitor who came in. For the manner in which a young man . . . addressed young ladies was a marked manner. . . . [I]f Ronny Norman said that, one had to reply in the same style. Nobody ever broke the convention. (149–50)

This manner is exemplified in Woolf's second novel, *Night and Day* (1919), by the heroine, Katherine Hilbery, who reminds the reader of Jane Austen's Emma Woodhouse. Late in her life, Woolf noted herself still occasionally playing "the game of Victorian society" and finding it useful:

> We still play the game. It is useful. It has also its beauty, for it is founded upon restraint, sympathy, unselfishness—all civilized qualities. It is helpful in making something seemly out of raw odds and ends. Major Gardner, Mrs Chavasse, and Mr Dutton need some solving to make it into a sociable party. ("A Sketch of the Past" 150)

From Helen Ambrose in *The Voyage Out* (1915) through Clarissa Dalloway and Mrs. Ramsay to Lucy Swithin and Mrs. Manresa in *Between the Acts,* Woolf created characters who smooth society's rough edges, bring people together, and help promote moments of harmony. The comfortable surface of "society" is part of the texture of all Woolf's novels. The privileged, "civilized" milieu of her books (and, indeed, of her own life) was scorned by critics such as the Leavises, who wrote in *Scrutiny* of her distance from the harsh actualities of what they deemed "real life."

The Marxist critic Georg Lukács singles Woolf out in *The Meaning of Contemporary Realism* as an extreme example of the modernist tendency to identify "what is necessarily a subjective experience with reality as such, thus giving a distorted picture of reality as a whole" (51). In line with Lukács's complaint about the "attenuation of actuality" (25) in modernist writing, many critics—particularly in England—have seen Woolf as an aloof and exquisite stylist, spinning gossamer fictions about the semitransparent envelope of consciousness. In recent years, however, particularly in the U.S., she has begun to be read as a politically radical, subversive writer. Her constant concern with how the individual's shaping of experience into the life of "Monday or Tuesday" becomes the fabric of our world has been recognized as having political and philosophical implications that are now being explored. Recent (mainly feminist) critics have understood that the "inner life" of her characters always exists in dialectical tension with a social circumference and that her focus on the individual is actually always on the individual *in relationship* with a much larger world.

Woolf was always concerned with "lives of the obscure" and with the minute transactions of social intercourse. In *The Voyage Out*, Terence Hewet wants to write a novel "about Silence . . . the things people don't say" (262). Woolf's concern with what goes unspoken had become almost obsessive by the time she wrote *Between the Acts*. Her diary, her letters, many of her essays, and the texture of the novels all demonstrate a lifelong concern with the exchanges between public and private worlds, with convention and how it is breached, with self and society.

Woolf's ideas about identity as dynamic process have perhaps distracted readers from the realization of social context in her fiction; the inward-looking tendency of most of her characters does seem to preclude any direct view of society at large. Nevertheless, as I have remarked elsewhere (Hussey 132), it is almost redundant now to point out that Woolf was aware throughout her life of the pressure of tradition, convention, and cultural memory on an individual consciousness. It seems reasonable to say that Woolf is always a "novelist of manners" in the light of her preoccupation with the way the smallest details of daily life reveal "cosmic immensities." Judy Little notes Woolf's concern "with the mythic paradigm behind the mores and institutions. . . . She examines the imagery and ritual of various modern festivities, of those liminal and renewing occasions, such as dinners, parties, and pageants. Her social criticism is perhaps too radical to be obvious; nevertheless, her laughter touches the deepest nerves of Western culture" (23).

To read Woolf is to experience a polar tension between center and circumference. The "center," corresponding to various articulations of the individual self, has received most critical attention, to the detriment of the "circumference." This latter we might say corresponds to "society," but in Woolf the forces with which an individual interacts are not limited to convention, custom, politics, and history: at times, self and "society" seem to merge; her work is characterized by rhythmic movement, and this makes the closure offered by definitions extremely difficult to achieve. Essential to Woolf's art is a tension between "I" and "We," a dynamic interplay between the inner voice and the world of relationship; the one and the many; part and whole; ontogeny and phylogeny.

Woolf's perspective on this interplay seems to me to have shifted after she wrote *To the Lighthouse* (1927). In order to put my reading of *Between the Acts* into context, I will briefly sketch some elements of that perspectival shift. Woolf, always acutely conscious of her own creative processes and practice, wondered in 1925 what she should call her fictions: "A new — by Virginia Woolf. But what? Elegy?" (*Diary* 27 June 1925). "Novel," she understood, brought to mind the solid constructions of Arnold Bennett, John Galsworthy, and Hugh Walpole, which, while "[v]ery different in detail," all shared "a common belief that there is only one view of the world, and one family" ("The Green Mirror" 71). Two years later, she described the "novel" of the future in her essay "The Narrow Bridge of Art." The essay sets out dimensions and concerns that are realized in *Between the Acts*. Woolf complains that modern novelists, focused too specifically and intensely on the personal, have "come to forget that a large and important part of life consists in our emotions toward such things as roses and nightingales, the dawn, the sunset, life, death, and fate" ("Narrow Bridge of Art" 19). The writer of the future would expand

> the scope of his interest so as to dramatize some of those influences which play so large a part in life, yet have so far escaped the novelist—the power of music, the stimulus of sight, the effect on us of the shape of trees or the play of colour, the emotions bred in us by crowds, the obscure terrors and hatreds which come so irrationally in certain places or from certain places or from certain people, the delight of movement, the intoxication of wine. (23)

In reading *Between the Acts*, these elements are recalled in so precise a way that it seems almost as if Woolf wrote the book with the essay of 1927 before her.

As she began to stand back, "to see the outline rather than the detail," the pressure of what she called the "common voice" came into the foreground of Woolf's work. In *A Room of One's Own* (1929), for example, she wrote that "masterpieces are not single and solitary births; they are the outcome of many years of thinking in common, of thinking by the body of the people, so that the experience of the mass is behind the single voice" (68–69). Such a tribute to the importance of the creative spirit of the masses would have cheered Lukács had he heard this note of historical materialism in Woolf. She wrote in the same text that she was "talking of the common life which is the real life and not of the little separate lives which we lead as individuals" (117).

In *The Years* (1937), too, the shift from the individual to the communal in Woolf's perspective is evident. *The Years* and *Three Guineas* (1938) shared a common impulse; Woolf said that the novel and the feminist polemic should, in fact, be taken as a single work. It is in *Three Guineas* that she makes an explicit statement of the political philosophy that is implied in all her fiction and that particularly informs the "little language" of *Between the Acts.* She brings before her readers' imagination a picture of a tyrant, "the figure of a man; some say, others deny, that he is Man himself, the quintessence of virility. . . . He is called in German and Italian Führer or Duce; in our own language Tyrant or Dictator":

> It [this image] suggests that the public and private worlds are inseparably connected; that the tyrannies and servilities of the one are the tyrannies and servilities of the other. But the human figure even in a photograph suggests other and more complex emotions. It suggests that we cannot dissociate ourselves from that figure but are ourselves that figure. It suggests that we are not passive spectators doomed to unresisting obedience but by our thoughts and actions can ourselves change that figure. A common interest unites us; it is one world, one life. How essential it is that we should realise that unity the dead bodies, the ruined houses prove. For such will be our ruin if you in the immensity of your public abstractions forget the private figure, or if we in the intensity of our private emotions forget the public world. Both houses will be ruined, the public and the private, the material and the spiritual, for they are inseparably connected. (*Three Guineas* 142–43)

The message is echoed at the close of the pageant of *Between the Acts: "Consider the gun slayers, bomb droppers here or there. They do openly what we do slyly"* (187). It seems, however, that the private house has been ruined at the end of *Between the Acts,* for its shelter disappears, leaving the figures of Isa and Giles exposed in a hostile world. This politics stresses unity and wholeness but preserves difference, the individual. It speaks of a *rhythm* between the individual center and the public circumference, each inseparably connected with the other. Even the image of actor and audience is that which structures *Between the Acts.* It is in the extraordinarily complex movements and utterly simple "plot" of *Between the Acts* that Virginia Woolf's concern with human "manners"—how each person lives in the world as a whole—can be seen to exemplify her radical political thought, thought that connects an individual bullying official (for example, a village police officer) with far larger tyrannies. There is always the temptation of resolving individuality into a "crowd" mentality, but this is not the "common life" of which Woolf speaks. Lucio Ruotolo has recently noted this: *"Between the Acts* postulates a series of temptations for the author and her readers, from the consolation of art to the nostalgia for rural England, only to leave us all without a center, equally dispersed, equally open to the impact of interruption" (16).

There is an extraordinary congruence of theme in the writings of the last few years of Woolf's life. The notions of commonality and of the persistence of the past in the present appear in her diary, in "A Sketch of the Past," in *Between the Acts,* and in her projected literary history (see Silver, "'Anon'"). The dynamic between individual and cultural consciousness is mapped in various registers: I and We; personal myth and archetype; outsider and collective mind; autobiography and the history of the race; unity and dispersity. The forms of the works of 1939–41 seem to emphasize this tension between center and circumference, present and past: a memoir, a biography (*Roger Fry*), a critical history of English literature, and a novel that reviews hundreds of years of English history in a single afternoon. In 1935, Woolf had noted "a further stage" in her development as a writer: "I see that there are 4? dimensions; all to be produced; in human life; & that leads to a far richer grouping & proportion: I mean: I: & the not I: & the outer & the inner." She thought this discovery would influence her biography of Roger Fry and found it "very exciting: to grope on like this. New combinations in psychology & body—rather like painting. This will be the next novel, after The Years" (*Diary* 18 November 1935).

The next novel, *Between the Acts,* opens with a group of people at Pointz Hall one summer's night, "talking, in the big room with the windows open to the garden" (3). By the close of this very brief, framing scene, several of the major characters and many of the concerns of the book have been introduced. Bart, Lucy, and Isa sit talking with Mr. and Mrs. Haines. Pleasantries are exchanged; idle talk; memories. The whole scene is permeated with the passion Isa feels for Haines; her emotion makes words "lie between them like a wire, tingling, tangling, vibrating" (15). The world of *Between the Acts* is immediately established as one in which the past is always just below the surface of the present; deep pools of silence threaten the conventional manners that keep "society" running smoothly; people respond consciously and unconsciously to myriad influences of sight, sound, environment, and emotion; and the materiality of language is made apparent.

The structure of *Between the Acts* is extremely simple: in a "remote village in the very heart of England" (16), people gather to watch the annual pageant, which this year consists of scenes from English literary history performed by the villagers and written by Miss La Trobe. The pageant is performed in the grounds of Pointz Hall, where Bart Oliver lives with his sister Lucy Swithin. Bart's son Giles is there with his wife, Isa; their relationship is "strained." Mrs. Manresa, a friend of the family, joins them on this June afternoon in 1939, bringing with her a young man, William Dodge. At the end of the pageant, everyone leaves the family alone again in Pointz Hall. Within this simple framework, Woolf puts in question the notion of history and its concomitant, a unified self. She demonstrates the interconnectedness of all things and radically questions the power of language to signify.[1]

Between the Acts is made out of voices. Memories, "scars," names, and "common emotion" are concerns and functions of language. The book gives a sense of being afloat on a sea of words. Words and phrases reverberate throughout, slipping in and out of different consciousnesses, reflected sometimes by the actors, sometimes by the audience. Language is several times referred to as an "infection," and everyone and everything seems to catch it. On this particular day, words will not stay still: to Giles Oliver, they rise up and become "menacing" (59) or scornful (149); to William Dodge, they become symbolical (73). Words are substantial, rolled and thinned on the children's nurses' tongues like sweets (10) or peppering the audience at the pageant "as with a shower of hard little stones" (78). Words evidently cannot be trusted to peg down reality; they are treacherous and shifty, acting differently on the mental substance of each person who hears or utters them. Nevertheless, they are the vehicle of our emotions and in some sense the matter by and in which we create ourselves and life moves. The echoes and fragments of *Between the Acts* bind the book together, making of it an enclosed world, a "re-created world" (153) at the same time as it is, of course, part of the world of all its readers.

There is a definite sense in the novel of a voice "behind" the many voices that we hear, an unconscious source of the plethora of words. Woolf's concern with the spaces between words and events, with silence, gesture, nature, and emptiness, recalls her blueprint for a new fiction in "The Narrow Bridge of Art." In "A Sketch of the Past," she made notes toward an analysis of the "many other than human forces" that affect every person. The colors of elm leaves, "the apples in the orchard; the murmur and rustle of the leaves" have an influence on the perceiver that is beyond description: "I could snapshot what I mean by some image; I am a porous vessel afloat on sensation; a sensitive plate exposed to invisible rays" ("A Sketch of the Past" 133). Woolf referred to these "invisible rays" as a "third voice" and felt that it was connected with art and religion.

In *Between the Acts,* she refers to a "third voice" (115) and to "another voice speaking" (117) seemingly to suggest felt influences, emphasizing that "life is not confined to one's body and what one says and does" ("A Sketch of the Past" 73). The "third voice" makes itself heard *in between* people, in the gaps and interruptions of their dialogue. There are many instances in *Between the Acts* of felt influences that pass between people without words. People "hear" when no words have been spoken; silence makes an "unmistakable contribution" to talk (39). Lucy Swithin twice gets up—once to show William the house (67), once to return with Bart to the pageant (118)—as if a signal had been given, though nothing has been said. Isa silently questions Mrs. Manresa; Giles silently condemns William. Isa, Giles, and William each say "without words" that they are desperately unhappy (176). "Thoughts without words," wonders Bart, the exemplar of Reason—"Can that be?" (55). *Between the Acts* most certainly answers "yes" to his question. The "third voice" is brought into being by the interactions of people with each other and with the natural world. Woolf's description of it in "The Narrow Bridge of Art" and in "A Sketch of the Past" reminds me of Trilling's definition of "manners" as "the whole evanescent context" within which the explicit statements of a culture are made (200).

Woolf's fiction, following the project she outlined in her essay of 1927, encompasses and goes well beyond Trilling's definition in its rendering of the many subtle influences at work on her characters.

When Giles Oliver arrives at Pointz Hall from London, bringing with him the first hint that there is a world beyond the village, the first thing he sees is Mrs. Manresa's car at the door "with the initials R.M. twisted so as to look at a distance like a coronet" (46). Enraged as he is at what he sees as the complacency of old fogies like his Aunt Lucy, and at his own sense of powerlessness as the war approaches, the presence of visitors touches his "tea-table training," and he changes his clothes before joining the others at lunch: "So one thing led to another; and the conglomeration of things pressed you flat; held you fast, like a fish in water" (47). Woolf used the same image in "A Sketch of the Past" when discussing her own sense of "invisible presences":

> the consciousness of other groups impinging upon ourselves; public opinion; what other people say and think; all those magnets which attract us this way to be like that, or repel us the other and make us different from that. . . . Consider what immense forces society brings to play upon each of us, how that society changes from decade to decade; and also from class to class; . . . I see myself as a fish in a stream; deflected; held in place; but cannot describe the stream. (80)

In *Between the Acts,* she doesn't so much *describe* the stream as show it at work. It is the "stream" that makes itself felt in the interactions and between the words of the characters, and in the sense of interconnection that is derived from the role of the natural world in the movement of the book.

The device of a play to represent human life is commonplace; all the world is, after all, a stage. Miss La Trobe's pageant, however, is a confusing jumble much of the time. The audience gets a little help from the blurred carbon-copy program, but it is never enough to provide the security they expect as an audience. Some of them grumble as they leave, "I must say I like to feel sure if I go to the theatre, that I've grasped the meaning" (200). Even the beginning of the pageant is obscured: "Was it, or was it not, the play?" (76). The confusion of the audience often becomes the confusion of the reader. No new paragraph, for example, announces the start of the pageant, and thus the question arises of whether we, as readers, should see it as not separate from the lives of the audience (as Miss La Trobe would seem to insist is the case in "Present time"). There is no beginning, perhaps, because that would suggest a point of origin for a neat and comforting narrative line; in *Between the Acts,* Woolf works "not to create and sustain but to subvert illusion" (Wilde 158).

By putting the reader often into the position of the audience, Woolf's metafictional shifts become very unsettling. Hana Wirth-Nesher has pointed out the blurring of distinctions between drama and "real" life that disorients both audience and reader as Woolf asks us to look at the mind looking at itself. The structure of audience and actors mirrors that of reader and text. With the confusing beginning of the pageant, the reader's consciousness shifts to a double perspective. Having watched the family at Pointz Hall with its guests and shared in their private troubles and tortures, we now look at the pageant *and* at the family and others watching the pageant. If words will not "lie flat in the sentence," and phrases such as "We are the audience" are threatening (59), a sentence such as "They were singing, but not a word reached the audience" (78) is loaded with suggestion for each of the book's audiences—i.e. those watching the pageant, and the readers.

Isa finds the pageant's Globe Theatre scene a confusing jumble; she can "make nothing of it." Her thoughts seem to reflect as much on *Between the Acts* as upon Miss La Trobe's pageant:

> Did the plot matter? . . . The plot was only there to beget emotion. There were only two emotions: love; and hate. There was no need to puzzle out the plot. Perhaps Miss La Trobe meant that when she cut this knot in the centre?
> Don't bother about the plot: the plot's nothing. (90–91)

In *Erring,* his intriguing book on the "time between times" of postmodernism, Mark Taylor explains that "the plot of a narrative . . . can be understood as the ground-plan or secret scheme devised by the A/author to fashion otherwise disparate episodes into a coherent literary creation" (63–64). If there is no plot, history becomes meaningless. History, in the conventional terms of Miss La Trobe's pageant, is the story of ourselves, "our island history," a narrative that represents the linear progress and development of ourselves. Taylor notes that "there can be no individual self apart from history and no history without the individual subject" (54); his observation makes clear the deconstructive implications of Woolf's narrative strategies. However, Miss La Trobe seems to have in mind another play behind the play she shows her audience.

"You don't," says William Dodge to Lucy, "believe in history" (175). Lucy seems not to believe in the progress of events, of one "period" leading to another. "The Victorians," she muses—"I don't believe . . . that there ever were such people. Only you and me and William dressed differently" (174–75). "We've only the present" is Lucy's challenge to the narrative of history: everything exists simultaneously in consciousness. The audience at the pageant is distressed by its questioning of historical narration, a human ordering principle that "reflects the effort to ease the trauma of dislocation by weaving scattered events into a seamless web" (Taylor 71). The import of the pageant is that the audience should not see the various "ages" as stages in a process of development; the actors merely play different parts while the love and hate that structure the world remain essentially the same. The pageant cuts its audience adrift from the easy identity afforded them by clothes and other external trappings:

> Yet somehow they felt—how could one put it—a little not quite here or there. As if the play had jerked the ball out of the cup; as if what I call myself was still floating unattached, and didn't settle. Not quite themselves, they felt. (149)

> They were neither one thing nor the other; neither Victorians nor themselves. They were suspended, without being, in limbo. (178)

In her playful presentation of ordinary minds on an ordinary day, Woolf "touches the deepest nerves of Western culture" (Little 23) and disturbs them. Taylor, again, sums up what *Between the Acts* implies: "Suspended between a past that has been lost and a future not yet possessed, history is the domain of discontent and restlessness, of striving and strife" (68).

Such discontent is most acutely experienced by Isa, who is 39, "the age of the century" (19). The book—representative of that narrative wholeness of beginning, middle, and end—has been replaced for her generation by the newspaper: each day is supplanted by the next, with no sense of continuity or connection between them. Sitting with William Dodge in the greenhouse during one of the intervals of the pageant, Isa and he are aware of the "doom of sudden death hanging over us"; "[t]he future shadowed their present, . . . a criss-cross of lines making no pattern" (114). For the old, like Bart and Lucy, there is "retreating and advancing" (114), dipping into the past from the present; Lucy, for example, is given to "increasing the bounds of the moment" (9) by excursions into the past in her imagination. For those of Isa and William's generation, the present is pre-history to catastrophic conflict. Gillian Beer has written that the present here is pre-history "in a double sense":

> Whenever the action of the historical pageant falters it is saved by the unwilled resurgence of the primeval: the shower of rain, the idiot, the cows bellowing for their lost calves. At the same time, the book describes a moment which may be the last of this culture. The planes swoop overhead. June 1939 is pre-history to a coming war which, this book makes clear without hysteria, may mark the end of this society. (112)

If history has been dissolved, "the 'final' plot seems to be 'that there is no plot'" (Taylor 73).

Most of the characters of *Between the Acts* experience this sense of dislocation. As several readers have noticed, the book actually moves *backwards* although it is apparently progressing. At the close, Isa and Giles have been abandoned by their "island history"; having become figures in "another play," they appear as pre-historic people in a world without shelter. In *The Waves*, Rhoda was terrified at the thought of "being blown for ever outside the loop of time!" (15): this is the fate of Giles and Isa.

Beginning to think about her new work of fiction, Woolf wrote in her diary:

> But to amuse myself, let me note: why not Poyntzet Hall: a centre: all lit. discussed in connection with real little incongruous living humour; & anything that comes into my head; but "I" rejected: "We" substituted: to whom at the end there shall be an invocation? "We" . . . the composed of many different things . . . we all life, all art, all waifs & strays—a rambling capricious but somehow unified whole—the present state of my mind? (*Diary* 26 April 1938; ellipses in original).

Between the Acts is Woolf's "moment of glory" and in many ways her most brilliant novel in that it gathers up the threads of all her previous fictions and points forward to new forms and concerns. The common, little life of the village merges with the *Spiritus Mundi,* a union intuited only in the act of reading, which blurs distinctions between spectacle and spectator, actor and audience, text and reader. Like her character Miss La Trobe, Woolf "seethes wandering bodies and floating voices in a cauldron, and makes rise up from its amorphous mass a re-created world" (153). Each individual consciousness, each subjectivity, is like a vortex in a stream; subjectivity extends to all the creatures of the world—even the "empty" barn is crisscrossed by myriad eyebeams looking from every edge and angle (100). *Between the Acts* presents both vortex (self, center) and stream (society, circumference) and shows them as thoroughly interdependent.

The work buzzes with gossip, with fragments of idle talk. It is shot through with complex emotions: William Dodge is attracted to Giles, who despises him; Isa and Giles are tangled in love and hate; Manresa and Giles are attracted to each other; Isa feels passion for Haines, maternal love for her children, conventional ties to Giles, the father of her children; she understands William and can (silently) confide in him; he, in turn, feels Lucy's empathy for his pain. These intensely personal emotions are founded in fully realized characters and yet treated at the same time as merely those universal feelings of love and hate that have structured relationships throughout time. Even Woolf herself, reading "Freud for the first time," discovered "that this violently disturbing conflict of love and hate is a common feeling; and is called ambivalence" ("A Sketch of the Past" 108). *Between the Acts* spans literary history; it is infused with the rhythms of Chaucer and Shakespeare, yet it is also "modern." Time, in other words, has been unravelled: "1830 was true in 1939" (52).

Virginia Woolf has not usually been thought of as celebrating communal life, although several critics have begun to explore this theme (see, for example, Silver, "Virginia Woolf"). In all her fiction, the "whole evanescent context" (Trilling, "Manners, Morals, and the Novel," 200) within which any personal act is performed is always present to the reader's consciousness. In *Between the*

Acts, the "third voice" is in effect the "culture's hum and buzz of implication"—Trilling's definition of manners. Woolf's works seem always expressive of a particular view of individual identity as constitutive of history. The personal is the world-historical in Woolf's fiction, each subjectivity a locus from which is produced not a distortion of objective reality, but, rather, a particular dynamic construction of the whole. In the loss of the center, of the ego-bound, death-tending "self" that has structured and been structured by history as a patterned narrative, the possibility of a truly communal life that does not erase difference is realized. The "rambling capricious but somehow unified whole" that is *Between the Acts* sees in the "little incongruous living humour" of daily existence the possibility of "a unity that rubs out divisions as if they were chalk marks only" (*Three Guineas* 143). With "megaphonic, anonymous" voices (*BTA* 186) urging the public to don their gas masks, the buzz of bombers overhead, and everywhere a sense that a world was passing, Woolf created a testament of hope in her final elegy, embodying her most profound visionary creativity in "scraps, orts and fragments" who are capable of coming together, if only for a moment, in harmony. At the end of the day, audience and actors departed, Lucy stands alone by the lily pool and pays tribute to the ordinary, to the possibility of community that any moment of any day holds:

> "Ourselves," she murmured. And retrieving some glint of faith from the grey waters, hopefully, without much help from reason, she followed the fish; the speckled, streaked, and blotched; seeing in that vision beauty, power, and glory in ourselves. (205)

Looking at *Between the Acts* through the lens of a revised theory of the novel of manners has the effect of concentrating reading on the outline rather than the detail. If Woolf in "The Narrow Bridge of Art" is to be believed, this is what she wanted. To consider Woolf's oeuvre in the light of this particular tradition is to modify retrospectively all those readings that have concentrated on the individual, the "self," and to see clearly that "ourselves" is always the necessary condition for the emergence of any sense of identity in Woolf's fiction. Reading *Between the Acts* in this context reinforces many recent readings of Woolf that demonstrate her concern with community, with the political, and with the possibility of recognizing in (and affecting by) the slightest personal gesture the social world.

Notes

1. Alan Wilde, "Touching Earth: Virginia Woolf and the Prose of the World": "Working in her last novel not to create and sustain but to subvert illusion, Woolf uses language in such a way—incessantly mocking, playing, teasing—as to call into question, it would seem, not only its representational and mimetic force but even its power to signify" (158).

9

Love, Marriage, and Manners in the Novels of Barbara Pym

Barbara Brothers

Least of all will a course of novels prepare a young lady for the neglect and tedium of life which she is perhaps doomed to encounter.

Mrs. Anna Letitia Barbauld

While marriage was frequently depicted as a stultifying experience in the seventeenth-century comedy of manners (see John Wilkinson's essay in this volume), it supplied the happy ending—the promise of a life of mutual love and fulfillment—from Fanny Burney's *Evelina* through the long list of nineteenth-century domestic novels or novels of manners. So strong was the tradition that Trollope assured readers of *Barchester Towers* (1857) that they need not worry about Eleanor Bold's choosing the wrong suitor; he just could not have Eleanor cry or Mr. Arabin "melt" too soon, or "where would have been my novel?" (32; vol. 2, ch. 30). Who in the nineteenth century but Trollope's dissolute Signora Madeline would dare to comment that "There is no happiness in love, except at the end of an English novel" (274; vol. 1, ch. 27)?[1]

Some in the eighteenth century had been skeptical of the emerging idea that a love match would produce marital happiness: Lawrence Stone quotes Oliver Goldsmith's observation on "[h]ow delusive, how destructive are those pictures of consummate bliss" (396) provided by literature. Nevertheless, by 1780, "romantic love became a respectable motive for marriage among the propertied classes" (284). What Swift had dismissed in 1723 as "a ridiculous passion which hath no being but in plays and romances" (Stone 283) became not just *a* reason but *the* socially sanctioned reason for marriage in the postromantic world that shifted the emphasis for achieving success and happiness

Figure 8. Isabel Bishop (1902–), *Two Girls*
(*Collection of the Butler Institute of American Art,
Youngstown, Ohio*)

to the individual. Thus, self-questioning, self-doubting Mr. Arabin would examine his conscience to determine whether he "in truth . . . did love" Elizabeth or whether "he did not also love her money," a quite "impure" reason for marrying (73; vol. 2, ch. 34). Love was deemed to be a selfless emotion, and a "gentleman," the right sort of man, married for love.

Perhaps nothing so much as the fact that Barbara Pym's novels are from the first to the last about love places them in the tradition of the novel of manners, the fictional form that encapsulated and gave expression to nineteenth-century attitudes toward the individual in love and marriage.[2] From *Some Tame Gazelle* with its epigraph of "Some tame gazelle, or some gentle dove: Something to love, oh, something to love!" to the last novel published and written during her life, *The Sweet Dove Died,* the title echoing that epigraph, Pym's novels explore the world of loving. However, unlike the endings of courtship novels of the nineteenth century, the endings of Pym's novels do not hold forth the promise of fulfillment through mutual love and sharing. Nor do her novels partake of that other strain of the novel of manners, popular in the 1850s and introduced according to Monica Correa Fryckstedt and Vineta Colby by Harriet Martineau's *Deerbrook,* in which the wife was fulfilled through "a pattern of endurance, self-sacrifice, duty, and honesty" (Fryckstedt 20).[3] Yet, Pym's novels are "domestic," their subject, like that of her predecessors in the novel of manners, the relationship between men and women.

Examining Pym's novels within the tradition of the novel of manners sheds light on her novels and on the novels of her predecessors as well. For many critics and literary historians, the substance of these novels is merely their descriptive and accurate recording of the details of everyday life, the novels raising no more serious issues than matters of social propriety. Reading backwards and forwards through these novels, however, helps us to understand that the novel of manners not only paints the "social customs, manners, conventions, and habits of a definite social class at a particular time and place" (Holman) but also both exposes and espouses particular value systems and ideologies that underlie the surface details of life.

True, the relationship between men and women, not politics, is the subject of the novel of manners; nevertheless, by depicting heroes and heroines who marry for love and affection and not for economic or social reasons, the nineteenth-century novel of manners served to promulgate the very values that led ever so slowly to the demise of the class system. Even as early as Fanny Burney's *Evelina,* the rightness of the love and marriage of Evelina and Lord Orville is a matter of the rightness of individual judgment and choice, though Burney chose not to confront the values of the class system directly, instead resolving the issue of Evelina's parentage in the denouement through Sir Belmont's recognizing Evelina as his daughter. Ironically, the novel of manners is identified with the English class system, but the ideology that informs these

Figure 9. Louis Ritman (1892–1963), *Jullien*
(Collection of the Butler Institute of American Art,
Youngstown, Ohio)

novels is the romantic belief in the power and potential of the individual that challenges birth and class as the determiners of worth and value. Austen's novels are as "bourgeois" as Martineau's *Deerbrook,* and Martineau's as "romantic" as Austen's. Colby infers a difference when she labels the "domestic novel" "bourgeois and anti-romantic . . . glorif[ying] the solid values of home and family" (212); she fails to apprehend the connection between romantic love, the idealization of the beloved, and romanticism, the idealization of individual.

Mary Poovey points out in *"Persuasion* and the Promises of Love" the relationship between the "triumph" in late eighteenth- and early nineteenth-century England of the "values and practices associated with bourgeois individualism" and the concept of romantic love (153, 152): "the fundamental assumption of romantic love—and the reason it is so compatible with bourgeois society—is that the personal can be kept separate from the social"; "one's 'self' can be fulfilled in spite of—and in isolation from—the demands of the marketplace" (172). In the nineteenth century, the institution of marriage was conflated with the illusion of romantic love; the loved one was all, and nothing of "self-interest and calculation" determined one's personal choice of a partner (see Poovey 172). Love and marriage, not class and marriage, were to go together like a horse and carriage.

Specifically, Poovey examines the ways in which the aesthetic conclusions of Austen's novels upheld bourgeois ideology through "repressing or displacing those questions which might jeopardize" (176) the myth of the family as accommodating "personal desire" and able to "yield personal fulfillment," a myth predicated upon the belief that "personal feeling can be a moral force within society" (171). Nor does our society, as Poovey notes, conceive of the family differently; and thus, she suggests, we place even more stress on the family as the source of fulfillment as our programs for social reform fail and the need for them increases (173). Some marriage counselors and clinical psychologists claim that the rising number of divorces and persons seeking family counseling results from our heightened expectations of the satisfaction to be found in human relationships, specifically those between men and women. Whatever the reasons, we value marriage, or perhaps more precisely the ideal that it represents, more, not less, than our nineteenth-century ancestors valued it; we want more, not less, from it.

Though authors of the nineteenth-century novel of manners, as James Kincaid points out in his essay in this volume, may have found it increasingly difficult to sustain the myth of the separable and distinct worlds of private and public upon which the Victorian ideal of the family depended, their depiction of character within those novels left both that myth and the one of the family as the embodiment of love unimpaired. The novels might sometimes raise questions or occasionally end tragically, but individuals, not the myths, were wanting. For example, Arabin does have self-doubts, posing to himself the possibility that not even love is free from commercial self-interest and social convenience, but the narrator comically dismisses them: "it was and ever had been his weakness to look for impure motives for his own conduct" (73; vol. 2, ch. 34). Arabin is overly scrupulous, or at least Trollope leaves this as one possible reading of Arabin's doubts. On the other hand, tragic or unhappy relationships in nineteenth-century fiction are the result of an individual's poor judgment, most frequently of the heroine's misinterpreting manners: Eliot's Dorothea Brooke accepts the wrong man for her first husband because she misreads his letters, his demeanor, and thus his character (see Bege Bowers's essay in this volume; Lydgate's tragedy might also be dismissed as a case of bad judgment).

Pym does not satirize love, family, or marriage, but her novels do demonstrate the absurdity of the Victorian *ideal* of the family, an ideal that Austen and the domestic novelists of the nineteenth century upheld through celebrating the "ultimate victory of personal needs and desires over social conventions" (Poovey 162) and the rewards of service in the name of love. Pym makes the ideal absurd by mocking romantic love and depicting the many forms that loving takes—platonic, love between men, friendship between women. In Pym's novels, romantic love provides no more personal gratification than the comfort of a cup of tea or the solace of a good book.

Pym also makes the ideal absurd through her characters. She has no romantic heroes or heroines in either of the senses of romantic—no Emmas, Mr. Knightleys, Cecilias, Eleanors, Arabins, Dorotheas, or Lydgates; her characters are quite self-interested and self-absorbed. For in Pym's novels, this is the nature of being human. Pym mocks the foibles of her characters and spoofs social pretentiousness and other aberrations of human behavior like so many of her predecessors in the novel of manners, at least in its comic as opposed to its moralistic, didactic version, and her characters lead quiet, ordinary lives. But in Pym's novels, the eccentric and idiosyncratic—the Mrs. Bateses, Bertie Stanhopes, and Mrs. Cadwalladers—have become the leading characters. Her characters' dress, manners, pastimes, and concerns are comic; that is, much importance is attached to appearance and trivialities—to what one drinks or eats, to who leaves the office first. Yet, these differences in individual behavior reflect merely personal proclivities, not the nuances or demarcations of social class or moral choice. Pym's conception of human beings—of what a man wants and what a woman wants—makes them unfit for parts in a narrative informed by a belief in the potential or desire of men or women to be little less than angels (see Brothers 79).

In commenting ironically on nineteenth-century conceptions of character, Pym's novels mock the nineteenth-century view of marriage as well. In the 1950s, when Pym published her first five novels, marriage was no longer an economic or social necessity. Women could and did "fulfill" themselves in ways other than marriage and a family, though work was still not viewed by that society as "ample compensation for [a woman's] not being married"; Prudence's classmate is "patronising" in her statement that it is (*Jane and Prudence* 10). Contributing to the powerful hold that the ideal of love and marriage has on our imaginations are, first, the way in which the gender roles sanctified by the Victorian marriage make for the comfort and well-being of those who control social, economic, religious, and legal institutions and, second, the fact that the ideal is bound up with our conceptions of self, particularly a woman's sense of personhood. As Lawrence Stone notes in his history of the family, the "shift of motives for marriage from the concrete ones of power, status and money to the imponderable one of affection" did not serve to improve the status of women; indeed, it may have "worked to the benefit" of men (398). A woman might now address her husband by his first name instead of Master or Sir as earlier wives had done even in their personal correspondence, but the hierarchy of family merely replaced the hierarchy of class (see Stone).

What is more, women found their position in the pecking order of workplaces and educational institutions the same as it had been in the home. As it is in the private sphere, so it is in the public: a woman serves a man. Or at least such is the case in Pym's novels. In the bourgeois world of the self-made man, a woman "achieved" her place in society through love, chosen not by virtue of her father's land, titles, or pocketbook but by virtue of *her* beauty, *her* graciousness, *her* purity of mind and body. As a loving helpmate, a woman was held responsible for fulfilling the desires of private gratification that family, within which women were imprisoned, represented. Not for himself did a man struggle, but for his family, an illusion that ennobled the gender roles of the Victorian patriarchy and the Victorian bourgeois conception of the family. Women have borne the responsibility for sustaining that illusion; indeed, a woman's selfhood has been measured by her ability to do so.

Like earlier novels of manners, Barbara Pym's novels record with "fidelity . . . minute social truths," what Henry James called attention to as constituting the art of the novel of manners (*Literary Criticism: Essays* 612).[4] Her novels reflect the British society of the 1950s and the two succeeding decades, from the ritual and rhythms of village life and the unmarried women who dote upon curates to the city and its offices that replicate the rituals of the family, including the making of tea and the expectation that women will make the tea. Pym notes everything from changes in eating and drinking habits and in courting rituals to the influx of blacks and Asians into the communities and work establishments of London.

As in earlier novels of manners, however, the domestic reflects the values of the society in which the individual lives, values the individual internalizes and through which he or she passes judgment upon the self as well as upon others. Men and women are still divided into two classes—those served and those who serve. Does that mean that men want one thing? And if so, what, indeed, is it that a man wants? It may be as pertinent for a woman to ask this question as it has been for a man to ask what a woman wants. And what if a woman were daring enough to depict what a *woman* wants? Would we at last learn the secrets of the "feminine soul" that refused to yield its secret to Freud after thirty years of research? Or would we learn how varied are the desires and souls of women? of men?

To read Pym's novels is not just to be made aware that the surface of things is not all, that a frumpy and inept woman may be the "right" woman for some man to share a life with, but to experience what John Bayley has called the "duality" of existence: "her novels take entirely for granted the fact that we live in two worlds" (53), though her two worlds are not the public and private spheres of the nineteenth-century novel of manners. For Pym, reality is located neither just in the tangible outer world—one's work, one's love, one's family—nor solely within the desires and fantasies of the individual. The ironic and the comic in Pym's novels expose not only the artificiality of the manners, the artificiality of the rituals and social institutions through which human beings attempt to express themselves, but also the gap between human desire and fulfillment.

I have chosen to focus on Pym's *Jane and Prudence* not because the novel fits better into the category of the novel of manners than any other novel written by Pym but because it specifically examines love, family, marriage, and work through the expectations and fantasies of women, counterpointing the past and the present, the "young" and the middle-aged, the married and the unmarried, village social life and the city's office life, and the world of men and the world of women. Pym sets the past against the present not only through the reflections of Jane and Prudence on their "lost youth" (7), evoked by their return to Oxford for a reunion in the opening scene of the novel, but also through placing her story of love, of a clergyman's wife and her unmarried friend, in relation to the stories of Austen and to those told by Gaskell, Trollope, Yonge, and other Victorian novelists. She also alludes through her setting to Woolf's factual fantasy about women's lives and writing—*A Room of One's Own*, a book Pym records as reading during the time she was rewriting *Jane and Prudence* (*A Very Private Eye* 159)—and to the celebration of love in the poetry of John Cleveland, Andrew Marvell, and other metaphysical poets. These allusions remind the reader that, as Woolf objects, women, both their characters and their lives, have been depicted almost exclusively through the conventions and illusions of romantic heterosexual love and marriage.

Trilling remarks that some twentieth-century novels of manners "evoke the question of reality by contriving a meeting and conflict of diverse social classes" (212). I doubt that Trilling had thought of a novel's questioning what is real, as does *Jane and Prudence*, by "contriving a meeting and conflict" of the two genders and taking "scrupulous note" of their "differences of manners." Gender may not have been what Trilling had in mind when he spoke of "diverse social classes," but the characters (men and women) in Pym's novels are as shackled by the social codes of gender as earlier men and women were by the practices, expectations, and alliances of the vertical class system. Though Pym does not let her readers overlook the greater prominence and power of men in society, her women struggle not with society and its political and economic discriminations but with the expectations and stereotyping of desire that are inherent in the designations of masculine and feminine.

I would not, however, fix the scene of that conflict where John Halperin does in his essay "Barbara Pym and the War of the Sexes." Her novels are not a twentieth-century version of *The Taming of the Shrew* with Katharina playing the role of Petruchio, her women conquering not by force but by their "unselfish and untiring support" of "overbearing and egotistical" men (Halperin 89). Rather than doing battle with men, Pym's women, like Don Quixote, must do battle with the windmills of their imaginations. The locus of conflict in Pym's novels is within the individual. The "ambivalent attitude toward marriage" expressed in *Jane and Prudence* (Strauss-Noll 79) emerges from the depiction of its "ordinary reality," much in contrast to idealized and genderized versions of it, and from the fact that the judgments made and the feelings expressed are those of individuals with quite different fantasies and expectations. Not only, as Jane observes and as the novel demonstrates, do people not "show their feelings in the same way, [but also] . . . they don't have the feelings one would expect" (105). The happy endings of Pym's novels result from her characters' accepting the rightness of their feelings over the correctness of social expectations; the old social order is not overturned but shown to be ineffectual and inaccurate in its assessment of what a woman or a man wants.

The Oxford reunion that Prudence and Jane attend makes Prudence uneasy with her life and shakes her self-confidence; she is still unmarried. Though Prudence does have a job in London and a nice flat and though she still has her unsatisfactory "love affairs," she is made to feel somewhat inadequate, not "labelled" and thus "fulfilled" as Miss Birkinshaw "liked her Old Students to be" (10). Certainly, as she realizes, her mother and her mother's friends feel it is time for her to marry. At twenty-nine, she is reminded that she cannot "be eighteen again and starting out on a long series of love affairs of varying degrees of intensity," the life she imagines for Jane's daughter Flora at Oxford and that she finds "entirely enviable" (158–59). Given Prudence's beauty, is it not "odd, really, that she should not yet have married," reflects Jane. Her thoughts replicate those of Prudence as Prudence, too, looks about her "at the odd garments and odder wearers of them, the eager, unpainted faces, the wispy hair, the dowdy clothes" of the other "university women" gathered at the dinner table—"and yet most of them had married—that was the strange and disconcerting thing" (9). She replies somewhat defensively to the pitying tone of a former classmate: "I often think being married would be rather a nuisance. I've got a nice flat and am so used to living on my own I should hardly know what to do with a husband" (10). Self-doubts, however, lead her to become a willing participant in her friend Jane's attempt at matchmaking.

Prudence is not alone in her self-doubts. Jane, forty-one, is also "conscious of failure." Jane worries that she has not been a "gallant, cheerful" wife, running a household efficiently while finding time to write. She has only one child, and her "outspokenness and her fantastic turn of mind" have not endeared her to the members of her husband's congregation (8). While being forty-one and married "may bring with it compensations unsuspected by the anxious woman of twenty-nine" (7), for so Prudence is described, it has not brought Jane a sense of fulfillment. Nicholas casts her "mild, kindly look[s]" (48), not "penetrating" glances (93) like those Prudence will receive from Fabian. Nor does he even listen to her quote poetry, much less send her a volume of poetry as Fabian sends one to Prudence. Nicholas may be "someone to tell one's silly jokes to, to carry suitcases and do the tipping at hotels" and "a great deal more than that" (10–11), but Jane wonders what she has done with her life. Her return to Oxford reminds her that she has not "really fulfilled her early promise" (11). She resolves to "dig out her notes" on a seventeenth-century poet, though she can't remember which one, and to become a matchmaker, like Pandarus or perhaps "much more like Emma Woodhouse" since she is adhering to "decorous conventions" of "lunches and dinners" (11, 96). Jane decides to win a widower for her friend Prudence, for Prudence needs *work* rather than "romantic" affairs. A "glance at Prudence's small, useless-looking hands with their long red nails" tells her that "satisfying work with her hands, digging, agriculture" will not be "suitable. Not agriculture then, but a widower, that was how it would have to be" (15).

The narrator, of course, is commenting comically on the unlikelihood of Jane's success in either writing a critical-scholarly book or making a match for Prudence. Jane's and Prudence's own uncertainties concerning the value of the lives they lead have been created by each looking at herself through the perspective of her youthful expectations as well as through her perceptions of what society expects of her. Yet, the doubts and discomforts they experience focus the novel on a fundamental human problem: its opening raises the questions of desire and fulfillment and of the individual's struggle with social expectations and personal fantasies. The anxieties that Jane expresses for Prudence stem from her uneasiness about her daughter's coming of age—from her lack of a defined role as Flora enters into relationships with men that may indeed involve sex. Prudence becomes surrogate daughter as well as friend, the object of Jane's displaced anxieties. The novel is as much about sexual desire and the social codes by which the individual's conduct is judged as it is about love, marriage, or a career. Rather than pitting married life against single life, the novel pits fantasy against the life one leads and desire against the opportunities for fulfillment. The merits of married life versus those of single life are a matter for the individual to judge, though, as in everything from how often one has sex to what one chooses to drink with dinner, society will be sure to have its say about what the individual does.

By sharply contrasting the ways Jane and Prudence each live and judge the life of the other while remaining exceptionally close friends, the novel emphasizes just how different one individual's perspective is from another's. The difference is not merely a matter of one's being so careless of her dress that she goes off for a day in London with her slip showing while the other chooses to wear a red velvet housecoat when alone. Nor that one decorates her home with linoleum and the other with a regency sofa. Each pities the other. Jane feels that "Prudence's flat [is] in the kind of block where . . . people might be found dead" (121), and Prudence feels that Jane has "missed something in life"— "Husbands took [one's] friends away," though even Prudence knows this is not quite true in Jane's case (83). Nor has a husband kept Jane from "her research" (83); Prudence merely likes to think it has. Prudence herself has hardly committed her life to scholarship or novel writing or something else that might be labeled "meaningful" work. What becomes apparent through their thoughts about each other is Jane's concern for Prudence's aloneness and Prudence's feeling that Jane's life lacks the independence Prudence values, even if, as Prudence observes when visiting the Clevelands, it makes a hot-water bottle unnecessary for Jane but highly desirable for Prudence.

The book abounds in mistaken interpretations that expose Pym's perspective on how difficult it is to know the truths of the human heart and on how different those truths are for each individual. In the eyes of the world, Prudence and Fabian are a good match, both quite handsome and meticulous about their dress and appearance, both seemingly cultured, at least in their choice of food and drink. But appearances are deceiving, for Fabian is dull, unread, and unintelligent. His letters are a bore. The match that Jessie Morrow—the plain, sharp-tongued eater of fish and chips who does not "intend to be a distressed gentlewoman" (125)—effects with Fabian is after all a good one, in spite of its seeming so impossible to Miss Doggett, who employs her as a companion, and to Mrs. Pritchard, who is sure Fabian "would have to look further afield" than the women who reside in the village (148).

Just how mistaken our perceptions can be even in day-to-day matters is the focus of chapter 16, which follows Jessie Morrow's entrance into Fabian's home and arms. Jane is first startled by a face she does not recognize at the second story window, but it is only the window washer's. Mr. Mortlake then appears at the vicarage, and Jane thinks with sinking heart that he has come to lecture her for her interference at a church council meeting. But he has come only to tune the piano. As she opens the front door, a young man is standing on the doorstep and informs her that he is soliciting old clothes, obviously unaware that he is at the vicarage. The Pritchards come to call, and Mrs. Pritchard comments to Jane upon there being "nobody here for him [Fabian]" (148). Ironically, Jessie had already "seduced" Fabian the evening before, dressed in a blue wool dress that had been his dead wife's. Jane even mistakes for a moment Canon Pritchard's holding out his hands in a "vague gesture" as his "attempting to give her some kind of a blessing" (149). He just wishes to wash his hands after all.

The constant misapprehenions or misjudgments of the characters in Pym's novel reflect their own conceptions of comfort or love, of seemly behavior or good food or drink. The members of the church council assume that the furnishings of the Clevelands are poor and disreputable, though the narrator comments that they are "in better taste" than the more costly chairs and tables of the members' homes (132). Viewed through the eyes of the young, Prudence, though still "quite attractive," is not youthful enough for a romantic heroine. As one of the office typists observes, "I hope I die before I'm thirty—it sounds so old" (97).

If one cannot judge others by their taste in furniture or clothes, perhaps one cannot judge another by demeanor either. Paul, the "mousy-looking young man" who discourses at length on "the higher flights of Geography" (158), does after all quote poetry to Flora in spite of Jane's certainty that he is not the type. Prudence's fifty-year-old boss (Grampian), with whom she has imagined a love affair, takes the tears in her eyes as tears for him: "he still retained his old power over women," he thinks at the men's club where he has gone for lunch (197). Yet, Prudence's tears were occasioned not by Grampian but by Fabian's desertion or Geoffrey Manifold's kindness to her, or a combination of both.

As Grampian's thoughts reveal, it is not just women in Pym's novels who seize on words or gestures and transform them in their imaginations, though critics seem to have noticed only how imaginative Pym's women characters are. *Jane and Prudence,* in fact, is frequently cited as an example of Pym's extolling women for the power of their imaginations: "that was why women were so wonderful; it was their love and imagination that transformed these unremarkable beings" (217). Jane often remarks that such is the case, but Pym has Jane herself call into question the truth of the observation. When Jane meets Arthur Grampian, another of those "negative" love affairs that has become a "habit" for Prudence, she notes how unimpressive he is—"middle size, almost short, and [giving] an impression of greyness, in his clothes and face and in the pebble-like eyes behind his spectacles." What "splendid . . . things women were doing for men all the time," thinks Jane, transforming an "insignificant-looking little man" by loving and admiring him. But even the fanciful Jane can see that "love didn't seem to have had any very noticeable effect on Arthur Grampian" (75). Of the two old clichés—the love of a woman transforms a man, and beauty is in the eyes of the beholder—only the latter would seem to be true. Since love lacks the power to "reform" the individual, it can hardly effect a transformation of society (compare Poovey 172–73 on the claims for romantic love).

That Pym's women are considered superior in imagination and in their powers of observation is the result of Pym's rarely making us privy to the thoughts of her male characters. The men in her novels, with the exception of *Quartet in Autumn,* only occasionally reveal what they are thinking or feeling. In Pym's novels, men—not women—are objectified and become the "other," the great enigma. Perhaps it is this perspective that accounts for some of her readers' believing she is misandrous. But Pym is bemused rather than offended by men, unlike Professor von X., who Woolf speculates may have been made so vicious in his attack on the "mental, moral and physical inferiority of women" by being "laughed at, to adopt the Freudian theory, in his cradle by a pretty girl" (31). Women are Pym's subjects; her readers, whether the narrative is first person as in *Excellent Women* or *A Glass of Blessings* or third person as in her other novels, share the perspective of her female characters. Her male characters are not equally and universally despicable, unfeeling, and uncaring, as some critics have stated; and though she has a true appreciation for the virtues of her "excellent" women, not all of her unmarried women are "angels," loving, self-less, and sympathetic.

The imagination of women is Pym's focus. She depicts the struggle of women to interpret themselves, others, and the culture that shapes them. What her women must come to terms with are the discrepancies between what society and fiction have portrayed as "feminine" desires, female roles, and the lives women find themselves leading, as well as the discrepancies between what women have understood as male desire and what they find the behavior of men to be like.

The question of what a man wants echoes explicitly and repeatedly in *Jane and Prudence.* Is it beauty? To be gazed at with "obvious devotion" of the kind Flora bestows first on Mr. Oliver and then on Paul (158)? To be fed meat and eggs as Mrs. Crampton and Mrs. Mayhew believe? To be served liquor (Jane wonders if men have stayed away from the literary society meeting because nothing but tea or coffee is served)? What do men want? Miss Doggett is the first to raise the question explicitly when she mentions Fabian's former habit of taking frequent trips to London: "Poor Constance was left alone a great deal. . . . They say, though, that men only want *one thing*—that's the truth of the matter" (70). But Jane's observations challenge Miss Doggett's surmise that it is sex when Jane concludes that Fabian "tended to make love to women—because he couldn't really think of much to say to them" (96). Perhaps the man who passes as philanderer is just a man without an imagination.

Earlier, at dinner that same evening, Nicholas had commented on Flora's skill as a cook: "She will make a good wife for somebody one of these days"

(82). Jane, remembering her conversation with Miss Doggett, exclaims: "But men don't want only that . . . though perhaps the better ones think they do." Yet, Jane "too had difficulty in remembering what it was that men wanted." The real irony of Nicholas's remark and Jane's response, however, is that Jane is as inept about meals as she is about her dress: "They say Mrs. Cleveland hardly knows how to open a tin," remarks a prominent parishioner (132). Such a judgment is more than confirmed by Jane's inability even to get lunch for herself and Nicholas. Perhaps Nicholas's remark reveals a certain yearning for the cook he did not marry.

Jane's later statement to Miss Doggett, that what a man wants is someone for typing his "thesis, correcting proofs, putting sheets sides-to-middle, bringing up children, balancing the house-keeping budget" (127), might seem to be the case for some men, at least for the ones Pym's "excellent women" like Mildred Lathbury do eventually marry. Yet, these things are certainly not what Jane does for Nicholas. She cannot even wash the dishes satisfactorily, do the laundry, or get curtains to fit the windows. At eighteen, Flora seems more mother than daughter to Jane. Nor does Jane fulfill well the role of the rector's wife; she goes to London to the meeting of a literary society rather than attending the meeting of the Parochial Church Council. Her deduction as to what a man wants—a helpmate—seems no more apropos than does Miss Doggett's suggestion that men want passion.[5]

Not even devotion would seem to be the correct answer to the question. In fact, Jane later agrees with Jessie Morrow that a woman's "devotion is worse than blackmail—a man has no escape from that" (126). But some men reject the entrapment of "devotion," finding it rather tiring and frightening to be made the object of such attention. At the end of the literary society meeting, the beautiful young poet flees from the admiring attentions of a serious young woman writer.

What a man wants remains a mystery. Sex, beauty, an angel of the house—none seems to fit. Nicholas seems to be quite contented with Jane, and their marriage a good one. He helps her to can plums, sees to the arranging of the flowers in the church, and accepts her forgetfulness and penchant for literary societies and trips to London. He does not notice her hanging slips or rumpled clothing. As Jane observes one morning when she discovers Nicholas putting four children's colored soap animals in the cloakroom downstairs, "If it is true that men only want one thing, . . . is it perhaps just to be left to themselves with their soap animals or some other harmless little trifle?" (129) Or, one might add, permitted to hang their tobacco leaves in the kitchen by an understanding or somewhat oblivious wife. Jane and Nicholas enjoy the "affectionate tolerance" (135) each seems to offer the other. Maybe what some men "desire" and what some women want is just that—"affectionate tolerance."

Pym undercuts by comic irony the stereotypical but conflicting accounts of what a man wants. She also mocks the assumptions of *essential* character upon which men's and women's roles are based. Men may expect the women they marry to be helpmates, but Jane is certainly not, and Nicholas is no more annoyed by Jane's lack of skill in the kitchen and in running the home than Jane is by his childlike and cluttering hobbies. Miss Doggett, who states "that men need company more than women do" since a "woman has a thousand and one little tasks in the house, and then her knitting or sewing" (113), expresses a cliché, not what is true for her or, for that matter, for any of the other women characters in the novel. Only the dead Constance seems to have been interested in or adept at the ways in which Miss Doggett feels women prove their self-sufficiency. Miss Doggett, an "old lady" but in reality a "vigorous" one, uses Miss Morrow as a "sparring partner," what Jessie tells Jane is the real "service" she provides (29). Nor do men seem to "need" company, Jane having herself speculated earlier that "men [might be] less gregarious" (117) than women since few men attended the literary society meeting. Fabian is certainly as "vain" as Prudence. And if Paul has made geography a "strange and wonderful" thing for Flora (158), as Jane observes, Flora has introduced him to the wonders of poetry. While men may expect women to do those things for a man that he does not want to do for himself, Pym demonstrates that women also expect others to do for them what they do not like to do for themselves. And it is not just the men who are sometimes boring or irritating in Pym's novels.

Pym makes the generalizations the characters mouth—"Men don't really go in for that sort of thing [in this case reading poetry]" (165)—as inappropriate as the quotations Jane remembers and occasionally blurts out to the discomfort and embarrassment of her companions. Prudence is wrong in her generalization and in her estimate of Geoffrey Manifold. He does indeed read poetry, and he imaginatively perceives that she might be lonely on a Sunday afternoon after the affair with Fabian has ended and appreciate an invitation to a quiet dinner at a lovely restaurant in Soho. A man, it seems, can be quite as sensitive as a woman. Indeed, the novel develops as a theme the error of all generalizations: "I thought people in the country were somehow noble, through contact with the earth and Nature . . . and all the time they're just worrying about petty details like water-tanks and magazine covers!—like people in the suburbs do" (137–38).[6] At the very least, we must be wary of attributing the comments of Pym's characters to Pym herself, mistaking an individual character's judgment for hers.

Pym's choice of Prudence as her coheroine marks a change in the ways in which a woman might choose to live her life. Prudence may go off on vacations with men to whom she is not married, and Jane wonders if Prudence entertains Fabian in her bedroom as well as her living room. Yet, even though a woman might at least take the "initiative" in a small matter such as asking to "see *him* [Fabian] home," as Jane suggests to Prudence (162), Pym's men and women are still divided into two distinct social classes. Throughout the novel, Pym calls attention to the fact that England is still a man's world in spite of the fact that Prudence and Jane's return to Oxford does not stir reflections of their exclusion from the lawns and libraries as it does for Virginia Woolf in *A Room of One's Own*. They recall their days at Oxford as ones of "wine and roses," spent in "the idyllic surroundings of ancient stone walls, rivers, gardens, and even the reading-rooms of the great libraries" (13). In their women's college at Oxford, a man existed in relation to a woman. But that is untrue outside the rooms of romance that Oxford represents for them. A few of Miss Birkinshaw's students chose to work rather than marry. Yet, whether they took a man's name or pursued a "brilliant" career, their work was for a man. They lived in relation to a man. Even Miss Birkinshaw's unfinished book on seventeenth-century metaphysical poets and Jane's "stillborn 'research'—'the influence of something upon somebody' hadn't Virginia Woolf called it?—" were studies of what men had done. Miss Birkinshaw, "a new woman enthusiastic for learning," had simply rejected one man for a number of men (11).

Certainly, the work that a man does seems vague. Even those who work in Grampian's office seem not to know the nature or significance of the research that he does. Perhaps that is because he writes "the kind of books that nobody could be expected to read" (11). His work is further trivialized by his office staff's having nothing more demanding to do than wait for their tea and decide what time it is proper for them to leave the office. Fabian Driver has no occupation; Edward Lyall of the Towers is the district's Member of Parliament, but his short speech to those gathered for the whist drive has as little substance as his comments at Fabian Driver's tea party, where not only he but Fabian and Nicholas as well try to outdo each other in claiming "weariness" from the demands of their jobs. But is not this what is expected of a man? Surely, men cannot be expected to talk about how "boring" their jobs frequently are.

Office hierarchies, which repeat the traditional Victorian roles for men and women, serve to keep women in their place and to continue the division of men and women into two social classes. But such distinctions, and the assumptions they are based on, are portrayed by Pym as "mannered," as affected as if Edward Lyall still ate an English country breakfast as his father did in Edwardian times. "There have [indeed] been many changes in the last few years," as Jane remarks. And "[e]specially since the war," Mrs. Lyall adds (90).

Pym is not writing a social protest novel. But she is observing the ways things are, and clearly she is bemused by the ways in which society acts and talks as if the Victorian world of men working and women serving as their helpmates still persists. Manners, rituals, and expectations have continued long after the system that gave them meaning has ceased to function, long after the only thing a woman could do was to marry. We cling to the myths of the past even when what they express is only such stuff as dreams are made of.

Pym's novel repeatedly takes note of the ways in which society still acts as if men were one kind of thing and women another. At the Parochial Church Council meeting, women's "voices" are "seldom heard," it being expected that they are unlikely "to have any sensible views" to offer, and even when they do comment, what they say is made "to seem slightly ridiculous by the men" (134). But how ironic since at one of these meetings the intelligent, rational men of the council are fighting over the cover for the parish magazine: If the high altar— more representative, as Miss Doggett observes, of their "beautiful old church"— were used instead of the lych-gate, someone might mistake their worship service for that of the Anglican high church, St. Stephen's, a perfectly "ridiculous" supposition as Jane observes (134–35).

Like Fabian's having settled on marriage to Jessie, Jane's and Prudence's acceptance of their lives as they are, of their own idiosyncracies, seems to be "the right thing" (215). Jane is just as much an ineffective wife and romantic at the end of the novel, forgetting the books she purchased for communion gifts, as she is at the beginning. Yet, she is obviously happy in the love she and Nicholas share, sitting by the fire eating the sandwiches that remain from the council meeting, Nicholas reading a book about tobacco-growing and Jane absorbed as always in her thoughts. Jane has her "work," her plans to act once more as a matchmaker for her friend Prudence rather than resuming her research, which would be "too much of an effort" (131). The greeting of the villagers when she and Nicholas return from a short vacation, so like the welcome she had anticipated when they first moved to the village but which they had not received, confirms that she has found "richness" (21) in her life. Prudence, too, sees the "richness of her life" (222), for she need be neither "the comfortable spinster or the contented or bored wife" (200). What has been resolved in the novel are the self-doubts of Jane and Prudence.[7] What has *not* changed in the world Pym mockingly depicts are the social expectations and mannerisms that grew out of the Victorian public text of work and the private text of marriage—the division of men and women into two distinct classes, the illusion that women might effect a change in that public sphere through their love and devotion, or that "one's own love" (Poovey 173) might fulfill all of human desire.

Notes

1. Henry James objected to the tradition that "a serious story of manners shall close with the factitious happiness of a fairy-tale." Yet, he also found "irritating" the "fatal" conclusion of *Mill on the Floss* (*Literary Criticism: Essays* 933).

2. In "Women Victimised by Fiction: Living and Loving in the Novels by Barbara Pym," I examined the challenge to the romantic paradigm that echoes in all of Pym's novels, though I focused on how she draws attention to the fact that literature sustains that paradigm through both "sins of omission and sins of commission" (63).

3. Fryckstedt excludes Jane Austen, though she does not state why, and uses the term *domestic novel* to discuss novelists whose "genre" reached "its height in novels by . . . Mrs. Gaskell, Trollope and George Eliot" (9). Does she consider the domestic novels that focused on courtship different in kind from those that related a "domestic love story" (9)? What else did courtship produce but "domesticity," marriage? Colby mentions Austen but makes clear that she excludes her because she "gave scant space to physical description of any kind" (15); in Martineau's *Deerbrook* one finds the "qualities that define the domestic novel."

4. Early reviewers of *Daisy Miller* stressed the moral lesson to be learned from the novelette, and one reviewer even suggested that the book be placed in the cabins of ocean steamers.

5. Nor are Pym's other wives efficacious angels of subservience and caring. Archdeacon Hoccleve's wife attends to her dress more than to running the home (*Some Tame Gazelle*); Rocky Napier's wife, Helena, ignores both house and husband to pursue anthropology and an anthropologist, Everard Bone (*Excellent Women*); Rhoda Wellcome performs the needed tasks of a mother better than her widowed sister, Mabel Swan, with whom she makes her home (*Less Than Angels*).

6. Pym also, of course, uses the generalizations and statements of her characters to depict their preoccupations and their efforts at self-protection. For example, when Prudence says that men do not read poetry, she is being defensive about Fabian's failure to quote poetry to her. When Prudence follows her generalization with the contradiction that Paul might quote poetry to Flora, Jane counters with her statement that "geographers don't read poetry" (165). Jane, "the anxious mother" (191), has linked Prudence's statement about poetry with Prudence's "assuring" comment to Jane earlier that Paul may have something more interesting to offer Flora than geography—"'Perhaps he is a wonderful lover'" (160). In fact, Jane's interest in how intimate the courting of Prudence by Fabian might have become may be traced to her concern for her daughter's embarking on a life of her own that now involves men. She hopes that Paul "will be the first of many" (160), but she is obviously made uncomfortable by the idea that "men may want only one thing."

7. For a bleak reading of the novel, see Jane Nardin, who states that it is "about disillusionment" (82). Such a reading ignores the comic tone and typical-Pym optimistic ending; Pym even has spring arrive to confirm her characters' resolutions of their problems. One does not need to turn to a source such as Pym's diaries and letters, *A Very Private Eye*, where she pronounces Wilmet and Prudence her two "favourite" heroines (223), to reject the strident tone in which Nardin judges and denounces both Prudence and Jane. One might indeed wish to aspire to something more in one's life, but Pym is not judgmental of her characters.

10

The View from the Outside: Black Novels of Manners

Mary F. Sisney

In 1853, when the first novel written by a black American was published in London, the novel of manners was flourishing. That year, two Elizabeth Gaskell novels—*Cranford* and *Ruth*—appeared, and a few years earlier (1848), Thackeray's *Vanity Fair* was published. But fugitive slave William Wells Brown's *Clotel* was not a novel of manners. It was a slave narrative written in the abolitionist tradition of Harriet Beecher Stowe's *Uncle Tom's Cabin* (1852).

Thackeray would no doubt have scoffed at the idea of a fugitive slave writing a novel comparable to *Vanity Fair*. Imagine Sambo as the protagonist in a novel of manners. That would be, to quote Thackeray, "entirely low" (54).[1] In the novel of manners, the lowest classes and the darker races provide background and often comic relief. They are the maids, butlers, cooks, and footmen for the middle- and upper-middle-class heroes and heroines.

Indeed, at first glance, the black novel, which usually calls for change in society—the abolition, first, of slavery, then, of Jim Crow and, finally, of racial oppression—appears to have little in common with the more conservative novel of manners, which generally accepts the mores of the society depicted and requires the individual to change in order to find her or his place in that society.

How could black Americans accept a society that rejected them? Why would they want to find their place in a social system that always placed them at the very bottom? And how could black American writers write about a society from which they were excluded? Even the characteristic tone and method of the novel of manners seem ill-suited to the black writer. Not all novels of manners follow the happy ending convention of high comedy, but the tone tends to be light—ironic, satirical.[2] And if there is political upheaval or violence, it usually takes place offstage. As Thackeray says, "Our place is with the non-combatants" (282). The only battles fought are domestic, taking place in the characteristic settings of the novel of manners—the drawing room, the opera, dances, weddings. Cruelty takes the form of slander and ostracism. There is no place in the novel of manners for the kind of brutality—rapes, lynching—that has been part of the black American experience.

And yet, the black novel and the novel of manners share at least three fundamental and related concerns—the fight for acceptance, the loss of identity, and the sense of oppression. In the black novel, the fight against Jim Crow and other forms of racism is, in part, a fight for acceptance. For characters in the so-called Talented Tenth novels (1890–1920), being accepted by the best of white society seemed to be the primary goal.[3] Such novelists as Charles Chesnutt and James Weldon Johnson created black heroes and heroines who differed from members of white society only in the degree of their suffering and in their capacity for compassion. These characters were usually white-skinned, middle-class blacks, sometimes, as in Chesnutt's *The Marrow of Tradition* (1901), closely resembling a white half-sibling and sometimes, as in Chesnutt's *The House behind the Cedars* (1900), and Johnson's *The Autobiography of an Ex-Coloured Man* (1912), choosing to pass as white in order to escape the brutality and oppression of racism.

"Passing" also occurs in the novel of manners. To pass is to deny one's true identity—family, heritage, class. Becky Sharp constantly attempts to pass for a lady in *Vanity Fair*. The daughter of an alcoholic artist and a French opera singer, she claims to be related to a "noble family of Gascony" (20). But passing can take more subtle forms than rewriting family histories. Becky is also passing when she assumes the role of a timid young maiden in a vain attempt to capture Joseph Sedley. And when the spirited Lily Bart, in Edith Wharton's *The House of Mirth* (1905), tries to mold herself into the image of a dull, dutiful wife so that she can attract Percy Gryce, "all on the bare chance that he might ultimately decide to do her the honour of boring her for life" (25), she, too, is passing.

In the rigidly structured, patriarchal societies depicted in novels of manners, there is only one place for a woman: beside or behind a man. And so women like Becky Sharp and Lily Bart must suppress their spirits and hide their true identities in order to trick men into marrying them. For Becky, marriage is a way to gain status and acceptance, to become a lady. For Lily, already a lady, marriage is a vocation:

> "Isn't marriage your vocation? Isn't it what you're all brought up for?"
> She [Lily] sighed. "I suppose so. What else is there?" (9)[4]

There is nothing else for the lady; she cannot work or live alone. Until she is married, a lady in the novel of manners has no security, no freedom, no identity.

Since there could be no black ladies and gentlemen in white society, the characters in early black novels had more in common with Becky Sharp than with Lily Bart. Just as Becky sought to marry a gentleman in order to become a lady, some of the blacks passing as white—the ex-coloured man, for instance—married whites in order to solidify their position in white society. There was no place in that society for any person known to be black, no matter how fair-skinned, wealthy, or genteel he or she might have been.

In the years following the Civil War, the newly emancipated and the already-free blacks who were educated and had acquired property began to form black societies. By the 1920s, close to sixty years after Emancipation, some very exclusive black societies existed in such cities as Charleston, Atlanta, New Orleans, Harlem, Chicago, Philadelphia, and Washington, D.C. (Frazier 196–200). These societies were generally as conservative and patriarchal as those depicted by Thackeray and Wharton. Although the black lady could work, usually as a teacher, a seamstress, or a secretary, her place in society was not secure until she married. For some of these women, marriage was the fulfillment of a dream, a long-awaited reward for a virtuous life. For others, it could be stifling and confining, even more unbearable than the life Lily Bart would lead as Mrs. Percy Gryce. But for all black society ladies of the twenties, marriage was a necessity.[5]

Although most black writers of the twenties—the Harlem Renaissance period of black literature—portrayed lower-class blacks, the so-called Rear Guard novelists focused on black society. Robert Bone describes these writers in his *Negro Novel in America* (1965):

> Fundamentally these novelists still wished to orient Negro art toward white opinion. They wished to apprise educated whites of the existence of respectable Negroes, and to call their attention—now politely, now indignantly—to the facts of racial injustice. From these nonliterary motives certain familiar consequences flowed. Where the Harlem School turned to the folk for literary material, these novelists continued to draw their characters from the Negro middle class. . . . Where the Harlem School emphasized "racial" differences, these authors suppressed them. (97)

Two of the more prominent members of the Rear Guard were women writers. One was Jessie Fauset, high school teacher, literary editor of the N.A.A.C.P. journal *The Crisis,* and member of the "Old Philadelphia" society; the other was Nella Larsen, nurse, librarian, wife of a physicist, and daughter of a Danish mother and black father. Both women were well educated, and both had traveled and lived in Europe. These cultured society women were the first black novelists of manners. Their novels, which focus on marriage as a means for the black woman to establish and maintain her place in society, have more in common with the works of such literary ancestors as Edith Wharton and Jane Austen than with those written by such black contemporaries as Claude McKay and Countee Cullen.[6]

Fauset, who wrote four novels between 1924 and 1933, explained her literary objectives in the foreword to her third novel, *The Chinaberry Tree* (1931):

> In the story of Aunt Sal, Laurentine, Melissa and the Chinaberry Tree I have depicted something of the homelife of the colored American who is not being pressed too hard by the Furies of Prejudice, Ignorance, and Economic Injustice. And behold he is not so vastly different from any other American, just distinctive. He is not rich but he moves in a society which has its spheres and alignments as definitely as any other society the world over. . . . He has seen, he has been the victim of many phases of immorality but he has his own ideas about certain "Thou shalt nots." And acts on them. . . . He boasts no Association of the Sons and Daughters of the Revolution, but he knows that as a matter of fact and quite inevitably his sons and daughters date their ancestry as far back as any. So quite as naturally as his white compatriots he speaks of his "old" Boston families, "old Philadelphians," "old Charlestonians." And he has a wholesome respect for family and education and labor and the fruits of labor. He is still sufficiently conservative to lay a slightly greater stress on the first two of these four. (ix–x)

The case of the aptly named Stranges, Aunt Sal and her daughter Laurentine, illustrates the importance of family and of "Thou Shalt Not's" to black society. Both women are "comely and upstanding" (1), and there is not a black or white woman in Red Brook more poised, talented, or rigidly moral than Laurentine Strange. But Aunt Sal has committed three of the most unpardonable "Thou Shalt Not's": She has borne a child out of wedlock, the child's father is already married, and he is a white man. To the respectable black citizens of Red Brook, the "sin" of miscegenation is just as objectionable as the sins of adultery and bastardy. Because of the "scandal" surrounding her birth, black children will not play with Laurentine when she is small, and she has trouble finding a suitable mate when she becomes an adult. Little Lucy Stone plays with her until Mrs. Stone intervenes: "My mumma say I dasn't. She say you got bad blood in your veins" (8). Phil Hackett, an early suitor, is also frightened away by the "bad blood" and hint of scandal. But as so often happens in the novel of manners, the virtuous woman is finally rewarded. At the end of the novel, Laurentine is marrying a doctor and entering the black society of Red Brook. Her cousin, Melissa Paul, is also rescued from scandal by marriage to a respected member of the Red Brook community. In the last sentence of the novel, the two women are compared to "spent swimmers, who had given up the hope of rescue and then had suddenly met with it . . . sensing with all their being, the feel of the solid ground beneath their feet, the grateful monotony of the skies above their heads" (340–41).

This ending is typical of Fauset's novels. Although her heroines are talented and self-sufficient, occasionally even prosperous, not one "feels the solid ground beneath her feet" until she finds the right man to love and marry. Critic Hiroko Sato describes the basic Fauset plot: "a beautiful heroine and a handsome hero are finally united after overcoming innumerable obstacles" (68). Most of those obstacles involve other handsome men, the heroes' rivals, the heroines' unworthy suitors. Before she marries the right man, the Fauset heroine must reject or be rejected by the wrong one. Thus, Laurentine Strange must be rejected by the selfish Phil Hackett before she can marry the loving Doctor Stephen Denleigh. And two other heroines fair enough to pass as white, Angela Murray in *Plum Bun* (1929) and Phebe Grant in *Comedy: American Style* (1933), must reject wealthy white suitors before they can find suitable black mates.[7]

In their depiction of marriage, Fauset's novels resemble those written by Jane Austen. The marriages are correct and proper. They bring order to the women's lives, ending long, sometimes painful, searches for love and acceptance. Through marriage, the Fauset heroine finds her place in society. She belongs.

Larsen's heroines, who also seek love and acceptance, have less success with marriage. Although it provides them with a place in society, marriage does not bring order, security, or peace to these women's lives. They have not married the right men; therefore, instead of finding themselves—their best selves—through marriage, like the heroines in Fauset's novels, these women, like Lily Bart and Rebecca Sharp, must deny their true selves. For Clare Kendry, Irene Redfield, and Helga Crane, marriage is a struggle, a trap, a dead end.

Helga Crane, the heroine of *Quicksand* (1928), the first of Larsen's two novels, has the same problem with black society as does Fauset's Laurentine Strange. Like Laurentine, Helga is the illegitimate daughter of one white parent (her mother) and one black (her father). Comparing black society to white, the narrator explains Helga's problem: "Negro society . . . was as complicated and as rigid in its ramifications as the highest strata of white society. If you couldn't prove your ancestry and connections, you were tolerated, but you didn't 'belong'" (8). Because she is more passionate and rebellious than the conservative Laurentine, Helga has even more trouble "belonging." Indeed, she is not certain that she wants to be accepted by black society since she does not completely accept its values.

When the novel opens, Helga is dissatisfied with her position as an English teacher at Naxos, a school for black girls: "Nor was the general atmosphere of Naxos, its air of self-righteousness and intolerant dislike of difference, the best of mediums for a pretty, solitary girl with no family connections" (5). She refuses to wear the subdued colors deemed respectable by the Dean of Women, "a woman from one of the 'first families'"; "'Bright colors are vulgar'—'Black, gray, brown, and navy blue are the most becoming colors for colored people'" (17–18). While the other women at the school wear "drab colors, mostly navy blue, black, brown, unrelieved, save for a scrap of white or tan about the hands and necks" (17), Helga chooses vivid colors and sensuous fabrics that reflect her more passionate nature: "dark purples, royal blues, rich greens, deep reds, in soft, luxurious woolens, or heavy, clinging silks" (18). In the opening scene, she is wearing a "vivid green and gold negligee and glistening brocaded mules" (2).[8]

Unhappy as an outcast and unwilling to conform, Helga escapes Naxos, leaving before the school term ends. Trying to explain why she must leave, she tells the principal: "But I—well—I don't seem to fit here. . . . Then, too, the people here don't like me. They don't think I'm in the spirit of the work. And I'm not, not if it means suppression of individuality and beauty" (19–20). Helga is so determined to escape the oppressive atmosphere at Naxos that she ends her engagement to fellow teacher James Vayle. Her rejection of this socially acceptable man clearly distinguishes Larsen's heroine from the women in Fauset's novels.

In a Fauset novel, James Vayle would be the handsome hero, "the right man." As a member of an Atlanta "first family," he belongs to the best of black society. And he is enough in love to risk alienating his family by marrying a socially obscure woman. Helga, however, is not impressed by Vayle. She finds him stuffy, and instead of allowing him to help her adjust to Naxos, she resents his easy acceptance of the school's restrictive environment. In fact, Helga is so certain that Vayle is the wrong man for her that she rejects him twice, once at Naxos and several years later in Harlem.

If James Vayle is the wrong man for Helga, certainly the man that she finally marries, the Reverend Mr. Pleasant Green, is not the right one. With Reverend Green, Helga finds passion, both in his sermons and in the bedroom. But she is even more out of place in "the tiny Alabama town where he was pastor to a scattered and primitive flock" (118) than she is at Naxos. The women in this town have no time to worry about the "suppression of individuality and beauty"; they are too busy cooking, cleaning, and having babies. Helga even has trouble handling these wifely duties. When her passionate nights with Reverend Green bring her three children in twenty months, she realizes that she is dying more than living, "too driven, too occupied, and too sick to carry out any of the things for which she had made such enthusiastic plans" (123). During the especially painful fourth delivery, she retreats into a weeks-long stupor: "Nothing penetrated the kind darkness into which her bruised spirit had retreated" (128). As her spirit and body recover, Helga plans her escape from the quicksand in which she is mired: "For in some way she was determined to get herself out of this bog into which she had strayed. Or—she would have to die. She couldn't endure it. Her suffocation and shrinking loathing were too great. Not to be borne" (134). But there is no escape, except perhaps through death. *Quicksand* ends with the following chilling sentence: "And hardly had she left her bed and become able to walk again without pain, hardly had the children returned from the homes of the neighbors, when she began to have her fifth child" (135).[9]

Helga's fate—slow death through painful childbirth and suffocation in an unfulfilling marriage to a fat, dirty man so egomaniacal and ignorant that he does not notice his wife's despair—is severe punishment for her failure to conform. And she is punished throughout the novel. Much of that punishment is self-inflicted, the result of ambivalence and inner conflict. As the narrator explains, Helga suffers because "she could neither conform, nor be happy in her unconformity" (7). Although she resents the restrictions placed on her by black society, she does not relish the role of rebel: "For Helga Crane wasn't, after all, a rebel from society, Negro society. It did mean something to her. She had no wish to stand alone" (107). As a wife, she is suffocated; as a single woman, she is isolated. Never at peace, Helga wanders almost literally around the world, searching for "a place for herself" (118). But there is no place for Helga Crane; she is condemned to be forever out of place.

The punishment for a woman "out of place" is even more severe in Larsen's second novel, *Passing* (1929). In that novel, Larsen contrasts two women, the very proper Irene Redfield and the very improper Clare Kendry. Each woman is fair enough to pass as white, but Irene, born into a middle-class family, has married a black doctor and become an important member of Harlem society while Clare, the daughter of an alcoholic janitor, has married a white business-man and become a wealthy, if isolated, white woman.

Irene leads a safe, morally upright life as a wife, mother, and socialite. She spends her time buying gifts for her family, having tea parties for her friends, and supporting her favorite charities by organizing such social events as the Negro Welfare League Dance. Above all else, she values security and tranquil-lity for herself and her family: "Yet all the while . . . she was aware that, to her, security was the most important and desired thing in life. . . . She wanted only to be tranquil. Only, unmolested, to be allowed to direct for their own best good the lives of her sons and her husband" (235). When she encounters Clare, a childhood acquaintance, Irene immediately recognizes the danger to her own security. She has "a natural and deeply rooted aversion to the kind of front-page notoriety that Clare Kendry's presence" (157) brings.

Clare is, as she herself confesses, "not safe." Her life is filled with intrigue, passion, and even terror. She is terrified that her husband will discover her racial identity. During the months before her only child is born, for example, she worries about its complexion: "I nearly died of terror the whole nine months before Margery was born for fear that she might be dark. Thank goodness, she turned out all right. But I'll never risk it again. Never! The strain is simply too—too hellish" (168). Yet, she dares to socialize in Harlem whenever her husband is out of town. And she does not hesitate to involve the clearly reluctant

Irene in her schemes, sending her "furtive" letters with no return address, crashing her parties, and perhaps (Irene believes) having an affair with her husband. In what could be taken as a warning, Clare explains to Irene that they are very different: "It's just that I haven't any proper morals or sense of duty, as you have, that makes me act as I do. . . . Can't you realize that I'm not like you a bit? Why, to get the things I want badly enough, I'd do anything, hurt anybody, throw anything away. Really, 'Rene, I'm not safe" (210).

Nevertheless, although Irene and Clare seem to be quite different, almost opposites, Larsen shows that they have more in common than either of them realizes. Each woman has married the wrong man and is denying some part of herself in order to maintain her marriage. The secretly black Clare has married an unrepentant bigot. Forced to listen without protest to her husband's constant abuse of her own people, she feels lonely and isolated: "I've been so lonely since! You can't know. Not close to a single soul. Never anyone to really talk to" (196). Inevitably, she begins to resent, even hate, the man who calls her "Nig" as a joke and who boasts, "No niggers in my family. Never have been and never will be" (171). Her marriage becomes like a prison with her husband as the jailer. And like many prisoners, Clare contemplates violent rebellion: "Damn Jack! He keeps me out of everything. Everything I want. I could kill him! I expect I shall, some day" (200).

Irene's marriage can also be compared to a prison, but she is the jailer, her husband the prisoner. Brian Redfield is a restless adventurer, trapped in a marriage to a woman who longs for security and stability. Irene struggles to placate her husband and keep him occupied so that he will forget his dream of moving to Brazil. She wants him to be happy, but only on her terms: "It was only that she wanted him to be happy, resenting, however, his inability to be so with things as they were, and never acknowledging that though she did want him to be happy, it was only in her own way and by some plan of hers for him that she truly desired him to be so" (190). Because of their conflicting needs, neither partner is happy in this marriage. Both are frustrated and resentful. And Brian is not the only prisoner; Irene has also imprisoned a part of herself. Although she feels strong emotions—frustration, jealousy, rage—she tries to hide them, clinging to her surface calm and struggling to remain in control. When she hears John Bellew's racist remarks, for example, she fears "that her self-control was about to prove too frail a bridge to support her mounting anger and indignation" (172), but her rage is "held by some dam of caution and allegiance to Clare" (173).

Exposure to such emotionally taxing situations as association with Clare brings is one reason Irene wants to avoid her. But there is another, more significant reason. As Deborah E. McDowell points out in the introduction to Quicksand *and* Passing, Clare disturbs Irene because she "is a reminder of that repressed and disowned part of Irene's self" (xxix). Clare represents the passion that Irene has suppressed in order to maintain her marriage and her place in society.

Apparently, Irene goes even further to save her marriage. There is a strong suggestion that she pushes Clare to her death in the climactic scene:

> She [Irene] ran across the room, her terror tinged with ferocity, and laid a hand on Clare's bare arm. One thought possessed her. She couldn't have Clare Kendry cast aside by Bellew. She couldn't have her free. . . . What happened next, Irene Redfield never afterwards allowed herself to remember. (239)

If Irene does push Clare, she is not just eliminating a potential rival for Brian. She is also putting an end to the confusion and chaos that Clare has brought into her life. And most important, she is pushing out, destroying that part of herself that Clare represents.

With the death of Clare, Irene can return to directing the lives of her husband and sons. The final scenes of the novel clearly indicate that her marriage will survive. When she goes outside to face the gruesome death scene, Irene takes Brian's coat, leaving hers behind: "Brian! He mustn't take cold. She took up his coat and left her own" (240). But Brian uses the coat to shield his wife: "Brian wrapped his coat about her" (241). They are protecting each other from the coldness of death and of the world. And when Irene faints at the end of the novel, she is "dimly conscious of strong arms lifting her up" (242). The reader understands that those strong arms belong to Brian.

Of course, the price paid to save the marriage is high. Passion, happiness, and Clare's life are sacrificed. And there is something in Irene's past that she can never allow herself to remember. But it is Clare who pays the ultimate price, just as it is Clare who suffers the most. Because she passes as white, she must endure isolation and humiliation. When she comes to Harlem to be with her own people, she meets death—severe punishment, indeed.

Although she presents a much harsher view of marriage, Larsen's treatment of Helga Crane and Clare Kendry shows that she shares Fauset's belief that the best place for a black woman is beside a black man within black society. Irene Redfield, the only Larsen heroine who marries within black society, can at least achieve an uneasy peace in her marriage. Helga Crane and Clare Kendry marry men outside black society and suffer the consequences.[10] Deborah McDowell comments on the apparent contradictions implicit in the punishment of Helga and Clare:

> While Larsen criticizes the cover of marriage, as well as other social scripts for women, she is unable in the end to extend that critique to its furthest reaches. In ending the novel with

Clare's death, Larsen repeats the narrative choice which *Quicksand* makes: to punish the very values the novel implicitly affirms, to honor the very value system the text implicitly satirizes. (xxx–xxxi)

McDowell suggests that Larsen's ambivalence results from her fear of openly condoning female sexuality. But I would argue that she is simply following the novel of manners tradition, the same tradition that Edith Wharton follows in *The House of Mirth*. Wharton can also be accused of sending conflicting signals in her novel. While criticizing New York society—and the marriages within it— she shows that Lily Bart cannot survive outside that society. In the traditional novel of manners, no lady can survive outside society.

The view of women in society is quite different in *Linden Hills* (1985), Gloria Naylor's contemporary novel of manners. In this her second novel,[11] Naylor depicts a middle-class black society that destroys the people—the women more relentlessly than the men—who belong to it.

The subjugation of women, particularly wives, is the foundation upon which this nightmarish society is built. Founder and patriarch Luther Nedeed buys his enslaved wife from her white owner but never sets her free. And each successive Luther Nedeed carefully selects a wife whom he can easily oppress and ignore. The early Mrs. Nedeeds are pale, "chosen for the color of their spirits, not their faces . . . brought to Tupelo Drive to fade against the white-washed boards of the Nedeed home after conceiving and giving over a son to the stamp and will of the father" (18). There is always only one son because after that child is conceived, the husband never sleeps with the wife again. Her only functions are to bear a son, to nurture him until he can walk beside his father, and then to fade quietly into the background. These dark-skinned sons show no signs of their mothers' influence. They look, walk, think, and act just like their fathers.

Naylor's fictional society is more conservative and rigidly conformist than either Fauset's Red Brook or Larsen's Naxos. Family and marriage are the cornerstones of the community. As Luther Nedeed explains, "No one's been able to make it down to Tupelo Drive without a stable life and a family" (75).[12] Love is not part of the formula for success in Linden Hills. Although Winston Alcott loves his best friend David, he must marry a woman—any well-bred woman—in order to prosper in Linden Hills. Uninterested in women, Alcott selects his wife the way he would choose any other necessary but undesirable household appliances: "She wanted a husband—I needed a wife. It's straight out of a soap opera. And they lived happily ever after until the next floor-wax commercial" (76). So unwanted is this new bride that even the jilted lover pities her: "David shook his head slowly. 'If that's your attitude, then I feel sorry for that girl. She's got some life waiting for her'" (76).

Any new wife in Linden Hills has "some life waiting for her." She must be prepared to give up her rights and her identity. The society is so patriarchal that a divorced woman is not allowed to live in her husband's ancestral home. When Laurel Dumont and her husband separate, Nedeed tells her that she must move: "Whatever is *in* this house and whatever you've added *to* this house is between you and your husband to divide by whatever laws of whatever century you choose. But Howard Dumont has decided that there are to be no more Dumonts at Seven Twenty-Two Tupelo Drive, and according to the original terms of the lease, that's how things must stand" (244–45). Laurel, who heads a division of men at IBM, cannot believe that she has no rights in her own home: "There is no way that this conversation is taking place in my living room, with this man looking me straight in the face and telling me that I don't exist. That *I* don't live in this house" (245).

Laurel Dumont is one of three women whose lives Naylor contrasts in the novel. At one point, Laurel reflects on her relationship to the other two women: "In desperation, she thought about the two people who had come the closest to being called friends. The three of them formed a strange triangle where she was in the middle between a woman who admired her and a woman she admired" (240). The woman who admires her is Willa Nedeed, the last of the oppressed Nedeed wives. Willa is a contemporary woman who has accepted the traditional roles of wife and mother: "There was one woman who never went anywhere. She seemed so content nested down there at the end of Tupelo Drive. No, it was more than contentment, a certain smugness as if it were a privilege to wait hand and foot on that prude, Luther. She didn't want a life of her own" (240). Nedeed rewards his wife's devotion by locking her and their son in the basement. Her crime? She gave birth to a pale son who otherwise looked exactly like his father. During her stay in the basement, Willa studies the notes, photo albums, and recipes of the other Nedeed wives. Understanding these records of her foremothers' suffering helps her to find the key to her own existence:

> Willa Nedeed was a good mother and a good wife. For six years, she could claim that identity without any reservations. But now Willa Nedeed sat on a cot in a basement, no longer anyone's mother or anyone's wife. So how did that happen? She stared at the concrete steps leading up to the kitchen door. It happened because she walked down into this basement. . . . She was sitting there now, filthy, cold, and hungry, because she, Willa Prescott Nedeed, had walked down twelve concrete steps. And since that was the truth—the pure irreducible truth—whenever she was good and ready, she could walk back up. (279–80)

Even though her child is dead and her husband does not want her, Willa is determined to reaffirm her identity as a wife and mother. Having accepted responsibility for her plight, she ascends those twelve concrete steps, carrying her dead child in her arms, moving toward one final tragic union with the father and husband.

While Willa's acceptance of her identity leads, at least indirectly, to her

Figure 10.   Harvey Dinnerstein (1928–   ), *Maggy*, 1986
             (Collection of the Butler Institute of American Art,
             Youngstown, Ohio)

death, Laurel Dumont dies because she has lost her identity. Laurel is an eighties' woman, an overachiever who has risen so swiftly and effortlessly that she has never stopped to think about who she is, where she is going, and why she is going there. She has "lost herself in people's minds" and, like the long-dead Nedeed women, has only faded photographs and newspaper clippings to prove she exists:

> the Phi Beta Kappa pictures in her yearbook, front page of the *New York Times* business section, the bridal pictures in the Dumont family album. All before her twenty-fifth birthday, and in all of them she had been smiling. No wonder the world pronounced her happy, and like a fool she had believed them. Perhaps, just once, if she had failed a course, missed a plane connection, or glittered less at Howard's parties, she might have had time to think about who she was and what she really wanted, but it never happened. And when she finally took a good look around, she found herself imprisoned within a chain of photographs and a life that had no point. (228)

Like Clare Kendry and Helga Crane, Laurel feels trapped, imprisoned in her high-profile, loveless marriage, in her prestigious but unfulfilling job, and in her impressive but hollow house. And like Helga, she searches in vain for a place to belong, a home:

> Georgia wasn't her home, nor Cleveland or California. They had been only way stations that she had passed through. The thought of her dislocation was stifling; the number of places she couldn't claim, dizzying. She had stopped at them all only long enough to get her pictures taken. And just maybe if she could freeze reality around her now, she'd know where she belonged. And with that reference point—with any point at all—she could discover what had gone wrong. (233)

The place where Laurel feels least at home is 722 Tupelo Drive, the house "that defied all their efforts to transform it into that nebulous creation called a home" (227–28). Her house has an emptiness that even her music cannot fill, and she feels utterly alone there. Eventually, she stops trying to find a place for herself; she stops caring. Laurel escapes from her pain in the same way that Helga escaped the pain of childbirth; she retreats from reality. And finally, she chooses the ultimate escape, leaping to her death at the bottom of an empty swimming pool.

Ruth Anderson, the third woman in the triangle, finds a less destructive way to escape the Linden Hills trap. She divorces her respectable husband, moves to an unfashionable neighborhood, and marries a mentally unstable, working-class man. At first, Laurel pities her friend, but she soon learns to admire her:

> Strange, she had started calling out of pity for Ruth: a broken marriage and losing that house on Fifth Crescent Drive. And then remarrying a man who was a mental patient and worked in

factories—when he could work. But slowly, very slowly, she began to sense that Ruth was actually pitying her—as if Laurel were mired down there on Tupelo Drive and the best thing that could have happened to Ruth was that divorce and moving back to Wayne Avenue. Laurel kept calling because she admired that in the woman: the ability to pretend with such ease. No, she kept calling because she admired *that* woman, *that* ease. And she became the pretender. (240–41)

There is certainly much to admire in Ruth. She stays with Norman Anderson even when he succumbs to the "pinks" (much more frightening than the blues) and smashes everything around him. And although she lives in a seedy apartment with only the few pieces of furniture that Norman has not smashed, she has created a home: "Visitors found themselves thinking, What a nice feeling to be allowed into a home. And it *was* a home with its bare wood floors, dusted and polished, and with the three pieces of furniture that sat in three large rooms: one sofa in the living room, one kitchenette set with plastic-bottomed chairs on uncertain chrome legs, one bed" (33). The Anderson apartment is a home because it is filled with love rather than with material possessions. Ruth and Norman take care of each other, and they care for each other. Their love will survive because it exists outside Linden Hills.

Although Ruth rejects her society husband and the Linden Hills society, she is not punished for her rebellion. On the contrary, she is the only woman in the novel who has found love and even some happiness. And significantly, of the three women contrasted, she is the only survivor.

In *Linden Hills,* the outsiders survive while the society is destroyed, its foundation, the Nedeed home, burning to the ground with the last Nedeed heirs inside. Clearly, Gloria Naylor is taking the novel of manners in a new direction. Her novel rejects the value system of the society depicted and affirms the values of the individual, the nonconformist. Ruth Anderson has chosen love and compassion instead of material possessions and success. She has chosen happiness instead of stability and security. And she has chosen wisely. As Laurel suspects, the best thing that happened to Ruth was moving back to unfashionable Wayne Avenue. It took her away from the living death, the nothingness of life in Linden Hills.[13] In this new novel of manners, the best place for a lady is outside society.

Notes

1. In chapter 6 of *Vanity Fair,* Thackeray's narrator describes how the novel might have been written:

    We might have treated this subject in the genteel, or in the romantic, or in the facetious manner. Suppose we had laid the scene in Grosvenor Square, with the very same adventures—would not some people have listened? Suppose we had shown how Lord Joseph Sedley fell in love, and the Marquis of Osborne became attached to Lady Amelia, with the full consent of the Duke, her noble father: or instead of the supremely genteel, suppose we had resorted to the entirely low, and described what was going on in Mr. Sedley's kitchen;—how black Sambo was in love with the cook (as indeed he was), and how he fought a battle with the coachman in her behalf. (54)

2. See James W. Tuttleton 127 and Richard Chase 157–58.

3. For a discussion of the Talented Tenth novelists, see Robert Bone 29–50.

4. Later in the novel, Wharton demonstrates that her heroine has no other vocation. When Lily tries working in a millinery establishment, she is a failure, much too slow and clumsy to compete with the sallow-faced working-class women whom she has pitied. Similarly, in *Vanity Fair,* Amelia Sedley tries in vain to market the skills that she acquired at Miss Pinkerton's "academy for young ladies." When she tries to sell some of her art, the response is scornful: " 'Don't want 'em,' says one. 'Be off,' says another fiercely" (476).

5. In "New Directions for Black Feminist Criticism," Deborah E. McDowell points out that the dominant attitude toward women expressed in the "little" magazines of the Harlem Renaissance period was "strikingly consistent with traditional middle-class expectations of women" (192). Most contributors "emphasized that a woman's place was in the home."

6. In "Patterns of the Harlem Renaissance," George Kent says of Nella Larsen, "Her work suggests that she had taken more than passing notice of Henry James and Edith Wharton" (43). And in "Under the Harlem Shadow: A Study of Jessie Fauset and Nella Larsen," Hiroko Sato says, "Jessie Fauset's novels can be regarded as novels of manners of the Negro upper class" (67). See Sato 71 for a discussion of the differences between Fauset and Jane Austen.

7. One Fauset woman does marry a white man. In *Comedy: American Style,* Teresa Cary yields to the pressures of her mother, who insists upon trying to pass, and marries a Frenchman. Teresa, who gave up a black man too dark to pass, does not have a successful marriage.

8. In her introduction to Quicksand *and* Passing, Deborah E. McDowell says that Larsen is using "clothing as iconography" to capture the conflicts between Helga and Naxos (xviii). See also "New Directions for Black Feminist Criticism," 194. For a discussion of the use of "dress or decoration" in the novel of manners, see Lionel Trilling, "Manners, Morals, and the Novel," included in *The Liberal Imagination.*

9. In her introduction to Quicksand *and* Passing, McDowell says, "Like so many novels by women, *Quicksand* likens marriage to death for women" (xxi).

10. It is significant that Irene is called by her husband's last name while Clare is always Kendry, never Bellew, and Helga is called Mrs. or "Mis" Green only by other characters, never by the narrator. Clearly, Larsen does not sanction the marriages of Helga and Clare.

11. Naylor's first novel, *The Women of Brewster Place* (1983), focuses on the lower class.

12. Naylor plays with "up" and "down" throughout the novel. Because the more exclusive houses in Linden Hills are down the hill, people on the way up move down. But as these people are moving up (which is down), they are also going down physically, morally, and spiritually. And so when they reach the bottom of the hill, they have also reached the "bottom" spiritually: "And whenever anyone reached the Tupelo area, they eventually disappeared. Finally, devoured by their own drives, there just wasn't enough humanity left to fill the rooms of a real home, and the property went up for sale" (17–18). Clearly, the move down toward Tupelo Drive is a descent into hell.

13. The concluding sentence of Frazier's *The Black Bourgeoisie* provides an apt description of Linden Hills: "The black bourgeoisie suffers from 'nothingness' because when Negroes attain middle-class status, their lives generally lose both content and significance" (238).

Figure 11. William Gropper (1897–1977), *Anniversary*
(*Collection of the Butler Institute of American Art,*
Youngstown, Ohio)

11

The Detective Novel of Manners

Carolyn G. Heilbrun

Until the day before yesterday, I would have defined the detective novel of manners with ease and certitude: its roots were the British golden age, late Victorian and Edwardian, when the only people worth writing about spent sunny afternoons at garden parties and cricket games, with an occasional amateur foray into the world of unexpected and quite unacceptable crime. Its setting was among intelligent people, comfortably surrounded by examples of dull rectitude, living a life readily evoked and encompassed in a recognizable community, in which murder was as outrageous as it was unusual. This detective novel of manners was never set in a world of criminals devoid of upper-class moral or social principles; its major story never encompassed those outside the bounds of the gentry, aristocracy, professional, or upper-middle classes. I would have said, in short, that the detective novel of manners consisted precisely of that: manners, displayed in a world where certain modes of behavior were trustfully anticipated, and murder or any other crime was reprehensible chiefly because it amounted to a betrayal of that trust. Definitions of the novel of manners, such as those that the writers of the introduction to this volume quote and to which they take exception—where questions of "social convention" predominate— these certainly suit the detective novel of manners if not the novel of manners generally. The nature of the "self" is hardly foremost in the detective novel of manners, and Tuttleton's description, quoted by Brothers and Bowers in the introductory chapter, would, I think, have nicely served to define the detective novel of manners until the day before yesterday.

What I have determined since yesterday is that the detective novel of manners is dependent upon class, particularly as class is embodied in British culture, and cannot survive without it. From the adventures of Sherlock Holmes

Copyright Carolyn G. Heilbrun.

to those of P. D. James's Adam Dalgliesh, the detective novel of manners has depended upon and would have been inconceivable without the clear class demarcations of English society: prep schools, public schools, university, small villages with their clear, unquestioned social hierarchy, and above all everybody's knowing his or her place. Whether English class distinctions were as clear in life as they appear in literature I am not historian enough to say, but my reading of modern British literature and my experience of England after World War II certainly suggest that class was palpable in that society. Noel Annan, in an article on the Leavises and the Bloomsbury Group whom they despised and attacked, mentions that "[i]f we are to isolate the most important element in Leavis's make-up, we must use the referent in British society which provides so many clues to British behaviour. We must observe class differences" (32). Annan continues:

> Bloomsbury addressed themselves to the English clerisy, to the elite who had been educated at public schools and at Oxbridge, together with any who had climbed the educational and social ladder and had assimilated to the upper middle class. The eclecticism of their approach to literature and their hatred of insularity made them assume that any educated person spoke and read French and also probably German, and was thoroughly acquainted with Russian literature in translation. That he had read the Greek and Latin classics in the original went without saying. . . .
>
> Leavis, on the other hand, was the son of a piano-dealer in Cambridge who was a vigorous rationalist and republican. He came, therefore, from lower-middle-class non-conformist stock, and went to the local grammar school. (33)

One need hardly add that both the Leavises detested detective fiction, detective novels of manners most of all, and that Dorothy Sayers is unique in receiving critical attacks as violent as those the Leavises mounted against Bloomsbury and especially Virginia Woolf.

Today, when England has many immigrants from its lost Empire who are not native, not white, and not imbued with centuries-old class feeling, when even Oxbridge graduates affect the lower-class accent of the Beatles, we must remember that the detective novel of manners was born and flourished at a time when everyone in England was white, most were Protestant, the richest were Church of England, and all belonged naturally to the class in which they had been born, a class marked not only by pedigree but also by distinctions of speech, height, dress, and demeanor. (As Annan notes, that some few men, by means of scholarships, or some women, by means of marriage, might move up within the class structure was, in great part, made possible exactly by the specific mannerisms that characterized each class.) As a reviewer wrote of a biography of Anthony Eden, comparing Eden's wealthy boyhood with his abandoned family estate:

[W]hat had been spacious and elegant was now gaunt and vacantly lonely. . . . Was not this ruin symbolic of a society's failure to grasp the kind of economic adjustments required by the harsh environment of the 20th century? The disappearance of Britain's world power is one of the most remarkable and, for some, melancholy features of this century. The causes—strategic, economic, demographic, social, psychological—are so complex and tangled that they have yet to find their Gibbon. (Smith 12)

With the disappearance of Britain's world power went, as a kind of footnote, the disappearance of the detective novel of manners. In so far as it persists, for example in Adam Dalgliesh, who went to public school and publishes poetry, or in the characters of a writer like June Thomson, it pictures the historical remnant of the British class system. P. D. James writes of what remains and is sharply aware of what is gone, but she is not nostalgic; John Le Carré writes of what is gone, and his public school and University graduates, like their real-life counterparts, become spies for the communist world. The detective novel of manners ends with British world power.

Think of Sherlock Holmes. He has been to public school and university. He is entitled, by class, to consult with royalty and to enter the most exclusive clubs. He has an unearned income. He is, unmistakably, inevitably, a gentleman. That he is so talented at imitating other classes, and disguising himself as someone less endowed, underlines the distinctive qualities that must be assumed for purposes of identification. (Think, for a moment, of how much easier it was for a man to pretend to be a woman in those days, as in *Charley's Aunt*. When the sexes dressed totally differently, and women in voluminous and inhibiting garments, one had only to put on women's clothes to become a woman; in the days of unisex wear—tee shirts and blue jeans—the male is less easily disguised.) Holmes's cases and clients are so embedded in the class system that there is scarcely a Holmes story that would be possible in today's world. There are many reasons for the continued popularity of the Holmes stories, but one certainly is the historical evocation of a world for which no one but a fundamentalist could have nostalgia, but which, because it is unconsciously honest about the class arrangements, is true to its own time. Nostalgia has no part in it; what is operating is the eternal fantasy of the time machine.

Class is at the very heart of the detective novel of manners, and the detective novel ceases to be a novel of manners precisely when class ceases to operate. The American school of tough guys walking mean streets created by Hammett, Chandler, MacDonald, and others does not produce detective novels of manners, not because no one in them has any manners but because everyone can be anyone: as Tocqueville long ago noted, if a gold watch chain marks a gentleman, in America one can get a brass watch chain and claim to be a gentleman. The very concepts of noblesse oblige and behaving honorably toward ladies, however more honored in the breach than in the observance, are hallmarks of the behavior of a gentleman and would be simply funny in an

American tough-guy detective novel. Julian Symons, who admires the American detective novel while castigating the likes of Sayers with a righteous Marxist scorn, nonetheless sets a recent story published in the *Ellery Queen* magazine in 1987, in a home of the upper classes, complete with snooty lady, servants, and a proper tea. Class is the clue. Not to put too fine a point on it, as they used to say in British detective fiction of the golden age, I have reluctantly come to recognize a simple and disturbing fact: the detective novel of manners is a novel of the white middle and upper classes, and it is perfectly defined by those attributes the editors of this volume, with good reason, wish to deny for the novel of manners in general.

In 1981, Hanna Charney published a book entitled *The Detective Novel of Manners: Hedonism, Morality, and the Life of Reason.* Her introduction defines the detective novel of manners succinctly as embodying the "yearning for premodern forms, nostalgia for a society that has disappeared" (xi). I would argue only that nostalgia is the wrong word, and that what Charney calls "a society that never was but only seemed to be" is a misnomer. On the contrary, the class society of the detective novel of manners did exist but has now definitely disappeared. Future detective novels of manners, if any there shall be, will, for the first time, be nostalgic. Just as fundamentalists today in the United States, in Iran and other Islamic countries, and in Israel think that they can revive the world of "old values," so the new detective novel of manners will strive to fill a need that Charney believes is reasserting itself. "Through the distancing of irony and a sharp self-consciousness, and the concern to revive a tradition boldly but without obsolescence, the detective novel has adopted the format of the novel of manners. The detective novel of manners shapes its own society, where understanding of social and moral norms is expected" (Charney xi). Well, as I hope to show, not quite.

Charney quotes John Cawelti thus: "Readers of classical detective stories, we hypothesize, shared a need for a temporary release from doubt and guilt, generated at least in part by the decline of traditional moral and spiritual authorities, and the rise of new social and intellectual movements that emphasized the hypocrisy and guilt of respectable middle-class society." But she quotes only to refute him: "There is undoubtedly truth in Cawelti's ideas, but what these ideas may mean specifically is another matter. The reassurance of the middle class is so vague a principle that it is almost impossible to evaluate in sociological or historical terms" (xvi). Far from impossible, it is a nonvague fact of English life upon which what came to be known as the detective novel of manners rested. If Cawelti's "view cannot elucidate the catharsis that the detective novel provides" (xvi), that is not because he overestimates class but because Charney has moved beyond a discussion of the detective novel of manners. However cathartic and, indeed, profound these detective novels of manners were at their best, their profundity rested on a world as clearly marked by class as Hamlet's.

We must notice that Cawelti speaks of the "classical detective story," another name for the detective novel of manners, while Charney has slipped into defining the detective novel tout court. Her introduction concludes triumphantly: "Evading the siren songs of psychoanalytic and sociological interpretations, this study assumes that the detective novel exists as a separate entity in varied and innovative, but conventionally discernible forms" (xviii). The "detective novel," yes, but not the detective novel of manners.

The Iran-Contra hearings of recent memory are not unconnected with this point. Even while they continued daily to fascinate, trouble, and astound me, I read Robin Winks's new book *Cloak & Gown: Scholars in the Secret War, 1939–1961,* which is about the development of the secret service and the beginnings of covert actions by the United States. Winks, himself no mean analyzer of the detective novel, here recounts how the agencies responsible for America's covert operations were founded and almost entirely staffed by men who were among Yale's most prestigious alumni, many of them members of Skull and Bones or other exclusive Yale clubs. Clearly, for a time, men highly placed socially, and working through networks of those similarly endowed, hoped simultaneously to maintain their elite ambiance and to develop covert actions. I found this history compelling and shocking, as was the author's intention. Nor could one read it without recalling the upper-class Cambridge network from which emerged—in England—McLean, Burgess, Philby, Blunt, and others, no doubt, with as yet less familiar names. The upper classes in both countries, the elite, deserted their house parties and other elegant pursuits and went in for spying (though in the case of the Americans, it was mostly spying for the home side).

Winks's covert actions are no longer run by Skull and Bones chaps from Yale, understanding each other, but by the likes of Oliver North, a born-again Christian altogether outside of the world that inspired the classical detective novel, the one with "manners." Which is to say that the detective novel of manners is finished, or if appearing in spectral form, giving the clues of its own demise in the rapidity with which it dates. The novels of Dorothy Sayers, which may be called the epitome of the detective novel of manners, are not dated: they are historical manifestations of a real time, when the upper classes were the model to which the middle classes aspired, when the British Empire was (apparently) intact, and the classes were accepted naturally, as though ordained by heaven. Sayers's novels, like Conan Doyle's, are documents as historical as Austen's novels, or Trollope's, or Pym's, and if we read them now from nostalgia, they were written not from nostalgia but from conviction and confidence. They are the product of a certain class, race, and empire that is done forever.

The heir to the true detective novel of manners, as opposed to its imitators, is John Le Carré, who has written best of the manners of a dissolving class and faith. In *Tinker, Tailor, Soldier, Spy,* Le Carré's hero, George Smiley, must determine which of the men within the inner circle of England's highest spy operation is a "mole," a double agent working for the Russians. The mole turns out to be a graduate of Eton and Cambridge, who has come to hate England: "He spoke not of the decline of the West, but of its death by greed and constipation. He hated America very deeply, he said, and Smiley supposed he did. Haydon also took it for granted that secret services were the only real measure of a nation's political health, the only real expression of its subconscious" (355). Haydon goes on to explain how "in the war it scarcely mattered where one stood as long as one was fighting the Germans"—

> For a while, after '45, he said, he had remained content with Britain's part in the world, till gradually it dawned on him just how trivial this was. How and when was a mystery. In the historical mayhem of his own lifetime he could point to no one occasion; simply he knew that if England were out of the game, the price of fish would not be altered by a farthing. He had often wondered which side he would be on if the test ever came; after prolonged reflection he had finally to admit that if either monolith had to win the day, he would prefer it to be the East. (356)

Smiley, when he has finally caught Haydon, feels little more triumph than Marlow feels in *Heart of Darkness* when he has found Kurtz and watched him die. "Leaving King's Cross, [Smiley] had had a wistful notion of liking Haydon and respecting him: Bill was a man, after all, who had had something to say and had said it" (366)—an exact quotation, conscious or not, from *Heart of Darkness,* that early analysis of imperialism. And when Le Carré came to write *The Little Drummer Girl,* only his naïve heroine was from an English-speaking country, without principle or purpose. The rest is the struggle of the Middle East, Israel against the PLO: class, empire, and the playing fields of England are quite out of it. Compare this to the easy racism of Sayers's novels, the anti-Semitism and anti-Black assumptions. Sayers was without nostalgia. She wrote of a world she believed was the best there was, one that could happily be assumed to endure.

Adrienne Rich, writing of the poetry she had been taught was universal but which she had come to recognize as white, male, and upper-class, nonetheless knows that it is often beautiful despite its lying claims to being universal. So it is with the detective novel of manners in its true form.

What we have today are not true detective novels of manners: they are imitation, they are nostalgia, and they succeed, I believe, only when their narration is able to encompass simultaneously the lost world and a new world, understood and welcome. Charney writes that the "detective novel of manners shapes its own society, where understanding of social and moral norms is expected" (xi). "The illusion," Charney claims, "depends on the cooperation of reader and narrator" (xii).

True enough. And for the nostalgic reader, like the nostalgic writer, the detective novel of manners that persisted beyond the time of the English system of class and race and gender is a nostalgic fake, depending on the cooperation of reader and narrator to pretend that they are not indulging in something similar to the Harlequin romance. Let us take a favorite example of Charney's, Robert Bernard's *Deadly Meeting,* an academic novel published in 1970. It serves Charney as an example of the closed society of the detective novel of manners. Encouraged by her book to read it, I was amazed to discover an English department wholly male, with a chairperson openly racist. There is a scene set at an MLA convention at which all the participants are men, with the exception of nuns in clerical garb. True, an English woman medievalist of advanced years is imported as a temporary stopgap. But the book assumes that all applicants for faculty positions will be men; in short, what is called a detective novel of manners is in fact a true exercise in nostalgia for the reader, and a misreading of "manners" for the writer. Class, gender, race must be firmly in place for the detective novel of manners to be written. Less than two decades after its publication, this so-called detective novel of manners jolts the reader with its inaccuracies. True writers of detective novels of manners are never inaccurate or dated: they are historical. That both Austen and Sayers, in their differing ways, criticized and subverted the gender and social arrangements of their society in no way disproves this rule.

Are there, then, no detective novels of manners being written today? Let me, before answering that question, swerve from a discussion of class, imperative to the creation of a true detective novel of manners, to gender, a much more slippery concept, though certainly connected to class and, like class, barely detachable from the detective novel of manners. A feminist since the dawn of the women's movement, I have recently been forced to realize how upper-class (perhaps upper-middle-class), white, and privileged a revolution feminism was in its second-wave beginnings. Recently, the women's movement has had to expand to become as aware of class and race as of gender, or, as I prefer to put it, of gender as it is played out among other cultures, races, societies, and classes. Students of mine in graduate school, now much more ethnically diverse than was the case a decade or two back, are studying literature through the lenses of class and race as well as gender and discovering what Woolf knew in the late thirties: that imperialism, patriarchy, and fascism are intimately related. This is a concept properly terrifying to the middle and upper classes of America and Europe. In England, which gave birth to the detective novel of manners, feminism is often feared by the upper, educated classes, who see it as lesbian—that is, opposed to the heterosexual plot on which the class system and patriarchy generally rested; devoted to the third world, and thus opposed to white supremacy in any form; and Marxist, or opposed to the power of private wealth. The question of how gender affects, reforms, and rewrites the class system upon which the detective novel of manners depends remains to be answered. As Virginia Woolf might have put it before World War I, "behold, literature was an elderly gentleman in a grey suit talking about duchesses" (*Orlando* 280).

Perhaps the least discussed aspect of the detective novel of manners is the position and role of women in these novels. Nothing so distinguishes the English detective novel from the American as the presence in the English novels of women of extraordinary vitality, intelligence, and individuality. This, of course, reflects a similar development in the English mainstream novel, particularly if, as should happen, Henry James is included in that canon.

I have written elsewhere about the development of the independent woman in the British detective novel of manners, reaching from Wilkie Collins through the women writers of the golden age, and including prominent male writers like Nicholas Blake and Dick Francis. Even Sherlock Holmes encountered a woman who defeated him, perhaps uniquely in the canon, who wore men's clothes when convenience dictated and remained for him *the* woman, suggesting that even this bachelor and reputed misogynist honored women of independent mien who had the intention and ability to control their own lives. There is no question, however, of the class of these independent women from Collins to the death of Sayers: they are all upper, or upper-middle class. That class divisions are occasionally flouted, as in the marriage of Lord Peter Wimsey's sister to a policeman, serves to emphasize the enormity of such a break with tradition. What is clear is that the class structure of the detective novel of manners allowed the emergence of women in a way that neither the American detective novel nor English and American imitations of the detective novel of manners were able to do. Robert Bernard's *Deadly Meeting* fails because it mistook a passing condition for solid structure and did not perceive the changing attitudes that were already undermining what turned out to be an ahistorical rendition: the sort of book that, when women write it, we call old-fashioned.

That John Le Carré is not a writer of detective novels of manners is evident; that P. D. James is not is less so. She has fashioned after her first novel, as Le Carré did after his, a world she recognizes and portrays as in a state of social transformation. While her detective is upper-middle class (the son of a parson), and some of her characters are upper-upper, these last come to sticky ends, wishing for death and expecting destruction. Compare her novels with those of Ngaio Marsh, for example, whose detective is the brother of an ambassador, chillingly upper-class, if gracious, and whose social world, as someone said of Jane Austen's, lies still beneath her glass. Since Marsh was from New Zealand, it is well to recall that the colonies were even more tightly class structured than the homeland. P. D. James, though she is profoundly influenced by detective novels of manners, as Henry James was by Austen, is notable for getting into the minds of her male characters in a way no detective novel of manners ever did, portraying against their expressed principles their deep resentment of women and often their efforts to manipulate women sexually, to use or avoid them.

Not only is Dorothy Sayers the best representative of the detective novel of manners, but in *Gaudy Night,* her most feminist novel and the one most rigorously attacked by the Leavises, she presents, without for a moment threatening the class structure, a rare community of women. I have heard many men sneer at this community, but for women it remains after fifty years encouraging and unique. In *Gaudy Night,* Sayers is writing, as Lee Edwards put it, of and for "an elite, an heroic cadre, a class of educated women (to use Virginia Woolf's phrase) whose education and intelligence demand that they choose, and that they understand their choice and its consequences" (295). She is not writing of those who have no choice. Choice is, indeed, the whole point of *Gaudy Night.* And choice is available only to those with the money and condition to make it. (That most women with the money and condition choose not to choose is true, but not the subject I am pursuing here.) P. D. James has written: "Like all good writers [Sayers] created a unique and instantly recognizable world into which we can still escape for our comfort, hearing again with relief and nostalgia her strongly individual, amused and confident voice" (xiii). But, she adds, "those of us who first enjoyed and were influenced by Dorothy L. Sayers in our youth, . . . still read her with something more than nostalgia" (xvi). American women read her with something more than nostalgia, since they can scarcely be nostalgic for something they have never had, nor even had the possibility of having in the years before 1970: the community of women scholars in Shrewsbury College in *Gaudy Night.*

Nina Auerbach has written: "The women of Shrewsbury—unlike many manless women in literature. . . . —are not defined by negation; they are seen vigorously, in terms of what they have, not of what they lack. . . . No other academic novel that I know of captures so well the fun that peers out from the methodological rigor and high seriousness of academic life, and the exhilarating privilege of belonging to it" (188). In the years following the publication of *Gaudy Night,* it continued to tell the only story available in which women lived lives defined not by negation, not by their lack of men, but by their commitment to and love for the work they had chosen, and their friendship and respect for one another. It is of the utmost importance to remember that the solution to the mystery of *Gaudy Night* does not involve massive ingenuity, but only a freedom on the part of the investigators from the internalization of sexual myths. It is, I believe, for this reason that it is not only necessary but wholly correct historically that Lord Peter should solve the mystery. For it is women, even women like Harriet Vane, who internalize the long-lived theories of women's dependence upon men and the accompanying doubts of female capacities, more than do highly intelligent and sensitive men, rare as these may be. Were Sayers writing today, Vane would be her own detective. But Sayers's novel is historically accurate about the complex ambiguities of educated women even as she created the only example of a true women's community.

Lord Peter, in propounding his solution to the mystery, understood the uniqueness of the Shrewsbury community. He says: the "one thing which frustrated the whole attack from first to last was the remarkable solidarity and public spirit displayed by your college as a body. I think that was the last obstacle that X expected to encounter in a community of women. . . . There was not a woman in this Common Room, married or single, who would be ready to place personal loyalties above professional honour" (ch. 22). And when, in Lee Edwards's words, "Annie attacks . . . the Shrewsbury community, she does so in the name of the old ideology of love" (186). But no one in the book attacks the ideology of class: quite the contrary. Sayers's vaunted defense of each person's doing her or his "proper job" was another way of reinforcing the Victorian concept of each adhering to the position in which it had pleased God to place one.

Let me here compare two episodes, one written by Virginia Woolf, the other by Sayers. Woolf, you will remember from *A Room of One's Own,* was wandering, lost in her thoughts, at Cambridge:

> It was thus that I found myself walking with extreme rapidity across a grass plot. Instantly a man's figure rose to intercept me. Nor did I at first understand that the gesticulations of a curious-looking object, in a cut-away coat and evening shirt, were aimed at me. His face expressed horror and indignation. Instinct rather than reason came to my help; he was a Beadle; I was a woman. This was the turf; there was the path. Only the Fellows and Scholars are allowed here; the gravel is the place for me. Such thoughts were the work of a moment. (5–6)

Here is Dorothy Sayers, from a letter to an Oxford friend written during the Easter break of 1913:

> The exam was so funny—I was the only woman taking it, and sat, severely isolated like a leper, in one corner of the T-room at the Schools, while the men occupied a quite different branch of it. The first day while looking for my desk, I wandered into the men's part of the room, whereupon the old chap who sees you settled (not the invigilator but the door-keeper sort of person) rushed at me with wildly waving arms and a terrified expression, and shooed me away to my seclusion like an intrusive hen.

You will have noted that Woolf, in 1928, and Sayers, in 1913, both knew "by instinct" what the trouble was at Cambridge and Oxford alike: they were women. Yet, Woolf's book was designed to challenge the class system, not only on behalf of women but also on behalf of working-class men whose chance to become great English writers was almost as bad as if they had been born female. Sayers's book, a genuine detective novel of manners, wishes to readjust the positions and expectations of women already enabled to receive an Oxbridge education.

Do I mean to assert that there will be no more detective novels of manners? Yes, unless we allow the definition to be so rubbery that it will fit any community with a clearly defined set of manners, in which case we should have detective novels of manners about the Mafia or about the members of municipal trade unions. The stories, for example, of whistle blowers, who go against the mores of their tribe, are profound and moral stories, but they are not detective novels of manners. The essential ingredient in detective novels of manners is class—and the unthinking acceptance of one's own class not only as having leisure, money, a certain education, and a clear path to the corridors of influence and power but also as deserving these privileges and seeing them as productive of a good world, perhaps the best possible world.

The feminist element in true detective novels of manners has perhaps been one of the attractions of this genre for the current generation of writers of detective fiction. If women writers are drawn to Peter Wimsey, his feminism is a large part of his appeal. The same can be said of the heroes and heroines of writers like Nicholas Blake, before he reverted to conventional English misogyny, Dick Francis, Robert Parker, and P. D. James. P. D. James has not only created a female private eye, Cordelia Gray, who is classless, however much her tasks may lie with the upper-middle classes, but also Kate Miskin, an equally classless policewoman from James's *A Taste for Death*. Similarly, the women police detectives, private eyes, and amateur sleuths created now and in recent years by women writers have been influenced by the English detective novels of manners, but these authors are not writing in that outmoded genre. It is questionable whether even a dyed-in-the-wool reactionary could write in that genre; even the most narrow-minded of the rich must perceive, if only dimly, that they are no longer the class that runs their world, and that entrance to any world—jet set, Brahmin, or Mayflower descendent—is possible to those with enough money, ambition, and what even the elegant today call chutzpah.

As for the traditional, tough-guy, nonfeminist, antiwoman American detective novel, that has never been a detective novel of manners. If those who eschew this genre of violence still write detective novels of moral people able to conceive of a moral universe, fighting for what seems right even when the system offers no rewards for such courage, they may be in the process of creating a new genre. The ancestry of that genre may include the detective novels of manners, but as with most ancestors, the influence will be fleeting and more and more difficult to recognize as time goes by.

Figure 12.   Chuck Close (1940–   ), *Georgia*, 1984
              (Collection of the Butler Institute of American Art,
              Youngstown, Ohio)

Conventions of Comedies of Manners and British Novels about Academic Life

John Wilkinson

If there are not so many approaches to *comedy of manners* as there are readers, there is yet sufficient variety of approach to cast doubt on the viability of any one interpretation, especially of an attempt to embrace examples of both drama and the novel separated by a gap of two hundred and fifty years. Nevertheless, it is my intention to show that the mode of Restoration comedies of manners can be found in a special type of novel of manners: contemporary British novels about academic life. Generally, I take it that *comedy of manners* identifies a literary mode the end of which is laughter and the substance of which concerns bourgeois social behavior. It is not melodrama, not farce, not satire, but may contain elements of these. It concerns bourgeois behavior since its protagonists are, in Restoration comedy, upper-middle class, nonworking yet nonaristocratic; and in British comic novels about academic life, educated people who are either already established as members of a bourgeoisie or who are seeking or repudiating membership. Essentially, both forms seem artificial rather than realistic, and in both the artificiality is a result of deliberate acts of exclusion, with what is excluded bringing pressure to bear on the artifice.

Although, as John T. Harwood points out in *Critics, Values, and Restoration Comedy*, arguments about Restoration comedies fall into two broad categories—whether the plays depend upon artifice or are mimetic—the two positions are not mutually exclusive. Both Restoration comedies and novels about academic life depend upon sets of conventions that presuppose audience tolerance for those conventions, and it is as important to understand that the artificiality of the plays and novels is a surface underneath which lie sharply observed studies of social life as it is to see that although both concern life in their respective contemporary worlds, they do so in a manner belied by surface frivolity. Since the "devices" of the plays and novels, their appearing to be artifice rather than mimesis, are apparent first, however, it makes good sense to look at the surface artifice before discussing what lies underneath.

The surface conventions of Restoration comedy are readily apparent and have been extensively recorded and discussed. That discussion need not be repeated here. Generally, the devices are evident in the comically exaggerated behavior of characters in plots that depend upon the complications attendant on seduction, disguise, and deceit. Behavior is often signaled by appropriate names. Old men, like Pinchwife in Wycherley's *The Country Wife* or like Sir Cautious Fulbank and Sir Feeble Fainwood of Aphra Behn's *The Lucky Chance*, are often jealous and avaricious. Situations, also, are stock ones. Young men are eager to seduce the daughters of the old. By convention, marriage is depicted as a stultifying experience best avoided. It is in order to escape such dullness that Millamant, vowing she will be "solicited to the very last, nay, and after-wards" (4.1.180–81), advances a series of requests in Congreve's *The Way of the World* before accepting Mirabell. Another convention of the plays is styl-ized, witty dialogue. Characters can often be divided on the basis of their wittiness into those likely to succeed and those eager to give the appearance of success, those who have wit triumphing over those who are pretenders to wit. Mirabell and Millamant possess wit and exercise it to the end of a marriage combined with the pleasures attendant upon an assured inheritance. On the other hand, Petulant and Witwoud, as their names suggest, lack wit and are the objects of the witticisms of others; they help define the nature of true wit by manifesting its opposite. As a true wit, Mirabell successfully schemes to gain Millamant without offending her guardian aunt; Petulant and Witwoud, however, lack true wit and scheme to no advantage.

Parallel devices can be found in British comic novels about academic life (called "campus novels" by David Lodge in "Robertson Davies and the Campus Novel" and by J. I. M. Stewart in his short story "Two Strings to His Bow"). In part, such devices are the result of comic writing that depends for some of its success on caricature and that, as in the plays, relies on deftness of plotting, the artifice of which leads to contrasts, turns, and surprises to comic effect. Not all of these novels are alike; neither are Restoration comedies. Tom Sharpe's novels about Wilt are more farcical than Kingsley Amis's *Lucky Jim* or John Wain's *Hurry on Down*. Nor do the novels use all of the devices associated with Restoration comedy. Some stock situations appear in other guises—for exam-ple, conflict between youth and age appears under the guise of conflict between the untenured and the established or between orthodox and fashionable writers, as in Lodge's *Changing Places* and *Small World*. There are sufficient devices in common, however, to establish a connection and to show that the two share at least surface similarities.

Caricature is the most apparent feature the novels share with the plays. *Wilt on High* and *Wilt* present caricatured Americans. In *Coming from Behind* (Howard Jacobson), Nick Lee, reminiscent of a Petulant in his apparent business, shares an office with Sefton Goldberg but is never available: "He kept a briefcase permanently on his desk and one of his jackets permanently over his chair so that by re-arranging them three or four times a day Sefton was able to make it appear that Nick was around somewhere but had just popped out—in all probability to the library" (25). Attached to the office door is "the usual message from Nick Lee explaining that he wasn't going to be able to get in today," with graded papers and reading lists available along with "detailed instructions for reaching him, should there be anything he was urgently required to talk over, via letter, telegram, telephone, telex and long wave radio" (101). Likewise, Wrottesley Polytechnic has a mysterious administrator, a Dr. Sidewinder: "No one knew who had appointed him. No one knew in which part of the building he had his room or what his secretary was called or what his internal telephone number was. No one knew how, officially, to address him, or in what place and on what matters" (32).

In Restoration comedies, names indicate character. The same device appears in the novels. Sharpe's *The Wilt Alternative* has a troublesome Mrs. De Fracas as a central character. Sometimes matters are more complex, however. In Malcolm Bradbury's *Rates of Exchange,* identification of name and character is combined with a Saussurian joke. The name on Petworth's luggage tag becomes his sign (48) and as parole is variously rendered as Pervert, Petworthim, Petwurt, Petwit, Patwat. About to deliver a lecture on the "English Language as a Medium of International Communication," he is introduced as Doctor Petworthi, a sociologist (190). In Jacobson's *Coming from Behind,* when Sefton Goldberg applies for a Disraeli Fellowship, he is interviewed by the Master of Holy Christ Hall, Woolfardisworthy, a man with a smell "of freshness—extreme immaculateness of flesh—and antiquity, not of person, but as it were of genealogy, of line" (164), who with unconscious anti-Semitism refers to him first as Goldman and then as Bergmann.

Such relationships, as I have pointed out, are surface parallels, matters of artifice, of comic structure. Concentration on those features and on eccentricities of character is an injustice to the plays and the novels, however, for it bypasses the extent to which both, as comedies about manners, suggest social ills evident beneath the surface. Critical emphasis upon the artifice exaggerates the farcical at the expense of the meaningfully comic. Restoration writers, at least, were careful to maintain a distinction between comedy and mere farce. Dryden, for example, argued in the "Preface to *An Evening's Love or, the Mock Astrologer"* that although comedy consisted of "low persons," it dealt with "such humours, adventures, and designs, as are to be found and met with in the world" (1:135–36), a criterion of "readability" he also appealed to in the epilogue he contributed to Etherege's *The Man of Mode.* It is an argument that allows simultaneously for caricature-like presentation and for the meaningfulness that separates comedy from farce. Indeed, underneath the surface conventions and the exaggerated behavior for comedy's sake lies a recognizable world the unpleasantness of which may, as it is glimpsed, run counter to the surface jollity, and it is this dissonance that such critics as Laura Brown and Rose Zimbardo have emphasized in their attention to the satiric elements in the Restoration plays. Although, then, the plays and the novels are funny, both also have more to them; both illustrate Aphra Behn's contention that it is not enough to make an audience laugh (Schneider 10, n.19).

In the Restoration comedies, unpleasantness and social maladies are generally evident in four areas. These are old age and its tyrannical hold over what the young seek; widowhood and its insecurity; violence between the sexes; and deceit.

The old are neither merely impotent, grumbling people nor conventional, comically removable obstacles in the path of romance. As Ben Ross Schneider explains, they tend to be avaricious: "[A]varice is more than a stage convention and rebellion against parents is more than simple insubordination. What we see again and again is a greedy parent forcing a generous child to marry an obnoxious person for money" (52). Lady Wishfort, for instance, with her heavily powdered face that threatens to crack, is an object of amusement, but she is also the grasping old person against whom the lovers must contend. The power she exercises within her household as the guardian of Millamant's finances is tyrannical.

There is more to Lady Wishfort, though, than this tyranny. Because she is a widow, she faces threats that have a real-life counterpart. Like contemporary Restoration women, as Pat Rogers explains, she would "[enjoy] minimal legal rights with regard to property and the like" (*Augustan Vision* 89). Women, he writes, "had few civic opportunities, no professional openings." Although with marriage "[t]heir social place was secure, or as secure as their husband's, . . . it does not seem to have struck them that this was a feebly vicarious hold on status" (89). Lady Wishfort has perceived that her grasp on her property is tenuous, and her behavior, then, is not a matter of caricature. Because she is a widow, that grasp is all that assures her status. Additionally, as Rogers argues, though murder was the crime that most horrified and fascinated the Victorians, for an inhabitant of Lady Wishfort's London the crime most feared was theft, reflecting, he writes, "the importance of property as a force in society" (99). In part, then, Lady Wishfort is to be laughed at, in part feared, and in part pitied, because she is aware of her insecure hold over her life and over her property. She serves to reveal, beneath the surface of the comedy directed against her foolish reception of the advances of the disguised Waitwell, the fear and insecurity of age and widowhood.

Moreover, relationships between the sexes can be violent and cruel in the plays. Pinchwife, in *The Country Wife,* appears, at first, as a type—the jealous old man—married to another type—the naïve country girl. His anxious protection of Margery from predatory London gallants is comic, yet his outburst in act 4, scene 2 is not merely the exercise of rights over what he calls his "freehold" (2.1.360): "Write as I bid you, or I will write 'whore' with this penknife in your face" (110–11). In *The Man of Mode,* Dorimant's behavior reveals a similar nastiness. His rejection of Loveit at first characterizes the indifference of the bored (and perhaps charming) roué. He says that "next to the coming to a good understanding with a new mistress, I love a quarrel with an old one" (1.1.216–18). Loveit's anger is not so amusing, though, for her words reveal her devastation:

DORIMANT. Spare your fan, madam, you are growing hot, and will want it to cool you.

MRS. LOVEIT. Horror and distraction seize you, sorrow and remorse gnaw your soul, and punish all your perjuries to me—*(Weeps).* (2.2.178–80)

Finally, the convention of disguise may reveal deceit. In Aphra Behn's *The Lucky Chance,* schemes involving disguise are successful because, by convention, disguises are always impenetrable. Likewise, those who should see through them are not perceptive. Bellmour plays Sir Feeble Fainwood's returning nephew in order to pay court to Sir Feeble's bride-to-be, Leticia. Later, he will appear before Sir Feeble as the ghost of himself. Gayman succeeds in hiding himself in the guise of a Mr. Wasteall. Bredwell, Leticia's brother, disguises himself as a devil on two occasions and appears once draped in a sheet to scare Sir Cautious and Sir Feeble out of their wits so that Gayman can enter Lady Fulbank's bedroom. The fop Bearjest loves Sir Feeble's daughter, Diana, but since she is claimed by Bredwell, he is married to Julia's maidservant, Pert, disguised as Diana. This is a great deal of frothy activity. Underneath it, however, is a world of arranged marriage, of adultery, of capricious exercise of power; and the amusing convention of disguise comes to signal deceit and treachery. Like Pinchwife, Sir Feeble is the "nauseous thing" of "an old man turned lover," as Leticia refers to him (1.3), but he is also the tyrant who arranged to promulgate the false news of Bellmour's death in Holland and who has in his possession, hidden away, Bellmour's pardon.

In the novels, the equivalents to those fearful and grasping worlds of the Restoration plays are problems and despairs sometimes peculiar to the academic world, sometimes suggestive of more intransigent post-World War II malaise. The novels show that underneath the comic surface all is not well. The following address by Morris Zapp, for example, is an instance of that contrast between wit and nonwit found in Restoration comedies, but it also serves to identify the uneasiness of a provincial academic community. Zapp explains that he "began a commentary on the works of Jane Austen, the aim of which was to be utterly exhaustive, to examine the novels from every conceivable angle—historical, biographical, rhetorical, mythical, structural, Freudian, Jungian, Marxist, existentialist, Christian, allegorical, ethical, phenomenological, archetypal, you name it" (Lodge, *Small World* 24). In keeping with the latest in critical theory, however, he has abandoned the project because *"every decoding is another encoding"* (25), so that a search for meaning is only an act of vanity. This remarkable instance of critical chutzpah and industry comically and conclusively demonstrates Zapp's superior wit. The reaction to his speech is one of puzzlement and anger, however, and this exposure of his audience's lesser wit also reveals the intellectual uneasiness of that audience.

This uneasiness is partly intellectual in origin, partly a matter of place. Restoration plays often oppose the delights of London life to the implied horrors of rustication. Occasionally, this contrast is purely comic. In *The Way of the World,* arriving from out of town, Sir Wilful Witoud is abused by Petulant for entering in boots. At the same time, Sir Wilful laments that Lady Wishfort should sleep late. Rural and urban values are both neatly lampooned, the joke depending upon a convention: London life is superior even while it is self-indulgent. In the campus novels, that felt superiority of London life over life in the provinces becomes the equally strongly felt superiority of Oxbridge, so that in *Small World,* life in the provinces presents instances of embarrassment that compound the intellectual uneasiness of Zapp's audience. The conference of University Teachers of English Language and Literature on the Rummidge campus at which Morris Zapp speaks is not full of filthy-booted participants, but those attending are housed in dormitories where "[e]ach room had a washbasin, though not every washbasin had a plug, or every plug a chain. Some taps could not be turned on, and some could not be turned off" (3). Other shortcomings of provincial life are evident in a sightseeing trip that does not go well: "the owners of George Eliot's childhood home had not been warned in advance, and would not let them inside the house, so they had had to content themselves with milling about in the garden and pressing their faces to the windows. Then Ann Hathaway's cottage proved to be closed for maintenance" (50).

Such instances of embarrassment, professional and circumstantial, would not in themselves amount to a great deal were they not two elements of a pattern identifying absurdity and despair widespread in the academic world. Jacobson describes Sefton Goldberg observing how Woolfardisworthy and his colleagues in Jacobson's *Coming from Behind* become caricature Oxbridge academics when they go in to dinner. Woolfardisworthy himself "began to take on an inky, careless look" (171) for the benefit of the students. Sefton Goldberg, though, is eager to participate in that comic drama of inky carelessness. He feels trapped at Wrottesley Polytechnic and spends most of his time filling out application forms for almost any other job in academe. In the novels by Tom Sharpe, his hero Wilt, employed in the department of Liberal Studies, has to exercise constant ingenuity catering to day-release apprentices indifferent to education. Although by the end of *Wilt* he has become the new head of Liberal Studies, Wilt is faced in *The Wilt Alternative* with budget cuts, and in *Wilt on High*, he has trouble explaining the function of his department to the County Advisor on Communication Skills (14–18). Ideals about "relevance" have led Wrottesley Polytechnic, at which Goldberg teaches, to offer lunchtime lectures on the "Microprocessor and You" and to try reaching the public through "sculptural forms in the Faculty of Purposeful Art and Design" (*Coming from Behind* 99). Although the proposed alliance of Wrottesley Polytechnic with Wrottesley Football Club in the same novel is a farcical nightmare, it has behind it the fundraising needs of an administration unmindful of education. Administrative regulations can be as bizarre as those in D. J. Enright's *Academic Year,* in which a decision is made that all examination-containing envelopes have to be signed with a red pencil, though no such pencil is available (193). Moreover, the academic life is evidently a financially impoverished one. Philip Swallow leads a life of genteel poverty in both of Lodge's novels.

Given the barely concealed sense of frustration and despair behind these matters, it is not surprising that some of the teachers should be as eccentric as Enderby in Anthony Burgess's *The Clockwork Testament, or Enderby's End,* reacting to administrative indifference to academic needs on one side and to impenetrable torpor on the part of students on the other. Beset by cultural philistinism at home and at college, in a moment of bleak insight Henry Wilt chooses *The Wind in the Willows* to illustrate English culture. The novel, he says facetiously,

> gives the finest description of English middle-class aspirations and attitudes to be found in English literature. You will find that it deals entirely with animals, and that these animals are all male. The only women in the book are minor characters, one a bargewoman and the others a jailer's daughter and her aunt, and strictly speaking they are irrelevant. The main characters are a Water Rat, a Mole, a Badger and a Toad, none of whom is married or evinces the slightest interest in the opposite sex. (*The Wilt Alternative* 35)

In like manner, and for like reasons of felt worthlessness, Sefton Goldberg teaches that the major English novelists are "Bulwer Lytton, Charles Lever, Harrison Ainsworth, Mrs. Henry Wood, and Angela Carter," while the greatest poets are "Francis Quarles and Namby-Pamby Philips" and the "greatest living critic . . . Bernard Levin" (39).

Finally, teachers in the novels labor under administrations that alienate them. The following exchange from *Wilt on High* between the Principal of the Technical College and Dr. Board shows the latter deliberately refusing to understand administrative language. Basically, Sharpe is using a device also found in the plays, opposition of wit to lack of wit. The committee meeting has replaced the London townhouse setting:

> "What puzzles me in the present instance is [the] use of the phrase 'real-time contact hours.' Now according to my vocabulary . . ."
>
> "Dr. Board," said the Principal, wishing to God he could sack the man, "what we want to know is quite simply the number of contact hours the members of your department do per week."
>
> Dr. Board made a show of consulting a small notebook. "None," he said finally. (3)

The episode is shrewdly observed and presented. The threat to the department is a familiar one, consisting in an administrative request for statistical evidence in language that obscures as it attempts to define. At the same time, the episode captures with exactness the pain associated with the codification of teaching's intangibles. The episode also suggests the looming and miasmic presence of a bureaucracy that has alienated those it seeks to control. The bureaucracy, in turn, represents one among many systems that fail to understand, and therefore threaten, Wilt's sanity.

The comic "worlds" of the novels and plays so far mentioned suggest other, less amusing worlds in which, in the instance of the plays, disguise and intrigue become deceit and in which, in the novels, the caricature of academic eccentricity becomes symptomatic of massive indifference. These comic worlds remain self-contained, however, demonstrating the truth of Dryden's argument that comedy deals with matters that may be "found and met with in the world," so that comedy brings actualities to mind. Provided that such a person as Wilt survives his hassles with the academic bureaucracy, police, wife, terrorists, and Americans, the reader can rest assured that somehow this larger world has not triumphed. These fictive and comic worlds of the plays and novels are very small, however, and in that smallness their fragility is evident. The worlds of the plays and novels endure despite, but under pressure from, threats to their continued existence.

These threats are of two kinds. First are those glimpsed as they are revealed from within the comic world itself. Such threats are contained, sometimes with difficulty, by resolution of the comic plot, so that the reader feels satisfied that difficulties have been overcome and problems settled. Second are those threats that derive from the larger world of which the fictive world represents only a very small part. These difficulties are not solved and are not capable of being absorbed by the comic world.

The difference between those works that suggest outside threat and yet manage to control it and those that are barely able to contain it can be shown by comparing *The Country Wife* to *The Way of the World*. In the former, Horner's threat to the social stability represented by marriage is restricted to the world of the play because the premise that a supposed castrato can entertain the disaffected wives of the gentry is sufficiently fantastic that it has reality only for the characters within the play itself. Although Pinchwife's cruel rage reminds us of actual domestic violence, the context of that rage counters the possibility of its being mistaken for actuality; the premise of the play has no readily perceived equivalent in reality. Sharpe's novels are roughly parallel to *The Country Wife* because Wilt lives in a world as fantastic as that of Pinchwife. Social horrors are not excluded, but they are brought to mind by the comic action; the comedy itself is primary. Fainall's aggressive needs in *The Way of the World,* on the other hand, bring into view a world that does threaten the comic. Although as a schemer and a deceptive man, and in his disdain for his wife and pursuit of Mrs. Marwood, Fainall might seem to be a character type, his threat to blackmail Lady Wishfort is outside the play's comic world; it constitutes true viciousness and greed in the context of a play that has otherwise only suggested real urgencies behind the intrigue: "You shall submit your own Estate to my management, and absolutely make over my Wife's to my sole use. . . . This, my Lady *Wishfort,* must be subscrib'd, or your darling Daughter's turn'd adrift, like a leaky hulk to sink or swim, as she and the Current of this lewd Town can agree" (5.1.476–88). Fainall's speech makes vivid the tenuousness of Lady Wishfort's hold on her property. It also demonstrates the fragility of the world of manners itself. Fainall threatens the viability of that exclusive artificial world, his speech affecting us like the information that within a world of sylphs, gnomes, and "cosmetic powers" in "The Rape of the Lock," "wretches hang that jury-men may dine." It forces us to judge the value of what is otherwise presented.

Even so, Fainall's is a threat to the comic world from inside, deriving from a character within the mannered and comic world. As such, it represents only one kind of pressure under which the comic world struggles. The comic realms of both Restoration drama and the academic novel of manners are also pressured from outside worlds that run counter to the enclosed world of mannered behavior and that define its smallness. In some instances, this outside world might be seen as part of the background of a work against which the comic plot is worked out. In other cases, the outside world consists of what has been excluded, and its absence delineates the small, mannered worlds of the works in question. In yet others, that outside world is part of the work but actively in conflict with the mannered world.

In Bradbury's *Rates of Exchange,* Petworth smuggles a novel out of Slaka in a briefcase that is accidentally unloaded at Frankfurt, taken for an incendiary device, and blown up by the authorities. The incident is grimly comic. Given that Bradbury wanted the novel to be lost, he clearly could have chosen other means of disposal. Since *Rates of Exchange* is about a linguist in a world having linguistic troubles, postal confusion over addresses would not have been inappropriate. The means of disposal of the novel, in other words, is deliberate. As an unpleasant act of destruction, the blowing up of the briefcase serves to define the preciosity of the academic world Petworth inhabits. Whatever the deficiencies of his private world and of the amusing problems associated with the odd gaps between *langue* and *parole,* they appear of little moment against the brutality of terrorism. Moreover, when he begins his British Council journey, Petworth leaves a London that provides examples of widespread shabbiness contrasting to the privileged world of Petworth the linguist:

> The bus pulls out into Sunday London streets, past pizza places, topless sauna parlours, unisex jeans outlets. Vandalism marks the spaces, graffiti the walls, where the council pulls down old substandard housing to replace it with new substandard housing. "Fly poundstretcher to Australia," cry the posters by the flyover, shining with sweatless girls in bikinis, drinking drinks with ice in other people's bright sunshine; rain falls over factories which stand empty with broken windows. (21–22)

The novel opens, then, in unpleasant shabbiness and concludes with an act of destruction necessitated by contemporary politics.

All works of art must exclude. The world of Restoration comedy is especially exclusive, though. Lamb, as Harwood points out, was able to praise the artifice of Restoration comedy by "denying any possible connection between Restoration life and his own London life" (37). The point is not, however, that the comedies are artificial by contrast to the world as perceived by a critic of a later time period, but that they are artificial because they are deliberately exclusive. That deliberately excluded world constitutes the second of the pressures on the mannered comic world.

The characters of Restoration comedies, with the exception of the servants and some few others such as the orange-woman and shoemaker of *The Man of Mode,* lack occupations and constitute a privileged group. Among the principal characters of *The Way of the World,* only the pretender to wit, Witwoud, has worked, as clerk to an attorney, and he is the object of Petulant's scornful amusement as a result. Judging by Pat Rogers's summary of the census made by Gregory King in the 1690s, the moneyed and nonworking types who inhabit the world of Restoration comedies would indeed represent a small fraction of the populace: "Out of a total population for England and Wales of five and a half million, [King] allots no less than 1,300,000 to the families of 'cottagers and paupers', with a close runner-up in the shape of 'labouring people and outservants', whose families comprised 1,275,000 persons." To be added to these groups, Rogers reports, there were 750,000 farmers, 700,000 "lesser freeholders," 280,000 larger freeholders, 240,000 artisans, 200,000 "shopkeepers, tradesmen, and innkeepers," and 220,000 making up the families "of common soldiers and seamen." Vagrants totaled 30,000; merchants, 60,000 (10).

None of these people need be included in a play, of course, but the census does reveal the extent to which the plays depict a small minority of especially favored people. The width of this gap between the propertied and others is illustrated in the comment by Rogers that "[i]t is not till we reach the 'better sort' of freeholders that the average income per household is put as high as £84" (11). By contrast, Gayman gambles £300 against Sir Cautious's wife for a single night in *The Lucky Chance*.

Both *Lucky Jim* and *Hurry on Down* are novels in which the impact of a large underclass can be felt. Both novels focus upon characters who represent this underclass, and both concern class distinctions. Such matters are also part of the other novels—Wilt's students are obviously working-class, as are Sefton Goldberg's. Petworth teaches in a Bradford college, and Swallow shares the provincial values evident in other novels by Lodge: *Ginger, You're Barmy, Out of the Shelter, The British Museum Is Falling Down*. Packet, in D. J. Enright's *Academic Year*, is from an impoverished "Methodist family" (41), and Louis Bates, in Bradbury's *Eating People Is Wrong*, is a working-class intellectual. Yet, in the novels by Amis and Wain, action is so motivated by differences of class that the world of "old-style unhurried academic privilege," to use Howard Jacobson's phrase from *Coming from Behind* (100), not only is threatened by an intrusive lower-class world or by disturbing changes in professional life but also has become the object of scorn and anger. The characteristics of the two novels are in part those identified by Lodge in the introduction to the reissue of *Ginger, You're Barmy*, in which he discusses briefly the Angry Young Man novel and lists its dominant features: "gritty realism, exact observation of class and regional differences in British society, a lower middle or working-class perspective, anti-establishment attitudes, hostility to all forms of cant and pretentiousness, a fondness of the first-person, confessional narrative technique" (5). *Ginger, You're Barmy*, based on Lodge's own National Service experiences, is a record of class distinctions within the mindlessness of army life. It is also a record of the disappointment felt in post–World War II England because of the failure of hoped-for social change: "meritocrats produced by free grammar schools and free university education were apt to find that the old-boy network, the lines of power and influence that connected London, Oxford and the public schools, the possession of the right accent, manners and style, still protected the interests of the hereditary upper-middle class" (5).

Professor Welch in *Lucky Jim* is self-involvedly bourgeois. He and his family represent those who aspire to power and influence. When we first meet Welch, he is complaining that a local reporter failed to note the difference between "flute and piano" and "recorder and piano" (9). The episode characterizes the infuriating way in which Welch sees his own activities as of supreme interest to others. The episode is a matter of caricature, as are his eccentric capabilities as a driver, but the episode is also indicative of the manner in which

Welch exercises power. He refuses by evasion to give Jim Dixon any clear indication of whether he will be retained at the university. He has asked Dixon to prepare a proposal for the honors course in history that Dixon in theory is scheduled to teach the following year, yet Dixon is fully aware that he must not attract students away from Welch. The latter's "Oh, Dixon, can I have a word with you?" reminds Dixon of the imperious manner of his flight-sergeant (83).

From Dixon's viewpoint, Welch belongs to a suffocating power structure that includes the mysterious Caton, the man who, having promised to publish what Dixon calls his piece of "niggling mindlessness" (16), steals the article. It is Welch who adheres to a "merrie" England theory of Medieval history, and whose manners are lampooned by the drunken Dixon in his final lecture, which reproduces Welch's "preludian blaring sound," begins to be repetitive, and uses Welch-like tags—"integration of social consciousness," "identification of work with craft" (227). Welch's son is as intolerable as Welch. Aside from being virulently anti-union, he has a stuffy sense of appropriate behavior, is full of self-advertising when he meets Gore-Urquhart, and tells Dixon that he does not "allow people of your sort to stand in my way" (212).

Dixon himself, of course, is no paragon of virtue. His cutting out of extensive cigarette burns in the sheets at Welch's house after an evening's drinking is funny, but one cannot admire his insistent deception about the matter. His frequent "girning," which perhaps can be seen as a working-class equivalent to disguise, is an immature response to frustration, and he has a tendency to silly acts of vengeance—the threatening letter to Johns, the disfiguring of the cover photograph on Johns's periodical. Yet, the mannered lifestyles of those around Dixon seem rule- and status-bound to the extent of being life-suppressing, so that we perceive Dixon's need for "a fierce purging draft of fury or contempt" (27) with sympathy. Moreover, Dixon's presence is physical, even if grotesquely so, with the result that his qualities of fallible humanity stand in sharp contrast to the stuffiness of Welch and his family, who act according to codes of mannered behavior.

The Welches are, then, the heirs of the bourgeoisie of Restoration comedy, an identification suggested by Wain's comment on *Lucky Jim:* "It is sometimes said . . . that there is currently an attempt by some writers to reaffirm the vitality and vigour of provincial life. I cannot say that I agree. The most successful product of that 'movement', so far, has been a satirical novel whose main butt is the aping of upper-class culture by the provincial bourgeoisie" (letter to *Encounter,* June 1955, quoted in Morrison 71). Dixon, though originating in caricature—Blake Morrison writes that the type, the "Yorkshire scholar," was created by Philip Larkin and that his hostility to "Filthy Mozart" is Larkin's taste (11)—is the means by which the numbing effects of that aping are exposed.

Although finally an outsider, Jim Dixon starts as a would-be participant in the world he allows us to judge. Before he makes his escape, he struggles against Welch to be admitted to the academic world, and in his escape he is helped as much by his disastrous lecture as by the good fortune of being offered a position with Gore-Urquhart. Wain's picaresque novel *Hurry on Down*, by contrast, is about an outsider who starts out and remains an outsider by choice and by bad fortune. The novel records Charles Lumley's progress from unemployed graduate in history, to window-cleaner, to member of a gang of drug runners, to hospital orderly, to chauffeur, to bouncer, and finally, to a three-year contract as a gag writer. The people who have power or position are less pleasant than Welch, whose oppressiveness is finally laughable, despite Dixon's suffering under it, because the world in which he, his family, and friends live is a small, impotent caricature that invites Dixon's vigorous responses to absurd power. In *Hurry on Down*, however, Charles Lumley is the victim of oppressions and deceits that constitute the world against which Lumley struggles. Dixon is a frustrated opposer of petty oppressions. Lumley is a victim of indifference and of his own failures.

The world in which Lumley lives can be seen as the obverse of a world of manners. Whereas other works have been shown to bring realities to mind, *Hurry on Down* can be seen as a novel that brings manners to mind. Three incidents allow the reader to glimpse the mannered world. In each instance, that world is judged as hypocritical because it is perceived as removed from the pressing needs of Lumley. In the first incident, Lumley takes Veronica to his former college and forces his tutor Lockwood to recognize him: "'Ah, yes, earning your living,' said Lockwood cautiously. 'We all have to come to it,' he added in a half-attempt at geniality. 'And in what, ah, sphere, in what . . . ?'" (121). In the second, working as chauffeur, Charles has to pick up Hutchins, a man he despises for having been educated into a snob embarrassed by his working-class parents. Hutchins "had his pipe at the ready in case it should be necessary to put on his don's act at short notice. Even at first glance Charles could see that the act had grown richer and more professional during his year of close contact with the real thing" (193). In the third, at the start of his short career as a window cleaner, Lumley needs to borrow five pounds for equipment, but he can borrow the money only by pretending to a solicitor uncle that the money is to cover a gambling debt. The first illustrates complacency and indifference; the second, snobbery; and the third suggests that success can be gained only by entering an irrelevant and fanciful world reminiscent of mannered Restoration behavior.

Unlike Jim Dixon, who is unable to conform to Welch's artificial world but happy to work for Gore-Urquhart, Lumley is trapped as much by his inability to enter the world of middle-class respectability as by his attempts to come to terms with the world that he has been educated away from. As Lumley sees matters, education has succeeded in removing his protective sharp edges and has inculcated cautiousness: "he saw himself bowed over books, listening to instruction, submitting to correction, being endlessly moulded and shaped" (21). He wishes he could "cast up and be rid of his class, his *milieu,* his insufferable load of presuppositions and reflexes" (23). When he does attempt to immerse himself in anonymity, however, matters do not work out simply. Although he lives a Bohemian life of near-desperate poverty with Froulish the writer, he discovers that life has been supported by money given to Froulish's girlfriend by Robert Tharkles in exchange for sex. After a near-fatal accident immediately following a failed drug run, he is cared for by Bernard Frederick's money on the understanding that he will stay away from Frederick's mistress, Veronica. The working-class life he looks for he finds in the father of a girl he courts, Rosa, but it is the life of an older person only. Rosa's brother Stan "was making a fairly determined effort to 'better himself' by rising out of the world of strictly manual work . . . into the circle immediately above it. This circle seemed, by all accounts, a good deal slimier" (175). And when, finally, Charles tries capitalism, selling single cigarettes to provincials left behind in London by their missed trains, one customer tries to rob him (220–21). In these ways, among others, he experiences what Alistair Davies and Peter Saunders call the "oppressive power of class, money and bureaucracy" (25).

Jim Dixon and Charles Lumley both escape from the worlds they first inhabit. Dixon frees himself from the university at the moment of impending expulsion and rescues for himself both the right woman and the right job. Charles Lumley, hostile to the university world of Lockwood and Hutchins from which he has emerged and facing a hostile world, finds employment and, though with ambiguity on Wain's part, Veronica. In both cases, the mannered worlds of middle-class respectability and of academe have rejected the outsider. The novels by Amis and Wain demonstrate clearly, therefore, what I have shown to be evident in the plays and the novels as a group, namely that the worlds of Restoration comedy and of the campus novels are carefully selective. Real-world counterparts may be suggested in the works, but the presence of those counterparts is disturbing, and their potentially forceful and destructive effects need to be controlled. Essentially, the world of manners operates by following rules that outsiders are unwilling either to perceive or to follow. That world needs to be self-enclosed to preserve itself, and it is, then, on behalf of this self-enclosure that Somerset Maugham can be viewed as having written when he judged that such people as Dixon "are scum" (quoted in Morrison 59). His assertion is not untrue provided one accepts its premise that the world of a Welch or a Lockwood or a Woolfardisworthy or even a Mirabell is the decent one. In a sense, of course, it is: were Fainall to triumph over Mirabell, treachery would win over amiable wit; Dixon's world would be self-indulgently chaotic; Lumley's would be a world of grim struggle; Goldberg's would be a world in which a place for oneself could not be found.

Yet, at the same time, one can see that these mannered worlds are extremely small. It is appropriate that one of Lodge's novels about academic life be titled *Small World*. Lodge no doubt refers to the smallness of the world represented in high-speed international travel from conference to conference on the part of a small band of academics. The title can also, however, be taken to suggest just how precarious that world is. The world of manners as microcosm brings to mind a larger and less pleasant one; occasionally that larger world threatens to overwhelm the enclosed, smaller one.

Contributors

BEGE K. BOWERS Associate Professor of English and Composition Coordinator, Youngstown State University. She is coeditor of the *CEA Critic* and *Forum*, chair of the Committee on Chaucer Bibliography and Research for the MLA Chaucer Division, assistant bibliographer for the New Chaucer Society, and special editor for theses and dissertations for the editorial board of *South Atlantic Review*. She has served as consultant for Duskin and Macmillan publishers and has worked as an editor for MLA.

BARBARA BROTHERS Professor and Chairperson of English, Youngstown State University. Her publications include essays on Sylvia Townsend Warner, Henry Green, Elizabeth Bowen, Barbara Pym, William Butler Yeats, and Margaret Kennedy. She is coeditor of the *CEA Critic* and *Forum*, on the editorial board of the *Barbara Pym Newsletter*, and president of the College English Association. She has served on the ADE executive committee and the Ohio Humanities Council and published articles on the profession.

GLORIA SYBIL GROSS Associate Professor of English, California State University, Northridge. She has published several articles on Samuel Johnson and eighteenth-century medical psychology including "Johnson and Psychopathology" in *Greene & Centennial Essays*, "Dr. Johnson's Practice: The Medical Context for *Rasselas*" in *Studies in Eighteenth-Century Culture*, and "Johnson and the Uses of Enchantment" and "'A Child Is Being Beaten': Suggestions Toward a Psychoanalytic Reading of Johnson," which are forthcoming. She is president of the Samuel Johnson Society of Southern California and serves on the Board of Directors of the Jane Austen Society of Southern California.

MARYLEA MEYERSOHN Assistant Professor of English and Women's Studies at City College of the City University of New York. She has published articles in *Jane Austen: New Perspectives*, *Notable American Women: The Modern Period*, and the *James Joyce Newsletter* and poetry in *The Thirteenth Moon*.

JANET EGLESON DUNLEAVY Professor of English, University of Wisconsin-Milwaukee. Her books include *George Moore: The Artist's Vision, the Storyteller's Art; The O'Conor Papers* (with G. W. Dunleavy); *George Moore in Perspective* (editor); and *Castle Richmond* (critical edition). She has written essays on Anthony Trollope, Mary Lavin, Elizabeth Bowen, George Moore, Flannery O'Connor, James Joyce, Lord Dunsany; on manuscript evidence of the oral tradition in Ireland; and on nineteenth-century America as seen by Irish and Irish-Americans. She has also published nonacademic books and magazine articles.

MAUREEN T. REDDY Assistant Professor of English and Women's Studies at Rhode Island College and director of the Women's Studies Program. She has published articles in *Studies in Short Fiction, The Journal of Narrative Technique,* and *Black American Literature Forum.* She is a contributing editor of *Hurricane Alice.* Her book, *Sisters in Crime: Feminism and the Crime Novel,* was nominated for the Edgar Award.

JAMES R. KINCAID Aerol Arnold Professor of English, University of Southern California. He is the author of books on Dickens, Tennyson, and Trollope, as well as several editions of and numerous essays on Victorian literature and on literary theory. He has just completed a book on Victorian pedophilia.

JOSEPH WIESENFARTH Professor of English, University of Wisconsin-Madison. In addition to *Gothic Manners and the Classic English Novel,* his books include *Henry James and Dramatic Analogy, The Errand of Form: An Assay of Jane Austen's Art,* and *George Eliot's Mythmaking.*

MARK HUSSEY The author of *The Singing of the Real World: The Philosophy of Virginia Woolf's Fiction.* He teaches at Pace University and at the New School for Social Research in New York City.

MARY F. SISNEY Professor of English, California State Polytechnic University, Pomona. She has published reviews and articles in *Explorations in Ethnic Literature* and *The CLA Journal.*

CAROLYN G. HEILBRUN Avalon Foundation Professor in the Humanities, Columbia University. She is the author of *The Garnett Family, Christopher Isherwood, Toward a Recognition of Androgyny,* and *Reinventing Womanhood.* Her latest book, *Writing a Woman's Life,* has recently been issued in paperback by Ballantine. She is the author of nine Amanda Cross detective novels.

JOHN WILKINSON   Associate Professor of English, Youngstown State University. He has published in *Restoration* and *Indiana English* and is a reviewer for *Choice*.

Works Cited

Amis, Kingsley. *Lucky Jim*. 1953. New York: Viking, 1958.

Annan, Noel. "Bloomsbury and the Leavises." *Virginia Woolf and Bloomsbury: A Centenary Celebration*. Ed. Jane Marcus. Bloomington: Indiana UP, 1987. 23–38.

apRoberts, Ruth. *The Moral Trollope*. Athens: Ohio UP, 1971.

Auerbach, Erich. *Mimesis: The Representation of Reality in Western Literature*. 1953. Trans. Willard Trask. Garden City, N.Y.: Anchor-Doubleday, 1957.

Auerbach, Nina. "Dorothy L. Sayers and the Amazons." *Romantic Imprisonment: Women and Other Glorified Outcasts*. Gender and Culture. New York: Columbia UP, 1985. 184–94.

Austen, Jane. *Minor Works*. Ed. R. W. Chapman. Vol. 6 of *The Works of Jane Austen*. 6 vols. Oxford: Oxford UP, 1954.

———. *The Novels of Jane Austen*. Ed. R. W. Chapman. 3rd ed. 5 vols. Oxford: Oxford UP, 1932–34.

Austen-Leigh, J. E. *A Memoir of Jane Austen*. 1872. Oxford: Clarendon, 1926.

Baker, Ernest. *The History of the English Novel*. Vol. 10. London: Witherby, 1939. 10 vols. 1924–39.

Banta, Martha. *Henry James and the Occult*. Bloomington: Indiana UP, 1972.

Bayley, John. "Where, Exactly, Is the Pym World?" Salwak 50–57.

Beaty, Jerome. *Middlemarch from Notebook to Novel: A Study of George Eliot's Creative Method*. Illinois Studies in Language and Literature 47. Urbana: U of Illinois P, 1960.

Beer, Gillian. "Virginia Woolf and Pre-History." *Virginia Woolf: A Centenary Perspective*. Ed. Eric Warner. New York: St. Martin's, 1984. 99–123.

Beer, Patricia. *Reader, I Married Him: A Study of the Women Characters of Jane Austen, Charlotte Brontë, Elizabeth Gaskell and George Eliot*. New York: Barnes, 1974.

Behn, Aphra. *The Lucky Chance, or The Alderman's Bargain*. [1686.] Ed. Fidelis Morgan. The Royal Court Writers Series. London: Methuen in Association with the Royal Court Theatre, 1984.

Berke, Jacqueline, and Laura Berke. "Mothers and Daughters in *Wives and Daughters:* A Study of Elizabeth Gaskell's Last Novel." *The Lost Tradition: Mothers and Daughters in Literature*. Ed. Cathy N. Davidson and E. M. Broner. New York: Ungar, 1980. 95–109.

Bernard, Robert. *Deadly Meeting*. New York: Perennial Library-Harper, 1986.

Blackwood, John. "To George Eliot." 8 June 1857. *The George Eliot Letters*. Ed. Gordon S. Haight. Vol. 2. New Haven: Yale UP; London: Oxford UP, 1954. 344–45. 9 vols. 1954–78.

Bone, Robert. *The Negro Novel in America*. Rev. ed. New Haven: Yale UP, 1965.

Boone, Joseph Allen. *Tradition Counter Tradition: Love and the Form of Fiction*. Chicago: U of Chicago P, 1987.

Booth, Bradford. *Anthony Trollope: Aspects of His Life and Art*. Bloomington: Indiana UP, 1958.

Bosanquet, Theodora. *Henry James at Work*. Washington: Folcroft, 1976.

Bradbrook, Frank W. *Jane Austen and Her Predecessors.* Cambridge: Cambridge UP, 1966.

Bradbury, Malcolm. *Eating People Is Wrong.* 1959. London: Secker, 1976.

———. *Rates of Exchange.* London: Secker, 1983.

Brothers, Barbara. "Women Victimised by Fiction: Living and Loving in the Novels by Barbara Pym." *Twentieth-Century Women Novelists.* Ed. Thomas F. Staley. London: Macmillan, 1982. 61–80.

Brown, Laura. *English Dramatic Form. 1660–1760: An Essay in Generic History.* New Haven: Yale UP, 1981.

Burgess, Anthony. *The Clockwork Testament, or Enderby's End.* New York: Knopf, 1974.

Burney, Fanny. *Evelina, or the History of a Young Lady's Entrance into the World.* 1788. Ed. Edward A. Bloom. Oxford: Oxford UP, 1968.

Burrows, J. F. *Computation into Criticism: A Study of Jane Austen's Novels and an Experiment in Method.* New York: Oxford UP-Clarendon, 1987.

Butler, Marilyn. *Jane Austen and the War of Ideas.* London: Oxford UP-Clarendon, 1975.

———. *Maria Edgeworth: A Literary Biography.* Oxford: Clarendon, 1972.

Cameron, Deborah. *Feminism and Linguistic Theory.* London: Macmillan, 1985.

Carlyle, Thomas. "Memoir of the Life of Sir Walter Scott, Baronet." *Westminster Review* (American ed.) 28 (January 1838): 154–82.

Cawelti, John G. *Adventure, Mystery, and Romance: Formula Stories as Art and Popular Culture.* Chicago: U of Chicago P, 1976.

Charney, Hanna. *The Detective Novel of Manners: Hedonism, Morality, and the Life of Reason.* Rutherford: Fairleigh Dickinson UP; London: Associated UP, 1981.

Chase, Richard. *The American Novel and Its Tradition.* Garden City, N.Y.: Anchor-Doubleday, 1957.

Ciplijauskaite, Birute. *La mujer insatisfecha: El adulterio en la novela realista.* Barcelona: Edhasa, 1984.

Clark, Katerina, and Michael Holquist. *Mikhail Bakhtin.* Cambridge: Harvard UP-Belknap, 1984.

Colby, Vineta. *Yesterday's Woman: Domestic Realism in the English Novel.* Princeton: Princeton UP, 1974.

Coleman, Linda. "Public Self, Private Self: Women's Life Writings 1600–1800." Diss. U of Wisconsin-Milwaukee, 1986.

Collins, K. K. "Prejudice, *Persuasion,* and the Puzzle of Mrs. Smith." *Persuasions* 6 (1984): 40–43.

[Colvin, Sidney.] Review of *Middlemarch,* by George Eliot. *Fortnightly Review* 19 Jan. 1873: 142–47. Rpt. in Bert G. Hornback, ed. *Middlemarch.* By George Eliot. Norton Critical Edition. New York: Norton, 1977. 648–52.

Congreve, William. *The Way of the World.* 1700. *The Comedies of William Congreve.* Ed. Anthony G. Henderson. Plays by Renaissance and Restoration Dramatists. Cambridge: Cambridge UP, 1982. 305–407.

Craik, W. A. *Elizabeth Gaskell and the English Provincial Novel.* London: Methuen, 1975.

Rev. of *Daisy Miller,* by Henry James. *Nation* 19 Dec. 1878: 386–89.

Davies, Alistair, and Peter Saunders. "Literature, Politics, and Society." *Society and Literature, 1945–1970.* Ed. Alan Sinfield. The Context of English Literature. New York: Holmes, 1983. 13–50.

Donadio, Stephen. *Nietzsche, Henry James, and the Artistic Will.* New York: Oxford UP, 1978.

Dryden, John. "Preface to *An Evening's Love or, The Mock Astrologer.*" 1671. *Essays of John Dryden.* Ed. W. P. Ker. Vol. 1. New York: Russell, 1961. 2 vols. 134–47.

Duthie, Enid L. *The Themes of Elizabeth Gaskell.* Totowa, N.J.: Rowman, 1980.

Eagleton, Terry. *The Function of Criticism: From* The Spectator *to Post-Structuralism.* London: Verso-New Left Books, 1984.

_____. *Literary Theory: An Introduction.* Oxford: Blackwell, 1983.

Easson, Angus. *Elizabeth Gaskell.* London: Routledge, 1979.

Edel, Leon. "The Myth of America in *The Portrait of a Lady.*" *Henry James Review* 7 (1986): 8–17.

Edgeworth, Maria. *Letters for Literary Ladies.* 1795. Ed. Gina Luria. *The Feminist Controversy in England 1788–1810.* New York: Garland, 1974.

_____. *Tales and Novels by Maria Edgeworth.* The Longford Edition. 10 vols. New York: AMS, 1967.

Edwards, Lee R. *Psyche as Hero: Female Heroism and Fictional Form.* Middletown, Conn.: Wesleyan UP, 1984.

Eliot, George. *Middlemarch: A Study of Provincial Life.* 1874. Afterword by Frank Kermode. New York: New American Library; London: New English Library, 1964.

_____. "To John Blackwood." 12 [July] 1857. *The George Eliot Letters.* Ed. Gordon S. Haight. Vol. 2. New Haven: Yale UP; London: Oxford UP, 1954. 361–62. 9 vols. 1954–78.

_____. "To John Blackwood." 24 July 1871. *The George Eliot Letters.* Ed. Gordon S. Haight. Vol. 5. New Haven: Yale UP; London: Oxford UP, 1955. 168–69. 9 vols. 1954–78.

_____. "To Mrs. Harriet Beecher Stowe." [October? 1872]. *The George Eliot Letters.* Ed. Gordon S. Haight. Vol. 5. New Haven: Yale UP; London: Oxford UP, 1955. 321–22. 9 vols. 1954–78.

_____. "The Sad Fortunes of the Reverend Amos Barton." *Scenes of Clerical Life.* 1858. Ed. Thomas A. Noble. Oxford: Clarendon, 1985.

Emerson, Ralph Waldo. *Journals of Ralph Waldo Emerson with Annotations.* Ed. Edward Waldo Emerson and Waldo Emerson Forbes. Vol. 9. Boston: Houghton, 1913. 10 vols. 1909–14.

Enright, D. J. *Academic Year: A Novel.* 1955. Oxford: Oxford UP, 1985.

Etherege, George. *The Man of Mode; or, Sir Fopling Flutter.* 1676. *The Plays of Sir George Etherege.* Ed. Michael Cordner. Plays by Renaissance and Restoration Dramatists. Cambridge: Cambridge UP, 1982. 209–333.

Faber, Richard. *Proper Stations: Class in Victorian Fiction.* London: Faber, 1971.

Farrell, Thomas J. "The Female and Male Modes of Rhetoric." *College English* 40 (1979): 909–21.

Fauset, Jessie. *The Chinaberry Tree: A Novel of American Life.* 1931. College Park, Md.: McGrath, 1969.

Fleishman, Avrom. "Two Faces of Emma." *Jane Austen: New Perspectives.* Ed. Janet Todd. Women & Literature New Series 3. New York and London: Holmes, 1983. 248–56.

Forsyth, William. *The Novels and Novelists of the Eighteenth Century, in Illustration of the Manners and Morals of the Age.* 1871. London: Kennikat, 1970.

Foster, Shirley. *Victorian Women's Fiction: Marriage, Freedom, and the Individual.* Totowa, N.J.: Barnes; London: Croom, 1985.

Frazier, E. Franklin. *Black Bourgeoisie.* New York: Free Press-Macmillan; London: Collier, 1957.

Fryckstedt, Monica Correa. "Defining the Domestic Genre: English Women Novelists of the 1850s." *Tulsa Studies in Women's Literature* 6.1 (1987): 9–25.

Frye, Northrop, Sheridan Baker, and George Perkins. *The Harper Handbook to Literature.* New York: Harper, 1985.

Gaskell, Elizabeth. *The Letters of Mrs. Gaskell.* Ed. J. A. V. Chapple and Arthur Pollard. Cambridge: Harvard UP, 1979.

_____. *Wives and Daughters: An Every-Day Story.* 1866. Ed. Frank Glover Smith. Middlesex: Penguin, 1975.

Gilbert, Sandra M., and Susan Gubar. *The Madwoman in the Attic: The Woman Writer and the Nineteenth-Century Literary Imagination.* New Haven: Yale UP, 1979.

Habermas, Jürgen. "Towards a Theory of Communicative Competence." *Inquiry* 13 (1970): 360–75.

Hagan, John H. "*The Duke's Children:* Trollope's Psychological Masterpiece." *Nineteenth-Century Fiction* 13 (1958–59): 1–21.

Hagstrum, Jean H. "Towards a Profile of the Word *Conscious* in Eighteenth-Century Literature." *Psychology and Literature in the Eighteenth Century*. Ed. Christopher Fox. New York: AMS, 1987.

Halperin, John. "Barbara Pym and the War of the Sexes." Salwak 88–100.

――――. *Egoism and Self-Discovery in the Victorian Novel: Studies in the Ordeal of Knowledge in the Nineteenth Century*. Studies in Literature and Criticism 1. New York: Franklin, 1974.

――――. *The Language of Meditation: Four Studies in Nineteenth-Century Fiction*. Elms Court: Stockwell, 1973.

――――. *The Life of Jane Austen*. Baltimore: Johns Hopkins UP, 1984.

Harden, O. Elizabeth McWhorter. *Maria Edgeworth's Art of Prose Fiction*. Studies in English Literature 62. The Hague: Mouton, 1971.

Harwood, John T. *Critics, Values, and Restoration Comedy*. Carbondale: Southern Illinois UP, 1982.

Hazlitt, William. *The Complete Works of William Hazlitt* [after the Edition of A. R. Waller and Arnold Glover]. Ed. P. P. Howe. 21 vols. New York: AMS, 1967.

Heilman, Robert B. "Two-Tone Fiction: Nineteenth-Century Types and Eighteenth-Century Problems." *The Theory of the Novel*. Ed. John Halperin. New York: Oxford UP, 1974. 305–22.

Hiatt, Mary. *The Way Women Write*. New York: Teachers College P, 1977.

Hill, George Birkbeck, ed. *Johnsonian Miscellanies*. 2 vols. 1897; rpt. New York: Barnes; London: Constable, 1966.

Holman, Hugh C. *A Handbook to Literature*. 3rd ed. Indianapolis: Odyssey, 1972.

Homans, Margaret. *Bearing the Word*. Chicago: U of Chicago P, 1986.

Hueffer, Ford Madox. *Henry James: A Critical Study*. New York: Boni, 1915.

Hurst, Michael. *Maria Edgeworth and the Public Scene: Intellect, Fine Feeling and Landlordism in the Age of Reform*. Coral Gables: U of Miami P, 1969.

Hussey, Mark. *The Singing of the Real World: The Philosophy of Virginia Woolf's Fiction*. Columbus: Ohio State UP, 1986.

Jacobson, Howard. *Coming from Behind*. London: Chatto, 1983.

James, Henry. *Literary Criticism: Essays on Literature, American Writers, English Writers*. Ed. Leon Edel. New York: Library of America, 1984.

――――. *Literary Criticism: French Writers, Other European Writers, The Prefaces to the New York Edition*. Ed. Leon Edel. New York: Library of America, 1984.

――――. "Mrs. Gaskell." In *Notes and Reviews*. 1921. Freeport, N.Y.: Books for Libraries, 1968. 153–59.

――――. *The Painter's Eye: Notes and Essays on the Pictorial Arts*. Ed. John L. Sweeney. London: Hart-Davis, 1956.

――――. *The Portrait of a Lady*. Harmondsworth: Penguin, 1978.

James, P. D. Foreword. *Dorothy L. Sayers*. Ed. James Brabazon. New York: Scribner's, 1981. xiii–xvi.

Johnson, Judy van Sickle. "The Bodily Frame: Learning Romance in *Persuasion*." *Nineteenth-Century Fiction* 38 (1983): 43–61.

Jolles, André. *Einfache Formen*. Trans. as *Formes simples* by André Marie Buguet. Paris: Seuil, 1972.

Jones, Ernest. *The Life and Work of Sigmund Freud*. 3 vols. New York: Basic, 1953–57.

Karl, Frederick R. *The Adversary Literature: The English Novel in the Eighteenth Century: A Study in Genre*. New York: Farrar, 1974.

Keener, Frederick M. *The Chain of Becoming: The Philosophical Tale, the Novel, and a Neglected Realism of the Enlightenment: Swift, Montesquieu, Voltaire, Johnson, and Austen*. New York: Columbia UP, 1983.

Kent, George E. "Patterns of the Harlem Renaissance." *The Harlem Renaissance Remembered.* Ed. Arna Bontemps. New York: Dodd, 1972. 27–50.

Kestner, Joseph A. *Mythology and Misogyny: The Social Discourse of Nineteenth-Century British Classical-Subject Painting.* Madison: U of Wisconsin P, 1989.

Key, Mary Ritchie. *Male/Female Language.* Metuchen, N.J.: Scarecrow, 1975.

Kierkegaard, Søren. *The Concluding Unscientific Postscript.* 1941. Trans. David F. Swenson. Princeton: Princeton UP, 1968.

Kincaid, James R. *The Novels of Anthony Trollope.* Oxford: Clarendon, 1977.

Klinkowitz, Jerome. *The New American Novel of Manners: The Fiction of Richard Yates, Dan Wakefield, and Thomas McGuane.* Athens: U of Georgia P, 1986.

Kraft, Quentin G. "On Character in the Novel: William Beatty Warner versus Samuel Richardson and the Humanists." *College English* 50 (1988): 32–47.

Labov, William. *Sociolinguistic Patterns.* 1972. Philadelphia: U of Pennsylvania P, 1975.

Lakoff, Robin Tolmach. *Language and Woman's Place.* 1972. New York: Harper, 1975.

Lansbury, Coral. *Elizabeth Gaskell.* Twayne's English Authors Series 371. Boston: Twayne, 1984.

Larsen, Nella. Quicksand *and* Passing. 1928, 1929. Ed. Deborah E. McDowell. American Women Writers Series. New Brunswick, N.J.: Rutgers UP, 1986.

Leavis, F. R. *The Great Tradition: George Eliot, Henry James, Joseph Conrad.* 1948. New York: New York UP, 1964.

Le Carré, John. *Tinker, Tailor, Soldier, Spy.* 1974. New York: Bantam, 1975.

Little, Judy. *Comedy and the Woman Writer: Woolf, Spark, and Feminism.* Lincoln: U of Nebraska P, 1983.

Litvak, Joseph. "Reading Characters: Self, Society, and Text in *Emma.*" *PMLA* 100 (1985): 763–73.

Locke, Elizabeth Hughes. "Anthony Trollope and the Novel of Manners." Diss. Duke U, 1972.

Lodge, David. *The British Museum Is Falling Down.* 1965. London: Secker, 1981.

_____. *Changing Places: A Tale of Two Campuses.* 1975. London: Secker, 1982.

_____. *Ginger, You're Barmy.* 1962. London: Secker, 1982.

_____. *Out of the Shelter.* 1970. Rev. ed. London: Secker, 1985.

_____. "Robertson Davies and the Campus Novel." 1982. *Write On: Occasional Essays '65-'85.* London: Secker, 1986. 169–73.

_____. *Small World: An Academic Romance.* London: Secker, 1984.

Long, Robert Emmet. *The Great Succession: Henry James and the Legacy of Hawthorne.* Pittsburgh: U of Pittsburgh P, 1979.

Lukács, Georg. *The Meaning of Contemporary Realism.* Trans. John and Necke Mander. London: Merlin, 1962.

Luria, Gina. Introduction. Edgeworth, *Letters for Literary Ladies* 5–9.

MacAndrew, Elizabeth. *The Gothic Tradition in Fiction.* New York: Columbia UP, 1979.

MacCarthy, Bridget G. *The Later Women Novelists, 1744–1818.* Cork: Cork UP, 1948.

McConnell-Ginet, Sally, Ruth Borker, and Nelly Furman, eds. *Women and Language in Literature and Society.* New York: Praeger, 1980.

McDowell, Deborah E. "New Directions for Black Feminist Criticism." *The New Feminist Criticism: Essays on Women, Literature, and Theory.* Ed. Elaine Showalter. New York: Pantheon, 1985. 186–99.

McKee, Patricia. *Heroic Commitment in Richardson, Eliot, and James.* Princeton: Princeton UP, 1986.

Mann, Thomas. *The Magic Mountain.* Trans. H. T. Lowe-Porter. Harmondsworth: Penguin, 1980.

Matthiessen, F. O. *Henry James: The Major Phase.* Galaxy, 1944; rpt. New York: Oxford UP, 1963.

Rev. of *Middlemarch,* by George Eliot. *Saturday Review* 7 Dec. 1872: 733–34. Rpt. in Bert C. Hornback, ed. *Middlemarch.* By George Eliot. Norton Critical Edition. New York: Norton, 1977. 645–48.

Miller, J. Hillis. "Optic and Semiotic in *Middlemarch.*" *The Worlds of Victorian Fiction.* Ed. Jerome Buckley. Cambridge: Harvard UP, 1975. 125–45.

Millett, Fred B., ed. *A History of English Literature* [by William Vaughn Moody and Robert Morss Lovett]. 8th ed. New York: Scribner's, 1964.

Milne, Gordon. *The Sense of Society: A History of the American Novel of Manners.* Rutherford: Fairleigh Dickinson UP; London: Associated UP, 1977.

Morgan, Charlotte E. *The Rise of the Novel of Manners: A Study of English Prose Fiction between 1600 and 1740.* 1911. New York: Russell, 1963.

Morrison, Blake. *The Movement: English Poetry and Fiction of the 1950s.* Oxford: Oxford UP, 1980.

Murray, Patrick. *Maria Edgeworth: A Study of the Novelist.* Cork: Mercier, 1971.

Nardin, Jane. *Barbara Pym.* Twayne's English Authors Series 406. Boston: Twayne, 1985.

Naylor, Gloria. *Linden Hills.* New York: Viking, 1985.

Nettels, Elsa. "*The Portrait of a Lady* and the Gothic Romance." *South Atlantic Bulletin* 39 (1974): 73–82.

Newby, P. H. *Maria Edgeworth.* The English Novelists. Denver: Swallow, 1950.

Newcomer, James. *Maria Edgeworth.* Irish Writers Series. Lewisburg: Bucknell UP, 1973.

———. *Maria Edgeworth the Novelist, 1767–1849: A Bicentennial Study.* Texas Christian U Monographs in History and Culture 2. Fort Worth: Texas Christian UP, 1967.

Newton, Judith Lowder. *Women, Power, and Subversion: Social Strategies in British Fiction, 1778–1860.* New York: Methuen, 1981.

O'Connor, Dennis L. "Intimacy and Spectatorship in *The Portrait of a Lady.*" *Henry James Review* 2 (1980): 25–35.

Paris, Bernard J. *Character and Conflict in Jane Austen's Novels: A Psychological Approach.* Detroit: Wayne State UP, 1978.

Pateman, Trevor. *Language, Truth and Politics.* Lewes, East Sussex: Stroud, 1980.

Phillipps, K. C. "Lucy Steele's English." *English Studies* (Anglo-American Supplement) 49 (1969): lv–lxi.

Pollard, Arthur. *Mrs Gaskell: Novelist and Biographer.* Manchester: Manchester UP, 1965.

Poovey, Mary. "*Persuasion* and the Promises of Love." *The Representation of Women in Fiction.* Ed. Carolyn G. Heilbrun and Margaret R. Higonnet. Selected Papers from the English Institute, 1981; New Series 7. Baltimore: Johns Hopkins UP, 1983. 152–79.

———. *The Proper Lady and the Woman Writer: Ideology as Style in the Works of Mary Wollstonecraft, Mary Shelley, and Jane Austen.* Chicago: U of Chicago P, 1984.

Price, Martin. "Manners, Morals, and Jane Austen." *Nineteenth-Century Fiction* 30 (1975): 261–80.

Pym, Barbara. *Jane and Prudence.* 1953. London: Cape, 1979.

———. *A Very Private Eye: An Autobiography in Diaries and Letters.* Ed. Hazel Holt and Hilary Pym. New York: Dutton, 1984.

Reeve, Clara. *The Progress of Romance and the History of Charoba, Queen of Aegypt, Reproduced from the Colchester Edition of 1785, with a Bibliographical Note by Esther M. McGill.* New York: Facsimile Text Society, 1930.

Rogers, Pat. *The Augustan Vision.* New York: Harper, 1974.

Rosmarin, Adena. "'Misreading' *Emma:* The Powers and Perfidies of Interpretive History." *ELH* 51 (1984): 315–42.

Routh, Michael. "Isabel Archer's Double Exposure: A Repeated Scene in *The Portrait of a Lady.*" *Henry James Review* 1 (1980): 262–63.

Ruddick, Sara. "Maternal Thinking." *Feminist Studies* 6.2 (1980): 342–67.

Ruotolo, Lucio P. *The Interrupted Moment: A View of Virginia Woolf's Novels.* Stanford: Stanford UP, 1986.

Sabiston, Elizabeth. "The Architecture of Consciousness and the International Theme." *Henry James Review* 7 (1986): 29–47.

Salwak, Dale, ed. *The Life and Work of Barbara Pym.* Iowa City: U of Iowa P, 1987.

Santos, Maria Irene Ramalho de Sousa. "Isabel's Freedom: Henry James's *The Portrait of a Lady.*" *Biblos* 56 (1980): 503–19.

Sato, Hiroko. "Under the Harlem Shadow: A Study of Jessie Fauset and Nella Larsen." *The Harlem Renaissance Remembered.* Ed. Arna Bontemps. New York: Dodd, 1972. 63–89.

Sattel, Jack W. "Men, Inexpressiveness, and Power." Thorne, Kramarae, Henley 118–24.

Sayers, Dorothy L. *Gaudy Night.* London: Gollancz, 1935.

_____ . Letters, ms. Sophia Smith Collection. Smith Library, Northampton, Mass.

Schneider, Ben Ross, Jr. *The Ethos of Restoration Comedy.* Urbana: U of Illinois P, 1971.

Scholes, Robert. "Dr. Johnson and Jane Austen." *Philological Quarterly* 54 (1975): 380–90.

Sharpe, Tom. *Wilt.* London: Secker, 1976.

_____ . *The Wilt Alternative.* London: Secker, 1979.

_____ . *Wilt on High.* New York: Random, 1984.

Silver, Brenda R., ed. "'Anon' and 'The Reader': Virginia Woolf's Last Essays." *Twentieth-Century Literature* 25.3–4 (1979): 356–444.

_____ . "Virginia Woolf and the Concept of Community: The Elizabethan Playhouse." *Women's Studies* 4.2–3 (1977): 291–98.

Silverman, Kaja. *The Subject of Semiotics.* New York: Oxford UP, 1983.

Smith, Gaddis. "A Gentleman and a Scapegoat." Rev. of *Anthony Eden,* by Robert Rhodes James. *New York Times Book Review* 23 August 1987: 12.

Southam, B. C., ed. *Jane Austen: The Critical Heritage.* London: Routledge; New York: Barnes, 1968.

_____ . *Jane Austen's Literary Manuscripts: A Study of the Novelist's Development through the Surviving Papers.* London: Oxford UP, 1964.

Spacks, Patricia Meyer. *The Female Imagination.* New York: Knopf, 1975.

Spender, Dale. *Man Made Language.* London: Routledge, 1980.

Stewart, J. I. M. "Two Strings to His Bow." *Parlour 4 and Other Stories.* London: Gollancz, 1986. 137–58.

Stone, Lawrence. *The Family, Sex and Marriage in England 1500–1800.* New York: Harper, 1977.

Stoneman, Patsy. *Elizabeth Gaskell.* Key Women Writers. Bloomington: Indiana UP, 1987.

Strauss-Noll, Mary. "Love and Marriage in the Novels." Salwak 72–87.

Swanson, Janice Bowman. "Toward a Rhetoric of Self: The Art of *Persuasion.*" *Nineteenth-Century Fiction* 36 (1981): 1–21.

Symons, Julian. "The Borgia Heirloom." *Ellery Queen* Nov. 1987: 52–56.

Tanner, Tony. "The Fearful Self: Henry James's *The Portrait of a Lady.*" *Henry James: Modern Judgments.* Ed. Tony Tanner. London: Macmillan, 1968. 143–59.

_____ . *Jane Austen.* Cambridge, Mass.: Harvard UP, 1986.

Taylor, Mark C. *Erring: A Postmodern A/theology.* Chicago: U of Chicago P, 1984.

Thackeray, William Makepeace. *Vanity Fair: A Novel Without a Hero.* 1848. Ed. Geoffrey and Kathleen Tillotson. Boston: Houghton, 1963.

Thorne, Barrie, Cheris Kramarae, and Nancy Henley, eds. *Language, Gender and Society.* Rowley, Mass.: Newbury, 1983.

Tomlinson, T. B. *The English Middle-Class Novel.* New York: Barnes, 1976.

Tracy, Ann B. *The Gothic Novel, 1790–1830: Plot Summaries and Index to Motifs.* Lexington: U of Kentucky P, 1981.

Trilling, Lionel. "Manners, Morals, and the Novel." *The Liberal Imagination: Essays on Literature and Society.* 1950. Garden City, N.Y.: Anchor-Doubleday, 1957. 199–215.

———— . *The Opposing Self*. 1950. New York: Viking; Toronto: MacMillan, 1955.

Trollope, Anthony. *Barchester Towers*. James R. Kincaid, ed. 1857. The World's Classics. Oxford: Oxford UP, 1983.

———— . *Clergymen of the Church of England*. Rpt. from the *Pall Mall Gazette*. London: Chapman, 1866.

———— . *The Duke's Children*. 1880. Oxford: Oxford UP, 1973.

———— . *Four Lectures*. Ed. Morris L. Parrish. London: Constable; Toronto: MacMillan, 1938.

———— . *He Knew He Was Right*. 1869. The World's Classics 507. Oxford: Oxford UP, 1948.

———— . *The Letters of Anthony Trollope*. Ed. N. John Hall. 2 vols. Stanford: Stanford UP, 1983.

———— . *Phineas Redux*. 1873. Oxford: Oxford UP, 1973.

———— . *South Africa*. Ed. D. H. Simpson. 2 vols. The Colonial History Series. 1878. London: Dawsons, 1968.

———— . *The Tireless Traveller: Twenty Letters to the* Liverpool Mercury *by Anthony Trollope, 1875*. 1941. Ed. Bradford Allen Booth. Berkeley: U of California P, 1941.

Trudgill, Peter. "Sex, Covert Prestige and Linguistic Changes in the Urban British English of Norwich." *Language in Society* 1 (1972): 179–95.

Tuttleton, James W. *The Novel of Manners in America*. Chapel Hill: U of North Carolina P, 1972.

Voss-Clesly, Patricia. *Tendencies of Character Depiction in the Domestic Novels of Burney, Edgeworth, and Austen: A Consideration of* Subjective *and* Objective *World*. Vol. 1. Salzburg Studies in English Literature 95. Salzburg, Austria: Institut für Anglistik und Amerikanistik, 1979. 2 vols.

Wagenknecht, Edward. *Cavalcade of the English Novel*. New York: Holt, 1954.

Wain, John. *Hurry on Down*. 1953. London: Secker, 1978.

Ward, J. A. "The Portraits of Henry James." *Henry James Review* 10 (1989): 1–14.

Watt, Ian. *The Rise of the Novel: Studies in Defoe, Richardson and Fielding*. 1957; rpt. Berkeley: U of California P, 1971.

Wharton, Edith. *The House of Mirth*. 1905. New York: Scribner's, 1975.

White, Robert. "The Matter of Sexuality in *The Portrait of a Lady*." *Henry James Review* 7 (1986): 59–71.

Wiesenfarth, Joseph. *Gothic Manners and the Classic English Novel*. Madison: U of Wisconsin P, 1988.

Wilde, Alan. "Touching Earth: Virginia Woolf and the Prose of the World." *Philosophical Approaches to Literature: New Essays on Nineteenth- and Twentieth-Century Texts*. Ed. William E. Cain. London: Associated UP; Lewisburg: Bucknell UP, 1984. 140–64.

Williams, Raymond. *The English Novel from Dickens to Lawrence*. 1970. London: Hogarth, 1984.

Winks, Robin W. *Cloak & Gown: Scholars in the Secret War, 1939–1961*. New York: Morrow, 1987.

Wirth-Nesher, Hana. "Figure and Ground in *Between the Acts*." MLA Convention, New York, 29 December 1986.

Wollstonecraft, Mary. *Thoughts on the Education of Daughters, with Reflections on Female Conduct in the More Important Duties of Life*. 1787. New York: Garland, 1974.

———— . *A Vindication of the Rights of Woman*. 1792. Ed. Carol H. Poston. New York: Norton, 1975.

Woolf, Virginia. *Between the Acts*. New York: Harcourt, 1941.

———— . *The Diary of Virginia Woolf*. Ed. Anne Olivier Bell. 5 vols. London: Hogarth; Toronto: Clarke, 1977–84.

———— . "The Green Mirror." Rev. of *The Green Mirror*, by Hugh Walpole. *Contemporary Writers*. London: Hogarth, 1965. 71–73.

———— . "Jane Austen." *The Common Reader*. 1925. First Series. London: Hogarth, 1975. 178.

———— . "The Leaning Tower." *Collected Essays II*. London: Hogarth, 1966. 162–81.

———. "The Narrow Bridge of Art." *Granite and Rainbow.* 1958. New York: Harcourt, 1975. 11–23.

———. *Orlando: A Biography.* 1928. New York: Harvest-Harcourt, 1956.

———. *A Room of One's Own.* 1929. New York: Harbinger-Harcourt, 1957.

———. "A Sketch of the Past." *Moments of Being.* Ed. Jeanne Schulkind. 1976. London: Hogarth, 1987. 61–159.

———. *Three Guineas.* 1938. London: Hogarth, 1952.

———. *The Voyage Out.* 1915. London: Hogarth, 1975.

———. *The Waves.* 1931. London: Hogarth, 1976.

Wright, Edgar. *Mrs. Gaskell: The Basis for Reassessment.* London: Oxford UP, 1965.

Wycherley, William. *The Country Wife.* 1675. *The Plays of William Wycherley.* Ed. Peter Holland. Plays by Renaissance and Restoration Dramatists. Cambridge: Cambridge UP, 1981. 227–341.

Zimbardo, Rose A. *A Mirror to Nature: Transformations in Drama and Aesthetics 1660–1732.* Lexington: U of Kentucky P, 1986.

Index